D1054913

YOUR VOICE

YOUR VOTE

YOUR VOICE

YOUR VOTE

The Savvy Woman's Guide to Power, Politics, and the Change We Need

◊ ◊ ◊

Martha Burk, Ph.D.

A.U. PUBLISHING
AUSTIN, TEXAS

Your Voice, Your Vote: The Savvy Woman's Guide to Power, Politics, and the Change We Need

Published by A.U. Publishing
Austin, Texas 78613

Ordering Information:

Quantity sales

Baker & Taylor, Inc.
2550 West Tyvola Road, Suite 300
Charlotte, NC 28217
Phone: 800-775-1800
http://www.btol.com

Ingram Content Group Inc.
1 Ingram Blvd.
La Vergne, TN 37086
Phone: 615.793.5000

CreateSpace Direct
www.createspace.com/info/createspacedirect

Library of Congress Control Number:

ISBN-13: 978-1470165536
ISBN-10: 1470165538

9 8 7 6 5 4 3 2 1

Printed in the United States of America
Distributed by Baker & Taylor and CreateSpace Direct

Table of Contents

◊ ONE ◊

Change, No Change, or Short-Changed: What's at Stake for Women in 2014 and Beyond?

Elections are often characterized as the "election of the century," and billed as "the most significant election in our lifetime" for one group or another, including women. The last two U.S. presidential elections were no exception, and indeed had high drama and high expectations. What made them so significant?

In the eight years from 2001-2008, the U.S. had gone from record surpluses to record deficits. We were at war in two countries with no end in sight. Gasoline prices had doubled since 2000. Our country was flooded with contaminated products, including the toys our children play with and our very food supply. Climate change continued to threaten the planet, yet the government appeared unresponsive.

But most importantly, women's rights, for which we fought so hard in the 20th century, had been steadily eroded since 2001. The first federal ban in history on an abortion procedure became law in 2007. Title IX, the law requiring equal educational opportunities for girls and women, was greatly weakened. A woman-hostile majority on the Supreme Court seriously curtailed our right to challenge employment discrimination.

And while it is true that the 2008 election ushered in was a "regime change" in Washington that was reaffirmed at the presidential level in 2012, it would be a monumental mistake to assume our problems, particularly as women, have gone away or been solved magically. In fact, 2010 changed the balance of power when the House majority changed, and not for the better insofar as women are concerned. The government has been all but paralyzed, and anti-woman legislation has been introduced time and time again at the national level and in the states as well. That's why 2014 is so important.

Forward progress is stalled. The pay gap remains, there are unprecedented and growing assaults on reproductive freedom and medical privacy, and we are the only industrialized country on earth without some form of pregnancy leave or paid family leave.

The child care system in the U.S. is a patchwork of "make-do" arrangements that leaves families struggling, and the few federal child care programs that exist have been cut to the bone. Social Security, women's primary retirement program, is under constant pressure, and long-term care is an increasing problem that families must solve on their own.

There are many other pressing national issues we don't normally think about as "women's issues" – but that is indeed what they are. The faltering economy, the health care crisis, ongoing and potential wars, tax policies – all affect women in different ways than they affect men, and all are growing concerns.

If this sounds like a doomsday scenario, it's not, though it is a challenge. *Women are the majority, and we have the opportunity to take control and make the changes we need in every election* – but having the opportunity is not enough. We must have the will – firmly grounded in essential knowledge of the issues and a path ahead. That's what this book is about.

This book is *not* about any candidate or party. It's about the challenges we face from the setbacks since the turn of the 21st century, and what we can do about them as we go forward. But please don't think of this as just another "good citizens act – good citizens vote" sermon.

Voting and taking action doesn't help, and indeed can hurt, if women end up doing something against their own interests because they don't know the facts.

It is still true that knowledge is power. By the time you close this book you will know what's at stake for women as we navigate the most important opportunities for progress – or lack of it – in this election year. But knowledge won't bring change without action – and that means holding candidates and elected officials accountable for long-term solutions.

The first action we must take is confronting candidates – incumbents and challengers of both parties – with questions not only about their voting records, but also their future intentions on our most vital issues. At the end of each chapter, you will find just such questions. After all, there's a national election every two years, and every one is "the election of the century" for women. And when the election is over, the information here will help you hold those who got elected accountable.

Those who would roll back the progress we've made toward reaching economic, social, legal, and political equality have vast financial resources, are very well organized, and are too often driven by a misogyny that borders on outright hatred of women. They are not prone to participate in rational and reasonable discourse. They will usurp control of social policy at every opportunity, and block any positive steps they don't agree with. And by now we know that is no idle threat – women are suffering both attacks and setbacks. It's up to women to stop it, and we must start *right now* in public discourse, election campaigns, and in the voting booth.

> "We shall employ agents, circulate tracts, petition the State and national Legislatures, and endeavor to enlist the pulpit and the press in our behalf."

These words are contained in the final paragraph of the *Declaration of Sentiments* from the First Women's Rights Convention held in 1848. The ladies of 1848 were determined, and after 72 more years of struggle they got what they wanted most – the vote. If they were alive to exercise that right today, they might put it this way:

> Read their records. Go to town hall meetings and confront them. Call in when you hear them on the radio. If they don't mention women, ask why not. Spread the word when they say something about our issues, good or bad. Email. Blog. Facebook. Twitter. Raise hell. Don't be captivated by fancy speeches or red-hot rhetoric. Arm yourself with knowledge and *vote your own interests*.

How to Read This Book

The essential background you need to make a difference is found in the first six chapters of this book; we urge you to read them first. After that – well, women have differing concerns. So you'll probably want to read the chapters about your priority issues next. We do think there are eye-opening facts in every section, but skipping around won't hurt. It is not necessary to go straight through to get the most out of *Your Voice, Your Vote: The Savvy Woman's Guide to Politics, Power, and the Change We Need.*

When you're finished, pass this book along, or keep it for reference and encourage your friends to get a copy and read it too. After all, one woman *can* change the world – but it's easier when we combine our power into a force to be reckoned with.

◊ TWO ◊

Who's in Charge? Why Should Women Care?

The Guy (or Gal) at the Top . . .

Throughout much of our history it has often seemed that control in Washington doesn't matter much. The government pretty well rocked on regardless of who was in the White House or which party had the most members of Congress. After all, it's a huge bureaucracy, each department has its mission, and it looked like not much changed from administration to administration.

But recent political climates have shown that view is very wrong. Control matters enormously. Our government has been gridlocked to the point of being unable to make even the smallest decisions (much less fix the big problems), and in 2011 brought the United States to the brink of financial default for the first time in history – because the President and Congress could not agree or compromise.

We learned in civics classes that the federal government has three branches – executive (the president and his staff, including the cabinet, advisors, and other political appointees), judicial (courts and judges), and legislative (the Senate and House of Representatives) – and that the three have equal power and serve as "checks and balances" on each other. That's all true – up to a point. A lot depends on who's in charge of each branch at any given time.

In 2006, when answering a question about conduct of the Iraq war, President George W. Bush declared "I am the Decider." While pundits have often made light of the remark, the fact is that it's true a lot of the time. And usually it matters a great deal.

Though the constitution grants the power to declare war only to Congress, in reality it is presidents who decide. The president also gets to decide (with the advice and consent of the Senate) who will sit on the courts, and which individuals will head the cabinet departments.

Through these appointments, the president sets an agenda for the country, because appointees usually carry out their duties in accordance with the president's wishes. (The Supreme Court is sometimes an exception. While presidents mostly get who they want – if not the first choice then the second – justices can change their outlook over time. Of course, they're appointed for life and can't lose their jobs.)

Consider some of the consequences – good and bad – of presidential agenda-setting and appointments in the last few administrations:

Ronald Reagan

Anne M. Gorsuch, Environmental Protection Agency Director	A firm believer that the EPA, was too big, wasteful, and too restrictive of business. Gorsuch cut the EPA budget by 22 percent. She boasted that she reduced the thickness of the book of clean water regulations from six inches to a half-inch.[1]
Clarence Thomas, Equal Employment Opportunity Commission Director	Downsized the agency and all but eliminated class action suits for employment discrimination. Declared that sexual harassment claims were not a priority for the agency.[2]

George H.W. Bush

Clarence Thomas Supreme Court	Voted with the conservative majority to uphold a federal abortion ban, curb women's employment rights, and outlawed using race as a factor in school integration plans.
Antonia Novello, Surgeon General, first woman and first Hispanic to hold the position	Focused her attention on the health of women, children and minorities.

William J. Clinton

Donna Shalala Secretary Health and Human Services	Raised child immunization rates to the highest levels in history; created national initiatives to fight breast cancer and violence against women.[3]
Ruth Bader Ginsburg, Supreme Court	Consistent vote for the rights of women, strong believer in freedom of choice. Issued rare dissents from the bench in 2007 in the *Gonzales* federal abortion ban case, and in the *Ledbetter* case which curbed women's employment rights.[4]

George W. Bush

Eric Keroack followed by Susan Orr, Health and Human Services Family Planning	Both opposed birth control, even though the office oversees $283 million in annual grants to provide low-income families and others with contraceptive services and counseling.[5]

Wade Horn, Health and Human Services Assistant Secretary	Founded the National Fatherhood Initiative to promote marriage as the solution to poverty, then gave the group a $12.38 million contract. Openly stated his belief that "the husband is the head of the wife just as Christ is the head of the church." Increased "Abstinence Only" sex education funding in the schools to $176 million per year. Advocated that Head Start be available only to children of married couples, not single parents.[6]
John Roberts, Chief Justice, Supreme Court, and Samuel Alito, Supreme Court	Both credited with sharply turning the Court to the right, joining in 5-4 majorities upholding a federal abortion ban without a health exception, and curtailing women's employment rights.[7]

Barack Obama

Sonia Sotomayor, Elena Kagan, Supreme Court	Sotomayor first Hispanic woman appointed to the Court. Both advocates for rights of minorities and women.
Hilda Solis, Secretary of Labor	First Hispanic Secretary of Labor. Declared women's employment and pay equity a priority for the department.
Hillary Clinton, Secretary of State	Elevated office of women's rights to ambassador status. Strong advocate for global women's rights.
Janet Napolitano, Secretary of Homeland Security	Pioneer in coordinating federal, state, local and bi-national homeland security efforts, and presided over large scale disaster relief efforts.

Kathleen Sebelius, Secretary of Health & Human Services	Presided over planning and implementation of the Affordable Care Act, the largest change in U.S. health care in history.
Janet Yellin, Chair of the Federal Reserve Board	First female chair pushed for more help for ordinary households, not just banks, in the economic downturn and financial crisis.

These high-level and very visible examples are only a small fraction of the number of appointments each president makes. Presidents infuse all government departments with appointees that will carry out their philosophy. If that philosophy is fairness and good government, women win. If that philosophy is anti-government, punitive toward the poor, sympathetic to the religious right, the very wealthy, and corporations, women lose.

Majorities Matter – Congress and Its Committees

Most business in Congress is done through a committee system, meaning that members can't automatically bring bills to the floor of the House or Senate for a vote. Bills are introduced, then they go to a committee for consideration. This is far from an orderly process, and what happens next almost always depends on which party is in the majority. That's because seats on each committee are determined by which party is in control.

If the Republicans are in control of the Senate or the House, they will have the majority of seats on *every committee* in that chamber, and the chairperson of *every committee* will be a Republican. The opposite is of course true if the Democrats are in the majority. The chairperson and majority members have control, so they are the decision makers as to which bills the committee will consider (and which bills it won't – those will "die in committee").

So back to that bill process. This is a shorthand explanation, but it will give you the basics. Suppose a bill is introduced that would make new law, or overturn an existing law. The bill is immediately sent to a committee that deals with the topic the bill addresses (e.g. education or energy), where the committee chair is in charge of its fate.

If the committee chair does not like the bill, it is never scheduled to come up for discussion. If the chair of the committee likes the bill, and thinks it ought to go to the floor for a vote, he or she schedules *hearings*, where advocates and experts come and talk to the committee about the pros and cons. Then the committee takes a vote on whether to send the bill to the full body (House or Senate) for a vote.

But the struggle isn't over, because the next step is getting it on the voting calendar, which is essentially a priority list. And guess who decides where it goes on the calendar? *The leaders from the majority party*. If a bill is placed too far down on the calendar, the clock may run out on the legislative session before it ever comes up for a vote, meaning the whole process has to be repeated by the next Congress.

Committees have another very important function – oversight. That means if something is going on in the government that they believe bears investigation, they can call witnesses before the committee to talk about it, and place them under oath if they want. Or not. And the "or not" is sometimes the more important part of the equation.

For example, when it became public in early 2006 that President Bush was conducting a program of wiretapping conversations of U.S. citizens without court warrants, the chairman of the Senate Select Committee on Intelligence, Senator Pat Roberts (R-KS) refused to hold hearings to investigate the legality of the program. When the Democrats gained power in the mid-term elections, the Senate Judiciary Committee issued subpoenas to the White House, Vice President Dick Cheney's office, and the Justice Department after what the panel's chairman Patrick Leahy (D-VT) called "stonewalling of the worst kind" of efforts to investigate the wiretapping.[8] Similarly, when the Obama Administration refused to hand over documents from the Department of Justice justifying the legality of drone strikes in 2013, the House Judiciary Committee obtained the material only after threatening a subpoena.[9]

Committees can also call people other than government employees before them to explain things that impact the public health, safety, or well-being.

In February 2012 House Republicans convened a hearing on whether contraception should be provided in insurance plans under health care reform, because Catholic bishops objected to the requirement being placed on any institution loosely affiliated with a church (e.g. a university or hospital). Because the committee majority has final say over who the witnesses will be in addition to whether to call a hearing in the first place, only men were allowed to testify. This caused a firestorm of protest from female members, and they walked out of the hearing.

An earlier (but still infamous) case is instructive. In 1994 the Democratic majority was investigating whether tobacco should be regulated as a drug. In an almost comical display, tobacco executives stood as a group before a congressional committee and swore under oath that they didn't believe tobacco was addictive. But before any action could be taken on regulation, control switched to the Republicans in the next election, and here's what happened: "Since the 1994 tobacco hearings the Republicans have taken control of the government majority, and the committee that investigated the tobacco companies is now headed by Thomas Bliley, a Republican from Virginia and one of the industry's strongest supporters."[10] In the decade since, hearings have never been reconvened – and tobacco has never been regulated.

Size (of the Majority) Matters – A Lot

It's fair to say the U.S. Congress has been gridlocked since 2010. Gridlock can be caused by an imbalance of power (one party having the overwhelming majority), recalcitrance (either party not wanting the other to claim victory), or hostility of one party to the agenda of whoever is in the White House. Though neither party has had an overwhelming majority, the balance has been such that very little has been accomplished. And it can happen even if one party is in control of both Congress and the White House. Here's an example: the number one priority of women (and men) in the 2006 mid-term election was ending the war in Iraq. According to all the polls, this was a the main factor in changing both the House and Senate from Republican to Democratic majorities. (Several races that gave control of the Senate to the Democrats were clearly decided by the women's vote.)

But even though the Democrats now had control, they could not end the war because they did not have enough votes. You might be wondering why not – they had majorities in both houses, didn't they?

In the easiest case, for a bill to become law, it must pass each house of Congress by a simple majority, and be signed by the president. But if the president wants to veto a bill to prevent it from becoming law after the Congress passes it, the path to enactment can be much harder – and this is indeed a situation where size matters.

Why? Two reasons: 1) not all members of a party can be counted on to vote together, so a few defections can make the difference between victory and defeat, and 2) a simple majority is not necessarily enough anyway, because if the president vetoes a bill (or announces he is planning to do so) a much larger majority (two-thirds of both houses) is needed to override. Most of the time, if party leaders know they can't override a threatened or promised veto, they won't even bring a bill up for a vote. The exception is when they want to embarrass the other party or the president on a measure that is popular with the people.

In the Senate, there is an additional hurdle to bill passage that is not found in the House – the filibuster. While House rules determine the amount of time a bill can be debated before it must be brought to a vote, there is no limit to the time a bill can be debated in the Senate. That means a bill can be filibustered, or debated so long that the other side gives up (the bill is literally "talked to death"). Ending a filibuster requires three-fifths of the full Senate (60 votes).

In the 2010 mid-term elections, control of the House turned over to Republicans, and they retained control in 2012. The Democrats still control the Senate, but by only 55 votes (counting two independents that vote with them) out of the 100 total. Republicans have 45 of the 100 members, and though it is not a majority, it is still enough to block important legislation through threats of a filibuster, because it takes 60 votes to end filibusters.

The filibuster threat has been used more since President Obama was elected than at any other time in history – to block votes on legislation and nominees to judgeships and various posts in the government. It was used repeatedly in the struggle over health care. Democrats needed 60 votes to overcome a threatened filibuster on a motion to begin debate (called *cloture*). In order to hold the party together and produce the winning majority, party leaders had to make some very expensive promises of federal dollars to the states of Senators in their own ranks.[11]

Four hundred and twenty bills passed the House but died in the Senate from 2008-2010.[12] The Democrats no longer even insisted that Republicans actually go to the floor and filibuster – the mere threat is enough to block a bill from coming up for a vote. After three more years of gridlock, Senate Majority Leader Harry Reid (D-NV) in 2013 invoked a rule change banning use of the filibuster on presidential nominees (except those for the courts). This move has been dubbed the "nuclear option," and it angered Republicans greatly. It remains to be seen what the GOP might do in retaliation should they once again gain control of the Senate in 2014.

All this means that "just a few seats" matter a great deal. If your incumbent "brings home the bacon" in road and bridge projects but votes against your basic rights on abortion, you can't look the other way. If a candidate promises to solve the environmental crisis but stands against women's access to paid family leave, child care, or fair pay, don't ignore it.

Small majorities fail. Women must give pro-woman candidates a *mandate* – by electing them in large enough numbers to insure victory when it counts.

The (Almost) Last Word – The Supreme Court

The job of the Supreme Court is to settle arguments about the law. They may be arguments about whether something like flag burning or the right to abortion is protected under the Constitution, arguments about whether laws passed by Congress are constitutional, or arguments about how laws should be interpreted.

Supreme Court appointments are for life, and they are extremely important. The decisions handed down are usually final, or at the very least can last for generations before new cases trigger a revisiting of a prior decision. Presidents appoint people to the Supreme Court that mirror the president's views about what the laws mean, or what they ought to mean.

Though everyone denies that "litmus tests" are used in appointments, this is simply not true. An anti-choice president is going to appoint anti-choice judges, and a pro-corporate president is going to appoint judges that he believes agree with him, whether or not the nominee is willing to say so publicly.

When it comes to women, past Supreme Courts have ruled that birth control is legal, that women have the right to abortion, that women have the right to equal educational opportunities, and that women have the right to be free from discrimination and sexual harassment at work, to cite just a few very important decisions.

But with new appointments of Justices Roberts and Alito to the Supreme Court under President George W. Bush, the tide turned against women (the Obama appointments did not change the conservative majority). The current Supreme Court has upheld a federal ban on one abortion procedure (with no exception for health of the woman), and severely curtailed the rights of women to take action when they learn they are being discriminated against in pay or promotion at work, overturning over forty years of precedent.

While the Supreme Court almost always has the last word, it can be overruled by Congress in some cases, usually those where the "intent" of a particular law is at issue. In reality, this happens very rarely – only twice in high profile cases affecting women in the past 50 years.

Title IX, the law prohibiting discrimination in education if an institution is receiving federal funds, is instructional. When the law was passed in 1972, Congress intended it to apply across the board to all programs in an educational institution getting federal dollars, regardless of where the money was spent. So women in a university couldn't be kept out of the law school, for example, even if all the federal money went to the medical school.

But in 1984, in a case called *Grove City v. Bell*, the Court issued a narrow interpretation of Title IX that opened a loophole. The justices ruled that colleges could discriminate against women in some programs (e.g. sports) if that particular program did not receive federal money, even if the school as a whole did get federal dollars.

Congress overturned the ruling four years later by passing a new law (the Civil Rights Restoration Act) explicitly stating that Title IX applies to all programs in any school receiving federal support, regardless of which department actually gets the money.

A similar fight was necessary to overturn the *Ledbetter v. Goodyear* decision in 2007, when the Supreme Court abandoned forty years of precedent and severely curtailed women's right to sue for sex discrimination in pay (see Pay Equity chapter for a full discussion). It took women's rights advocates two more years of lobbying Congress, and an election that produced a change in control of the White House, to get a new law passed that reversed the ruling.

But just because advocates succeeded after a several years of fighting in these very isolated cases, don't believe Congressional action is an easy or reliable safeguard against bad court opinions. As we saw above in the discussion of majorities and overrides, there is no guarantee that this process can succeed once the Supreme Court makes a ruling – most of the time Congress doesn't even try. That's why it is crucial that pro-woman judges be appointed to begin with, and that the Senate has enough votes to confirm them.

Over the next four years, the president could appoint at least two and perhaps as many as six Supreme Court justices, setting the course of law as it affects women for a generation or more. Justice Ruth Bader Ginsburg, a champion of women's rights, is 81. Three others are in their late seventies.

If those new justices do not believe in the basic rights of women, the right to abortion will be overturned, and other gains of the twentieth century, such as protection against discrimination in employment, education, pregnancy, and credit could be rolled back or eliminated, one by one.

It goes without saying that women must be the "Deciders" as to who will be in the White House making these appointments, and who will be in the Senate confirming them.

◊ THREE ◊

The Gender Gap – Women Can Control Any Election

The Long, Long Road to the Female Majority

When the Constitution was adopted in 1789, the ruling class was white, male, and land-owning. Rights of full citizenship were granted on that basis. It was never disputed that"persons" granted citizenship were understood to be white and male, but the framers could not agree on whether land ownership should also be a requirement for voting. Unable to resolve the issue, they left voting requirements to the states. None of the states allowed Indians, black men, or any women to vote.

The Fourteenth Amendment, ratified three years after the abolition of slavery in 1868, granted citizenship to "persons born or naturalized in the United States," and the right to vote to non-white men, but to no women, white or non-white. It also guaranteed "equal protection under the law," to all "persons."

The breathtaking hypocrisy of the federal government proposing a constitutional amendment guaranteeing equal protection for all citizens, while denying the female half the vote, was not lost on the suffragists. In the years before adoption controversy raged as to whether women should be included, with the formidable Susan B. Anthony on the side of women (black and white) and the equally formidable black leader Frederick Douglass against. Douglass's arguments were summed up by the influential newspaper editor Horace Greeley when he told the women:

> . . .hold your claims, though just and imperative. . .in abeyance until the negro is safe beyond peradventure, and your turn will come next. I conjure you to remember that this is "the negro's hour," and your first duty now is to go through the State and plead his claims.[13]

Of course he meant *male* negroes. Ultimately the guys won (surprise!), introducing the word "male" into the Constitution for the first time, and enshrining in that document that race discrimination is more serious than sex discrimination – a strange and enormously harmful notion that continues to be upheld by the courts to this day.

Women would have to work another 52 years, until 1920, to pass a separate amendment to get equal voting rights. Carrie Chapman Catt, one of the movement leaders, told just how hard it was:

> To get the word "male" in effect out of the Constitution cost the women of the country fifty-two years of pauseless campaign . . . During that time they were forced to conduct 56 campaigns of referenda to male voters; 480 campaigns to get Legislatures to submit suffrage amendments to voters; 47 campaigns to get state constitutional conventions to write woman suffrage into state constitutions; 277 campaigns to get state party conventions to include woman suffrage planks; 30 campaigns to get presidential party conventions to adopt woman suffrage planks in party platforms; and 19 campaigns with 19 successive Congresses.[14]

There were too many arguments against women's suffrage to count, but a frequent one was that women did not need the vote because they would just vote the same way their husbands did anyway. Another argument was the opposite: anti-suffragists, far from believing women would be so apathetic, feared that women would take over the nation and its politics. As a matter of fact, neither happened. For the next sixty years, though not necessarily casting their ballots in the same way as men, women voted in lower numbers, and certainly didn't take over the country.

But the 1980 election brought the "perfect storm" in terms of the women's vote. Women now outnumbered men in the population, and that year they surpassed men in both voter registration and turnout. *And for the first time in U.S. history, women voted in a markedly different way than men.*

The Equal Rights Amendment (ERA) granting equal constitutional rights to women was pending before the states, and the right to abortion had been upheld by the Supreme Court through the *Roe v. Wade* decision only seven years earlier. Ronald Reagan, the Republican candidate, ran on a platform that included opposition to both abortion rights and the ERA. His opponent, Democratic incumbent Jimmy Carter, was pro-choice and a strong ERA advocate. Reagan won the election, but his support split along gender lines, with 54 percent of men voting for him vs. 46 percent of women – a difference of eight percentage points.

This *gender gap,* named and identified by feminist political analyst Eleanor Smeal, has never gone away. Neither has women's majority in voting, and that's why change is possible.

Though it has never gone away, since 1980 the gender gap has been larger in some elections than others. It was smallest in 1992 (with women favoring Bill Clinton by 3 percent), when third party candidate Ross Perot siphoned votes from both major party candidates. The gap was largest in 2000 – women favored Al Gore over George W. Bush by 12 percentage points – in a contested election that was awarded to Bush by the Supreme Court with a 5-4 decision.[15]

There was a seven percent gender gap in the presidential election of 2008. Though Barack Obama won the majority of votes from both women and men, his margin among men was only one percent. Women voted for him by 56 percent to 43 percent over opponent John McCain. Unmarried women, who made up a fifth of the electorate, went for Obama by a whopping 70 percent.[16]

The gender gap in the 2012 presidential election was the largest on record. President Obama won women by 12 percentage points, while Mitt Romney won men by 8 - a 20-point gender gap. It was the fifth straight election to feature a double-digit gender gap.[17]

Women's votes have been decisive in a number of other close elections, such as contests in 2006 that turned over control of the Senate and the House of Representatives from majority Republican to majority Democratic. The war in Iraq was a hot issue–75 percent of voters overall cited ending it as a top priority. It was more important for women, with 80 percent rating it very high as opposed to 71 percent of men.[18] Since the Republicans in Congress continued to support the war, this was the biggest factor behind the voters overturning both the House and the Senate. Black women provided the winning margin (a gender gap of 10 points) for Jim Webb, the anti-war Democrat challenging incumbent Republican George Allen in Virginia.

If men had been the only voters, Republicans would have maintained their majority in Senate. Everyone also knew that if the Democrats took the majority in the House of Representatives, the first woman in history would be Speaker of the House, Nancy Pelosi of California. Women saw this as much more important than men (54 percent–43 percent).[19] The Democrats also achieved a filibuster-proof Senate majority in 2008, picking up eight seats. In all of these races except one there were substantial gender gaps, ranging from 4 percent to 16 percent.[20]

Women's votes were once again decisive in maintaining Democratic control of the Senate in 2012.

Some of the key Senate races where the gender gap made an impact were:

- Chris Murphy (D-CT) defeated Linda McMahon ® with an 11 percent gender gap, with 60 percent of women's votes to 49 percent of men's votes , despite McMahon's spending tens of millions of dollars;

- Elizabeth Warren (D-MA) won with a 12 percent gender gap, with 59 percent of women's votes and only 47 percent of men's votes;

- Martin Heinrich (D-NM) won with a 6 percent gender gap, with 54 percent of women's votes and 48 percent of men's votes;

- Sherrod Brown (D-OH) won with an 8 percent gender gap, with 56 percent of women's votes and 48 percent of men's votes;

- Bob Casey (D-PA) won with a 9 percent gender gap, with 58 percent of women's votes and 49 percent of men's votes; and

- Tim Kaine (D-VA) won with a 7 percent gender gap, with 56 percent of women's votes and 49 percent of men's votes.

If only men had voted in each of these races, according to exit polls, the Republican candidate would have won and the Senate majority would be Republican.

In the mid-term elections of 2010 the House of Representatives turned over and went to Republicans, with the women's vote shifting somewhat from the large majority they gave Democrats in 2008. Almost all of the dropoff of women's support for Democrats came from white women. African American women voted for Democrats 92 percent of the time, and Latinas 65 percent.[21] There were no analyses of individual House races in 2012, when Republicans maintained their majority, widely seen as the result of redistricting. The overall numbers from 2004-2012 indicate that the gender gap in House races has favored Democrats by 12.4 percent.[22]

Women are Democrats, Men are Republicans

There are growing gender gaps in party identification. For a number of years, women have not only been voting in greater numbers than men, but choosing more Democratic than Republican party candidates. Since 1972, both women and men have also switched to the independent category from one or the other parties. Men have migrated away from calling themselves Democrats, with more moving to the independent category than to the Republican ranks. Females have been more stable, the majority identifying as Democrats since 1972, and fewer leaving either party to become independents.

As of 2012, there was a 10 percent gender gap in Democratic party identification between women and men (37 percent-27 percent). The gender gap between females and males identifying as Republicans was only 1 percent (24 percent-25 percent). Both parties have lost members to the independent column.

The table below shows us how party identification has changed over the years.

Party Identification
Year-by-Year Party Identification By Gender[23]

	Male			Female		
	Dem.	Ind.	Rep.	Dem.	Ind.	Rep.
1972	44%	22%	34%	47%	17%	36%
1976	39%	38%	23%	43%	30%	27%
1980	42%	27%	31%	48%	24%	28%
1984	35%	29%	36%	41%	23%	35%
1988	33%	28%	39%	42%	25%	33%
1992	34%	30%	36%	41%	26%	34%
1996	34%	29%	37%	44%	23%	33%
2000	33%	29%	38%	44%	25%	32%
2004	31%	29%	39%	41%	24%	35%
2006	32%	31%	37%	43%	23%	34%
2009	32%	34%	28%	41%	26%	25%[24]
2010	30%	n/a	23%	38 %	n/a	25%
2011	27%	n/a	26%	36%	n/a	26%
2012	27%	43%	25%	37%	33%	24%[25]

Voting is not the only place where gender gaps have developed. Women and men differ substantially on many issues. You'll find examples throughout this book. Suffice it to say that if women did not vote at all or voted in lower numbers than men, different people would be elected, and different priorities would be emphasized by lawmakers.

Gender Gaps in Congress

Female elected leaders have also been responsible for making a difference in Congress on a variety of measures, from efforts to end the Iraq war to pushing for more money for breast cancer research and combating violence against women. Women are often in solidarity across party lines, and differ with men within their own parties.

In the House of Representatives, Democratic women are decidedly more liberal than Democratic men.[26] In the May, 2007 House vote to approve supplemental funding for continuing the war in Iraq without benchmarks for withdrawal, women accounted for about 26 percent of the "no" vote, even though they comprised only 16 percent of the House membership. More than half of the women members voted against open-ended funding of the war, compared to only 29 percent of the male representatives.

Votes on social issues are even more telling. Sixty four percent of the women in the Senate voted against the passage of the first federal abortion ban in history that became law in 2007, while 64 percent of the men in the Senate voted for it.[27]

(The law that passed is not a total ban on all abortions, but on certain late-term procedures, regardless of the health consequences for the woman. The official photo of the bill signing, with President Bush surrounded by a cadre of smiling older white men, caused outrage among abortion rights supporters.)

The women's vote did *not* split along party lines – both Democratic and Republican women voted against the ban. It is obvious that if there had been as many women in the Senate as there were men, the measure could have been defeated.

The same is true of the vote for the Stupak-Pitts amendment to outlaw abortion coverage in the health care overhaul that passed the House in November, 2009. The great majority of women voted against the restriction, but their numbers were not enough to prevail, since men constituted 83 percent of the House membership.

Republican and Democratic women also united in the Senate in 2009 to pass the Lilly Ledbetter Fair Pay Act, the first bill President Obama signed into law. All of the female Senators voted in favor of the bill. The men's vote split straight down party lines, with all of the Democrats supporting, and all of the Republican men voting "no." Similar gender solidarity across party lines has been shown on votes for a military children's health program and ratification of the United Nations treaty on the disabled (though the overall vote fell short).

These examples are just a small snapshot of why gender gaps do matter – whether in the voting booth or in the halls of Congress. If women want to make change, they must vote their priorities regardless of party, and they must support leaders who share those priorities – again regardless of party. The good news is that women are now a permanent majority – in the population, in voter registration, and it voter turnout. That means women can control any election.

Wouldn't it be great if the fears of the anti-suffragists weren't so far-fetched after all?

◊ FOUR ◊

Where We Stand: We've Come a Long Way. . .and Yet?

There is no question that women in the United States, whether rich, poor, or in between, enjoy a relatively high standard of living compared to many women worldwide. But among developed nations, U.S. women are far from being "number one" politically and socially. If we are to change things at the ballot box, we first have to know where we really stand in our own country, and in comparison to women in other parts of the world who live in industrialized countries with economies and governments similar to our own.

The Global Gender Gap Index[28] benchmarks national gender gaps on economic, political, education, and health-based criteria. We rank 23rd, just behind Burundi (22) and just ahead of Australia (24). And we're WAY behind the top four - Iceland, Finland, Norway and Sweden. What's more, were not getting better. We've been dropping for the past few years – we were 22nd in 2012 and 17th in 2011. On one of the issues that polls highest with American women, pay equity, we sink even further to 67th, right below Yemen. (We did beat out Saudi Arabia at 111th, no doubt because women in the U.S. are allowed to drive to work.)

But it's not all bad – our score is a mixed bag. We're number six in Economic Participation and Opportunity, and number one in Educational Attainment. But then we drop to 33rd in Health and Survival, and we're way down at 60th in Political Leadership.

In this chapter you will find a wealth of facts. They may look like dry statistics, but they are eye-opening. You can scan them now, or refer back as you read chapters on specific issues (some are repeated in issue chapters, but not all).

Constitutional Rights:

- Women do not have equal rights with men under the United States Constitution.

- Only 21 U.S. states have equal rights guarantees in their constitutions.

- Most individual countries in Europe have formalized equal rights for women in their constitutions, and equal rights are included in the Treaty of Lisbon, which is tantamount to a European Union constitution.

- Women have had equal constitutional rights in Japan since 1946, and the constitutions of many other countries worldwide declare women as legal equals to men.

- Since the 1990s, new constitutions in countries like Iraq, Mozambique, Namibia, Ethiopia, Malawi, Uganda, South Africa, Rwanda, Burundi, and Swaziland have included non-discrimination or equality provisions, prohibiting customary practices if they undermine the dignity, welfare or status of women.[29]

Political participation:

- In November 2013 the U.S. was tied with Albania at 79th in the world in the number of women in Congress (down from 69th in 2011), with 17.9 percent of the House of Representatives and 20 percent of the Senate. By contrast, among developed countries, Sweden ranked the highest, with women making up 44.7 percent in Parliament.[30]

- There are 125 countries where political quotas for women have been implemented in constitutions, regulations and laws, or where political parties have implemented their own internal quotas[31] – but not in the United States.

- The United States has never had a female president, vice president, chief justice, or Senate majority leader. The first female speaker of the House of Representatives was elected in 2006. In the 20th century, there were 46 female prime ministers or presidents in other countries. As of January 2014 there were 8 sitting female presidents and 10 female prime ministers worldwide.[32]

- Women are the majority in the United States, and outnumber men in voter registration and voter turnout. Fifty-five percent of voters in the 2012 presidential election were female, with women's turnout exceeding that of men by 4 percent.[33]

Earnings, Pay Gap:

- According to U.S. Bureau of Labor Statistics figures for full-time, year-round workers, the ratio of women's median annual earnings in 2012 (latest available) were 76.5 percent of men's for full-time/year-round work. That means the gender wage gap is 23.5 percent. When compared to white men (the highest earning group) African American women come in at 64.5 percent of men's earnings, and for Native American women the percentage is 60 cents. Latinas are at the bottom with only 54.1 percent. The gender wage gap has stayed essentially unchanged since 2001. In the previous decade, between 1991 and 2000, it closed by almost four percentage points, and in the decade prior to that, 1981 to 1990, by over ten percentage points. Progress is clearly stalled. If the pace of change in the annual earnings ratio continues at the same rate as it has since 1960, it will take another 45 years, until 2058, for men and women to reach parity.[34] By contrast, women in Australia, Belgium, Italy and Sweden reached 80 percent as early as 2003.[35] According to the 2013 Global Gender Gap Report, 66 countries rank above the U.S. in wage equality.[36]

- The poverty rate among women climbed to 14.5 percent in 2010 from 13.9 percent in 2009, the highest rate in 17 years. It remained at the same level through 2012. Men's poverty rate was lower, at 11.2 percent.[37]
- Adult women are nearly two-thirds of all U.S. minimum-wage workers. At the current $7.25 an hour, a full-time minimum-wage worker taking no vacation will earn just $15,080 a year. For tipped workers like waitresses and nail salon workers -- a group that is overwhelmingly female -- the federal minimum wage is a shockingly low $2.13 an hour.[38]

Workplace protection:

- Employers in the United States are prohibited by Title VII of the 1964 Civil Rights Act from discriminating on the basis of sex – but the burden of proof falls on the worker.

- Women (and men) in the U.S. have no legal right to sick leave. This puts us in stark contrast to other nations –145 countries provide for paid sick leave. Usually, provisions include both time for leave and wage replacement during sickness, which vary between lump sums and up to 100 percent of wages.[39]
- There is no legal right in the U.S. for paid maternity or paternity leave. By way of comparison, out of 167 nations cited in a United Nations 2010 report, 162 had some form of paid maternity leave, putting the United States in the company of Lesotho, Papua New Guinea and Swaziland.[40]
- While U.S. law guarantees 12 weeks of *unpaid* family leave for birth, adoption, or family illness, we lag behind other countries in paid family benefits. Ninety-eight of the 168 other countries that have guaranteed paid maternity leave offer 14 or more weeks off with pay, 66 provide paid paternal leave, and 37 ensure paid leave for illness of a child.[41]

Business:

- One-half of all U.S. workers are women, and mothers are the primary breadwinners or co-breadwinners in two-thirds of American families.[42] Despite this, there are a mere 23 women heading Fortune 500 companies in the U.S. – just 4.6 percent (and that was touted in the press as a record high!). In 2013 women held 16.9 percent of Fortune 500 board seats, 10 percent had *no* women on their boards, and women of color held only 3.2 percent, according to women's issues research group Catalyst.[43]

- Even though the number of women business owners is growing at twice the rate of other businesses, a large gap still exists in the share of federal dollars going to contracts with women-owned businesses. In the fiscal year ending September 2013, federal contracting went down for women-owned businesses as a share of all contracts, continued to fall short of the government's goal (a mere 5 percent set-aside, which was established *twenty years* ago), resulting in a several billion dollar shortfall. [44]

  In contrast, the six top recipients of federal contracts are Lockheed Martin, Boeing, Northrop Grumman, General Dynamics, Raytheon, and United Technologies. Collectively, they scoop up close to a quarter of all federal procurement spending, totaling almost $400 billion in the period between October 2006 and November 2011 alone.[45]

Higher Education/ Professions:

- Women now outnumber men in college enrollments, but they remain segregated by college major. Ninety-seven percent of early childhood education majors, with a median wage of $36,000, are women. Women also dominate such low-wage fields as medical assisting, student counseling, and other education fields. But in high-paying fields like mechanical ($80,000), electrical ($85,000), and marine ($82,000) engineering, more than 90 percent of students are male.[46]
- Women achieve slightly higher GPAs than men in every college major, including engineering, computer science, science and mathematics.

Despite the fact that women outperform men in school, pay gaps persist.[47]

- In the 20 years since 1991, the proportion of women in engineering has increased, although it still remains below 20 percent. Women's participation in computer sciences has increased considerably at the doctoral level (still below 30 percent) but has declined at the bachelor's level to under 20 percent.[48]
- Female enrollment in undergraduate business programs is 41 percent, but drops to just over a third at the MBA level.[49] According to the Graduate Management Admission Council, female students are more likely than men to carry educational debt prior to business school, making it a less affordable option for them than for men.
- Women's enrollment at law schools overall has been on a steady decline since 2002, when women constituted about 49.05 percent of law students. The American Bar Association's reports that ten years later women made up about 47 percent of all first-year law students and about the same percentage of law school graduates.[50] The all-time high was in 1993, when women's enrollment bumped just above 50 percent.[51]
- The percentage of female medical school students has declined from a high of 50 percent in 2003 to 46 percent in 2012.[52] The gender pay gap is growing, and exists even after accounting for such differences as medical specialty, hours worked, and practice type.[53]

Child care:

- U.S. parents pay almost all of their child care costs without state or federal assistance, amounting to a large portion of household income. The Organisation for Economic Co-operation and Development estimates that the cost of center-based care for two children in the U.S. could amount to as much as 37 percent of a single parent's income – a considerably larger portion than in almost all other countries.[54]
- Child care tends to be the first or second-largest household expenditure, running from $5,574 to $16,430 per child per year. According to the latest figures available, the average annual cost for an infant in center-based care was higher than a year's tuition and fees at a four-year public college in every region of the U.S.[55]
- Many countries in Europe have some form of national child care. For example, almost 100 percent of French three-, four-, and five-year-olds are enrolled in the full-day, free *écoles maternelles*; all are part of the same national system, with the same curriculum, staffed by teachers paid good wages by the same national ministry.[56]
- Most public child care funding in the U.S. goes to poor families – but according to the U.S. Department of Health and Human Services, funding levels for the Child Care and Development Block Grant provided for only one out of 10 eligible children even before the recession.[57]
- The passage of the American Recovery and Reinvestment Act (generally known as the stimulus package) passed in February 2009 provided an additional $2 billion in funding for the

Child Care and Development Block Grant to states. But according to news reports, by 2011 the money had all but dried up, and states were cutting back by as much as 30 percent.[58]

Health:

- Almost one in five women in the U.S. lacked health insurance in 2009 before passage of the Affordable Care Act (ACA). The numbers were miserable when broken down by race: 25 percent of African American women were without insurance, 30.5 percent of Native American women, and a whopping 40 percent of Hispanic women were not covered.[59] Due to the slow start of ACA enrollment, no updated numbers were available as of January 2014. Virtually every country in Europe has universal health care, as do Australia, Canada, and Japan.
- According to Amnesty International, the USA spends more than any other country on health care, and more on maternal health than any other type of hospital care. Despite this, women in the USA have a higher risk of dying of pregnancy-related complications than those in 49 other countries, including Kuwait, Bulgaria, and South Korea. African-American women are nearly four times more likely to die of pregnancy-related complications than white women. These rates and disparities have not improved in more than 20 years.[60]
- The most recent survey found that 88 percent of all U.S. counties have no identifiable abortion provider. In non-metropolitan areas, the figure rises to 97 percent.[61]

Long-term Care:

- Women are the primary recipients of long-term care services. That's because older women tend to have chronic health problems and consequently require more long-term care services than men, whose illnesses tend to be acute and short-term.[62]
- The majority of *unpaid* family caregivers are women providing assistance to individuals, usually relatives, who need long-term care. Sixty percent are wives of disabled, often older, husbands. Most of these women are 65 and older, and many are facing their own aging, physical illnesses, or financial burdens.[63]
- More than 90 percent of *paid* long-term care workers in the United States are female –about half are racial or ethnic minorities. Paid caregivers provide a remarkable array of services, while generally receiving low wages ($10 per hour or less) and few employee benefits.[64]
- In the U.S., there are few government resources for long-term care of the elderly, except for some elderly poor. Long-term and elder care varies in other countries, but many, such as Japan and the Netherlands, provide for assistance regardless of income. In Canada, 8 of the 10 provinces now provide some form of long-term care coverage for all citizens.[65]
- The Affordable Care Act bars sex discrimination in health insurance plans, but the long-term care industry has long maintained that the rules barring insurers from charging women more than men don't apply to them. The nation's largest long-term care insurer announced in 2013 that it would charge women between 20 and 40 percent more per month. Industry experts predicted the practice

would become a trend – a prediction that has proven true. The National Women's Law Center filed federal complaints charging sex discrimination in January 2014.[66]

Social Security Benefits:

- In the United States, both women and men are eligible for Social Security at age 62 (reduced lifetime benefit) or 66 (full lifetime benefit). Benefits are based on earnings of the worker (or if married, earnings of the spouse if the spouse's income is higher). There is no credit for time out of the workforce for caregiving.
- In the United Kingdom, the number of work years needed for a full pension is reduced if the insured is caring for a child or an elderly or disabled relative.[67]
- In France, pensioners are granted a child-rearing supplement equal to 10 percent of the pension if the insured has reared at least three children.[68]

Violence:

- According to the U.S. Department of Justice in 2013:
  - 25 percent of U.S. women have experienced domestic violence
  - 85 percent of domestic violence victims are female
  - Over 2 million women are assaulted by men each year
- The U.S. ranks fourth among developed countries in the number of rapes per thousand population.[69] The vast majority of victims are female.

- Women are five times more likely to be victims of domestic violence than men, and three times more likely to be murdered by an intimate partner.[70] Females are more than four times likelier to be sexually assaulted or raped, and black women are raped and murdered at higher rates than whites.[71]

International Treaties Affecting Women:

- The United States is the only industrialized country that has not ratified the international bill of rights for women, called The Convention on the Elimination of All Forms of Discrimination against Women (CEDAW). By not ratifying, the U.S. is in the company of countries like Iran, Sudan, and Somalia. The treaty must be ratified by the Senate. President Obama and Secretaries of State Clinton and Kerry have urged ratification.
- The Convention on the Rights of the Child is the most widely accepted human rights treaty. Of all the United Nations member states, only the United States and the collapsed states of Somalia and South Sudan have not ratified it. Although signed by the Clinton administration, the treaty has never been submitted to the Senate for consideration. The Obama administration has said that it intends to submit the treaty to the Senate, but with no firm timeline.[72]
- The Beijing Platform for Action, adopted in 1995 by the U.N. Fourth World Conference on Women, recognizes that women and children are particularly affected by the indiscriminate use of landmines. In December 1997, the treaty's banning of antipersonnel mines was signed by 122 countries.

Seventeen years later, in 2014, more than 80 percent of the world's states had ratified the treaty, including most members of NATO. Only 35 countries have not yet joined – including the only two in the western hemisphere, the United States and Cuba.[73]

◊ FIVE ◊

What *Do* Women Want? What *Are* We Thinking?

Women and men often think alike, but when it comes to politics and priorities, the book title *Men are from Mars, Women are from Venus* is often accurate. That's because women's life experiences are different, and that causes them to see things in a different way than men. G u n control is a good example. When asked about how available guns should be, men might think of hunting, "cleaning up Dodge City," or defending their households. Women think of getting raped at gunpoint or their children getting shot at school – a basic difference in point of view.

Even when women and men are on the same page, women may feel more strongly about an issue; e.g., both rate Medicare solvency high on the list of priorities, but women are more passionate about it. And women and men often rank issues differently when it comes to what is most important.

We've already seen how gender differences play out in the voting booth. Looking at what women and men tell pollsters is one way to get behind the voting numbers, to see what drives the gender gap. It's also a way to get a good idea of the values and opinions that shape priorities, and how women and men might view the issues that should be addressed by elected officials and candidates.

How Do We Rate National Priorities?

How people rate national priorities depends on a number of factors, including what the news media and candidates are hammering on at the time of a given poll, how the questions are asked, and what is included in lists of priorities that they are asked to rate. It is significant that asking people an open-ended question such as, "What do you think is the most important issue facing the country?" produces quite different answers than when people are presented with a "laundry list" and asked to rate each one in importance.

Nevertheless, we can tell from polls what is on the radar at any given moment, and some issues rate high in both types of polls.

The Economy

Women's concerns about the economy pre-date the Great Recession, going back at least as far as the 2006 elections. An election-eve poll conducted by Lake Research Partners for Ms magazine and the Women Donors Network asked people to assign a number of 0 (very low priority) to 10 (very high priority) to the several economic issues:[74]

Percent Rating "10" in Importance

Issue	Men	Women	Gender Gap
Economy/jobs	30	41	11
Social security & retirement	31	40	9
Raising minimum wage	22	31	9
Paid sick leave	10	16	6

On election eve in 2008, jobs and the economy were named the highest priority by very high percentages of both women and men in a survey by the Pew Research Center for People and the Press on top priorities for their upcoming votes. In 2011, as the jobless rate continued to hover above 9 percent, strengthening the economy was again rated highest priority overall by respondents, with no appreciable gender gaps.[75] By election season in 2012, the jobless rate had improved, and once again women's priorities diverged from those of men. When asked an open-ended question on what issues were most important, 39 percent of women named abortion first, followed by jobs (19 percent), healthcare (18 percent) and the economy (16 percent). By contrast, abortion didn't make the men's list at all, with 75 percent of them naming either the economy or the federal budget deficit as most important.[76]

The Worry Quotient

Before the recession had hit with full force in 2008, pollsters asked both women and men about national economic conditions and personal financial situations. Though very few people rated the economy "excellent" overall, twice as many men did so as women, producing a significant 6 point gender gap. Women also rated their personal financial situations worse than men.[77]

Results can be found on the following page.

National Economic Conditions	Male	Female	Gender Gap
Excellent	4%	2%	-2
Good	25%	21%	-4
Excellent/Good combined	29%	23%	-6 **
Only fair	42%	47%	-5
Poor	29%	28 %	-1

Personal Financial Situation	Male	Female	Gender Gap
Excellent	12%	8%	-4 **
Good	40%	39%	-1
Only fair	31%	37%	-6
Poor	15%	15%	–

**Statistically significant gender gaps

In a separate poll from the National Women's Law Center, women were much more likely to feel pessimistic about their economic futures. Some 59 percent were worried about reaching their economic and financial goals over the next five years, as compared to 46 percent of men. Many women felt they were losing ground economically. This was especially true for those at lower income levels (75 percent said they were falling behind), women with a high school degree or less education (68 percent falling behind). African-American women feel particularly vulnerable (70 percent behind).[78]

These findings were underscored again in 2011 when 71 percent of women reported still feeling the effects of the recession, as compared to 65 percent of men. Low income women, single mothers, and Latinas reported being particularly hard hit.[79]

Beyond the Economy

In 2008, just as they had before the 2006 elections, far more women than men (78 vs. 63 percent) named the Iraq War as one of their highest concerns, producing the second highest gender gap in voting priorities. Abortion produced the highest gender gap of all – a whopping 16 percent, with just under half of women naming it as a top priority compared with a third of men. Statistically significant gender gaps also emerged on other issues. A higher percentage of women (63 percent) vs. men (54 percent) rated reducing health care costs as a high priority. Women and men are about equally likely to rate energy, trade policy, immigration, and gay marriage as very important.

Priorities had shifted by 2012, on the eve of the presidential election. Perhaps because the candidates differed markedly on abortion, and women's job gains were stronger than those of men in the wake of the recession, women were more than twice as likely to name abortion than economic issues.

What do you consider the most important issue for women in this election?

Among female registered voters

	%
Abortion	39
Jobs	19
Healthcare	18
The economy	16
Equal rights/pay/opportunity	15
Government regulation	3
Education	2
Medicare/Care for the elderly	2
Social Security	2
Taxes	1

What do you consider the most important issue for men in this election?
Among male registered voters

	%
Jobs	38
The economy	37
Federal budget deficit/Balanced budget	10
Healthcare	10
Taxes	6
Government regulation	4
Defense/National security	4
Medicare/Care for the elderly	3
Foreign policy/International affairs	2
Honesty/Integrity	2

Asked of registered voters in 12 key swing states
Oct. 5-11, 2012

GALLUP

Are Women (and Men) Feminists? Are You?

The answer to this question seems to depend on whether women are asked about the *word* "feminist," or the *dictionary definition* of a feminist. When asked if they are feminists with no explanation – "Do you consider yourself a feminist?" – only about a fourth of women say yes. But when asked the question this way – "A feminist is someone who believes in social, political, and economic equality of the sexes. Do you think of yourself as a feminist or not?" – 65 percent of women identify as feminists, and so do 58 percent of men.[80]

When asked to rate the importance of women's equality from a list of issues for Congress to address after the 2006 elections, 34 percent of women and 26 percent of men rated it a top priority.[81] Even when asked an open-ended question (chart above) about the most important issues in the 2012 elections, 15 percent of women named equal rights/pay/opportunity, while none of the men did so.

Women believe strongly that the women's movement has made their lives better, with 65 percent saying agreeing. Men are about evenly divided on the question – maybe because some of them now have to wash more dishes. When asked *how* the women's movement has made their lives better, women cite better jobs, more choices, better pay, and more legal equality. Fifty-one percent of working women think there is still a need for a strong women's movement, compared to 39 percent of women not employed outside the home.[82]

Perhaps more women would think there is still a need for a strong women's movement if they realized that women do not have equal rights in the U.S. Constitution (see chapter 22). In the most recent poll conducted on equal rights between women and men, 97 percent of Americans, regardless of their sex, age, race, geographic region, or other demographic category, said they believed that male and female citizens should have equal rights.[83] In an earlier poll, 88 percent stated that the U.S. Constitution should make it clear that they are so entitled. (There is a gender gap on this, with 85 percent of men and 91 percent of women saying the Constitution should be clear on equal rights.) However, nearly three out of four Americans – 69 percent of women and over 75 percent of men – assume that the Constitution *already* includes that guarantee – and they're all wrong.[84]

While a strong majority of Americans overall (63 percent) agree that the U.S. still has a long way to go to reach complete gender quality, the total hides a huge gender gap. Three-quarters of women (74 percent) agree, just over half of men (52 percent) do. A similar situation is found regarding work. Over half of Americans overall (52 percent) say most employers are willing make the conditions of work flexible enough to help women with families who want to go to work. Again, the number hides a gender difference, as three in five men (60 percent) agree with this compared to less than half of women (46 percent).[85]

At substantially higher rates than men on every measure, women strongly support policies aimed at providing women with equal opportunities. Large majorities of women say that the following policies are extremely or very important for Congress and the administration to take up (more than half the men also strongly support these policies, just not by as large a majority):

- Provide women with the legal protections they need to get equal pay (77 percent of women).
- Make sure there are effective safeguards against discrimination in the workplace, including protections from sexual harassment (72 percent of women).

Women are also stronger than men in recognizing that there is still work to be done to pave the way for younger generations of women. Three in five women (compared with less than half of men) believe that we must do more to ensure that young women are protected from sexual harassment in schools, given equal opportunity in sports and education, and provided equal access to all career options.[86]

Women (and Men) Are Pro-Choice

Public divisions over access to abortion are long-standing, and have changed only slightly over the past two decades. Both women and men in the U.S. are pro-choice, with only small gender differences. Neither women nor men want *Roe v. Wade* overturned. Over 60 percent in both cases say the law should stay the same, and the great majority of those report feeling strongly about it.[87] Extremely large majorities (80 percent or above) of both sexes say abortion should be legal to save a woman's life or health, and in cases of rape or incest.[88]

In a poll conducted by Quinnipiac University in July 2013, 60 percent of women said abortion should be legal in all or most cases, and 54 percent of men agreed. This represents an increase in the numbers since 2010. However, when asked if they would rather have abortion legal without restriction for up to 20 weeks or 24 weeks as embodied in *Roe v. Wade*, large majorities of both women and men favored 20 weeks.[89]

In contrast, voter action over almost a decade indicates that people do not want more restrictions. In 2006, all state referenda restricting abortion were defeated, as were abortion-restriction ballot measures in California, Colorado and South Dakota in 2008. In 2010, parental notification was approved in Alaska, but a constitutional amendment declaring "personhood" at conception was once again defeated in Colorado. Voters also rejected a Mississippi "personhood" initiative, which would have granted citizenship to fertilized eggs. In 2013 the first city level referendum in the nation making abortion illegal after 20 weeks was soundly defeated by voters in Albuquerque, New Mexico.

There are gender gaps between women and men on abortion, and there are also divisions among women. Both pro-choice and anti-choice women have expressed significantly stronger feelings about the issue than men, and much more often said it could be a factor in their vote.

Not so for men. In the most recent polls available on whether abortion would influence their votes, nearly six in ten men who oppose further abortion restrictions nevertheless said they would vote for a candidate who disagrees with them on this matter, if they shared views with the candidate on most other issues.

There also is a sizable gender gap in abortion attitudes among younger adults. Women age 18 to 24 oppose further limits on abortion access by a wide margin (63 percent oppose -34 percent favor). But young men are less supportive of access to abortion – 50 percent of those polled in 2013 opposed more abortion restrictions, while 45 percent were in favor.[90] One unsettling poll in 2014 found that among adults under 30 years old, only 44 percent know that *Roe v. Wade* was a decision about abortion. Younger adults also are less likely to view abortion as an important issue: 62 percent of Americans ages 18-29 say it is "not that important" compared with other issues.[91] Perhaps this is because abortion has been legal all their lives, and they do not realize the threat to abortion rights.

In terms of activism, women seeking more restrictions on abortion have been somewhat more active. They stand out as one of the groups most engaged in the debate, with 21 percent reporting that they have actively expressed their views through donations, activities or letter writing in the previous year. Only 13 percent of women who opposed abortion restrictions had taken similar steps. (These results were reported before the House passed restrictions on abortion coverage in the proposed health care overhaul in November, 2009. Both sides of the debate reported surges in activism after that vote.) On both sides of the issue, men are less likely to have done anything to express their views.[92]

Women are More Supportive of Gay and Lesbian Rights

After many years of advocacy, support for gay marriage reached majority support in the U.S. in 2011.[93] However, there are still gender gaps on specifics. In 2013 when asked if they would vote to make gay marriage legal in all 50 states, 56 percent of women said yes, while only 48 percent of men did so.[94] Support for civil unions also stands at an all time high, with 60 percent of women and 54 percent of men favoring allowing gay and lesbian couples to enter into legal agreements with one another, giving them many of the same rights as married couples.[95]

When women and men were asked about support for allowing gay and lesbian adoption, 56 percent of women favored, half of men agreed. Both groups were much more favorable than they were a decade earlier, when 43 percent of women and 33 percent of men were in support. Similarly, women are more supportive of allowing gays to serve openly in the military: sixty-one percent of women are in favor, compared to 50 percent of men.[96]

There are gender gaps on other social issues, such as the death penalty, gun control, and women in the military. We'll take up some of these in later chapters.

◊ SIX ◊

Politicians With Forked Tongues: "Beware the False Prophets"

We know that women are the majority of voters, and can control any election. And we've seen what women care about. But do candidates and parties listen? Too often the answer is "no."

Legislators, candidates and parties, with a good deal of help from the media, are notorious for turning the debate away from issues people are most concerned about or emphasizing topics that stir up emotional reactions, oftentimes while misrepresenting the facts.

False prophet politicians concentrate on two categories: wedge issues and non-issues. Wedge issues are so-called "hot button" social issues, calculated to divide voters along false fault lines. They are almost always presented simplistically or outright dishonestly. Non-issues are those that actually affect only a small fraction of Americans, and either fall extremely low on the list of priorities for voters, or do not register all.

Both categories could also be called "bait and switch" issues, because candidates and parties talk a lot about them during the campaigns but do nothing once elected. (If they actually solved the "problem" they would not have the issue to run on again next time.) I've given some examples below. When you hear these come up, ask why they are talking about important issues in a misleading and divisive way, or why they seem obsessed with the non-issues while ignoring problems women really care about.

Wedge Issues

Banning Abortion: Conservative and religious right candidates often run with "ending abortion" as their number one priority, and say that's what the country wants. They present "abortion on demand" as a grave national problem, even though recent events indicate the opposite is true – access to abortion is more restricted now than it has been in the last 40 years, and the right to abortion is more threatened than at any time since it became legal in 1973 (see chapter 12).

As for the electorate, polls consistently show that the overwhelming majority of Americans do *not* want to ban abortion. The percentage who want abortion to be completely illegal varies between 15 percent and 20 percent, and the numbers have not changed since Gallup started tracking this issue in 1975.[97] And after several years when neither gender ranked abortion as one of their top five issues overall, prior to the 2012 election the issue emerged as women's primary concern in the 12 key swing states. When women were asked an open-ended question about what they considered the most important issue in the election, a whopping 39 percent rated it number one, no doubt because attacks on both abortion and birth control had ramped up in the preceding four years. Tellingly, abortion did not make the list of the 10 most important issues for men.[98]

Constitutional ban on gay marriage: Whether or not gay Americans should be able to marry or form same-sex legal unions first emerged as a major wedge issue in the 2002 elections, with conservative candidates stumping for a constitutional ban. President Bush took up the call in his State of the Union address of 2004.

National polls in 2011 showed majority support for gay marriage for the first time (53 percent - 45 percent), though there were sharp divisions between the parties. Only 28 percent of Republicans supported legalization, as opposed to 69 percent of Democrats and 59 percent of Independents.[99] Past polls have shown that women support gay marriage in greater numbers than men[100], and while fewer people oppose civil unions overall, there is a larger gender gap; women are considerably more inclined to support civil unions than men (60 percent-54 percent).[101]

And no poll has shown that a federal anti-gay amendment has anywhere near the level of support needed to secure two-thirds approval in both houses of Congress and ratification by three-quarters of the states.[102] In fact, the tide has definitely turned, not only on gay marriage but on other issues such as gay adoption and civil unions (see chapter 20). In 2013, a nationwide poll showed the majority of adults favored legalizing gay marriage in all 50 states, with women in favor outnumbering men by 8 percentage points.[103]

In any case, banning gay marriage through a constitutional amendment is extremely low on the priority list of most pressing issues facing the country – it doesn't make the list at all when pollsters ask the open-ended question, "What do you think is the most important problem facing this country today?"[104]

When the item "social issues such as abortion and gay marriage" is specifically included in a list of desirable top priorities for the federal government, only 2 percent choose that option.[105]

Deporting Immigrants: It is estimated that there are over 11 million illegal immigrants in the U.S. today, and illegal immigrants make up about 5 percent of the workforce.[106] Research has shown that politicians with the fewest immigrants in their states (Arizona the exception) are the most prone to "grandstand" on the issue with punitive anti-immigration votes, since they don't actually have to deal with it.[107]

Conservative candidates often hold that Americans want a "get-tough and get-tough-only" approach, but *public opinion research does not back them up*. The National Immigration Forum, after a compilation and analysis of polls from a number of sources such as *Time Magazine* and the Associated Press, concluded that the public wants a much less punitive solution, with "strong support for a more intelligent and realistic approach to controlling immigration, including enhanced border security, workplace and employer enforcement, earned legalization for undocumented immigrants with a path to citizenship, and expanded visas for future immigrant workers and families."

A consistent and solid majority of Americans – 63 percent – crossing party and religious lines, favors legislation to create a pathway to citizenship for immigrants living in the United States illegally, while only 14 percent support legal residency with no option for citizenship. Sixty percent of Republicans, 57 percent of independents and 73 percent of Democrats favor a pathway to citizenship. Only 18 percent favor a tough enforcement strategy of identifying and deporting undocumented immigrants.[108]

People on both sides of the aisle agree that our immigration policies are dysfunctional. However, debate continues over how to solve the illegal immigration problem, since the labor provided by these individuals is needed in many states. Proposals range from creating programs whereby those in the country illegally can start on a path to citizenship (with variations on how to accomplish this), to extremely unrealistic plans for deporting them all wholesale, asking them to "self deport," as candidate Mitt Romney suggested in the 2012 presidential race, using drones developed for the Iraq war, and building a fence along the entire 1,933-mile U.S.-Mexico border. (One wag asked how we can find 11 million people and deport them when we couldn't get one million out of New Orleans after Katrina, and we knew where *they* were.)

The U.S. Senate passed an immigration bill in 2013 which included completion of 700 miles of fencing along the border, and instituting a path to citizenship after the fence and other security measures are completed. However, the House leadership has strongly indicated that no action will be taken in the House prior to the 2014 elections, and some predict it will take even longer. There is also doubt that a path to citizenship will be part of any eventual House bill.

While most Americans have somewhat liberal opinions on how to solve our immigration problems, few rank it a priority for the country above other issues. When asked open-ended questions about priorities for the country or Congress, or what they consider the most important issues facing the country, the percentage of polling respondents naming immigration consistently varies between zero and 3 percent.[109]

Gun Control: Gun control is another area where politicians like to posture, and posturing has ramped up in the wake of mass shootings such as those in Aurora, Colorado and Newtown, Connecticut (the December 2012 mass shooting of 20 elementary school students and six adult staff members). Many will falsely assert that the public wants *less* gun control, saying voters are fearful of losing their right to tote guns everywhere from churches to grocery stores to national parks.

Newtown changed the debate. According to a March, 2013 issue brief – co-authored by a bipartisan team of pollsters who have each conducted public-opinion research on attitudes toward guns in recent years, there are four key points:

- The Newtown shooting had a greater impact on public opinion about guns than any other event in the past two decades—and led to a clear rise in public support for stronger gun laws.

- There is near unanimous support for universal background checks and clear majority support for high-capacity magazine and assault-weapons bans.

- There is almost as much support for stronger gun laws among gun owners as among the general public.

- There are large gender gaps in views on guns and violence.

In the wake of Newtown, four major polls each show a double-digit gender gap in support of stronger gun laws, with approximately 6 in 10 women supporting such a change. Both Pew and Gallup tracking suggest that this gender gap dates back to the 1990s.

The gap pervades every proposal tested. Support for a ban on assault weapons and high-capacity magazines runs 16 points and 15 points higher, respectively, among women than it does among men. In fact, majorities of women support every single specific stronger gun law tested, aside from arming teachers. And it is not true among women that the National Rifle Association is a well-liked organization. While men are slightly favorable toward the "NRA leadership," women are unfavorable by a nearly 2-1 ratio.[110]

But whether it is a top issue for voters is another matter, perhaps because they don't believe anything can be done, since even massacres like Newtown have not moved Congress to take action. When people were asked to name their most important issues in open-ended questions in a number of general polls between 2012-2014, gun control never made the list. When "gun policy" was presented in a laundry list of concerns, it rose above 3 percent only once, when it garnered 15 percent of respondents a month after the Newtown shooting.[111]

Non-Issues

Non-issues are those that are for all practical purposes "manufactured" by politicians. These non-issues usually sound good if presented in a simplistic (and often dishonest) way. They often represent a special interest group (e.g. corporations or the Catholic church) but are presented as a grave problem for ordinary citizens. Some may also affect only a tiny fraction of Americans, but are made to sound like all of society is threatened by them.

Death tax: This is a term false prophet politicians use to describe the estate or inheritance tax. Those who grandstand on this issue would have us believe that, because of the estate tax, we are all going to die paupers and be unable to leave any of our hard-earned dollars to our children and grandchildren. In reality, the estate tax is relevant to less than two-tenths of one percent of all U.S. estates.[112] Senator Bernie Sanders (I-VT) put it this way in a twitter post: "99.7 percent of American families will not pay one nickel in an estate tax. This is not a tax on the rich, this is a tax on the very, very, very rich."

The term refers to the federal tax on estates over $10 million for a married couple, or $5 million for an individual (adjusted upward each year for inflation beginning in 2013). But not the whole estate; a family's first 10 million is exempt. So repeal of the estate tax is of no benefit whatsoever to almost all Americans, because they are never going to reach the threshold for the tax in the first place.

While a very few quite wealthy families may indeed have some concern about the estate tax, it *never* gets mentioned by ordinary Americans when talking about their concerns and priorities – particularly not by women.

Tort Reform: The term "tort reform" is used as shorthand for limiting the ability of individuals to bring lawsuits for medical malpractice, nursing home abuse, harm from tainted or unsafe products, personal injury at unsafe workplaces, insurance abuse, and other wrongs, and to limit awards when such suits are successful.

Conservative think tanks and politicians have relentlessly pushed the idea that U.S. courts are hopelessly clogged because of "frivolous lawsuits," and that the awards are outrageously unfair to business.[113] In fact, the majority of lawsuits are filed by businesses against one another and do not originate with individuals.

An extensive poll of likely 2008 voters conducted by Peter D. Hart Associates found that "Americans are deeply worried about their nation's future, and corporate misconduct is a major source of their anxiety." The public is far more concerned with corporate abuse of workers and the public, than with abuse of the courts by individuals. This was borne out in the fall of 2011 when spontaneous demonstrations broke out on Wall Street and then spread nationwide to protest corporate power.

Voters also considered corporate misconduct much more important than "lawsuit abuse." Trial lawyers making too much money and victims getting too much award money ranked at the bottom of a list of concerns, behind 11 examples of corporate misconduct.[114] Neither "tort reform" or "lawsuit abuse" is mentioned at all when people are asked to name their top concerns with open-ended questions about their own priorities, or priorities the government ought to address.[115]

Religious Freedom: "Religious freedom" has cropped up as a false issue since passage of the Affordable Care Act. The ACA mandates coverage of birth control without co-pays in employer insurance plans, with some narrow exemptions for churches if birth control is against their core beliefs. But that is not good enough for the Catholic church or some corporate employers such as Hobby Lobby. Both have filed lawsuits seeking much broader exemptions from the requirement.

The U.S. Conference of Catholic Bishops wants to broaden the exemption to include church-affiliated institutions such as hospitals, child-care centers, and universities. Hobby Lobby and some other for-profit corporations want to exempt themselves. As of early 2014, these suits were pending before the U.S. Supreme Court. If successful, it could mean that any employer could refuse to cover any medical procedure on the grounds of the company's religious beliefs. Never mind that no one has ever seen a corporation, hospital, or university in church, nor do these organizations get down on their knees and pray.

Another more recent use of the "religious freedom" argument for exemption from the law has been used by businesses that do not want to serve gay people. The Arizona legislature passed such a law in 2014 allowing businesses to refuse service to gays and lesbians if it went against the beliefs of the business. After a national outcry and threats of business boycotts (and even the threat of moving the 2015 Super Bowl out of the state), the measure was vetoed by conservative Republican Governor Jan Brewer.

Deficit/Debt "Crisis": For the past few years, since early in the Great Recession in 2008, conservative politicians have been warning that yearly deficit spending and the ensuing national debt were going to bankrupt the country and every individual in it. Doomsday scenarios have been painted regularly, culminating in a Fall 2013 government shutdown forced by Republicans because they didn't want to raise the debt ceiling – the amount the U.S. is allowed to borrow to pay bills already incurred. For almost all of our history, the debt ceiling was routinely raised with bipartisan votes and no fanfare. But with the rise of the Tea Party wing of the Republican party, the vote is now routinely held hostage in an effort to force cuts to social programs such as Medicare, Social Security, and Medicaid, always accompanied by rhetoric about the debt "crisis."

Though deficits increase in bad times due to lower tax revenues and increased spending on unemployment and stimulus measures, there is no threat to the economy. In fact, according to leading economists like Nobel Prize winner and *New York Times* columnist Paul Krugman, deficit spending can improve ailing economies, and the U.S. should actually have more of it until the economy fully recovers from the deepest crisis we've seen since the Great Depression.[116] But expert opinion doesn't halt the grandstanding. After all, if you can get people worrying about a non-existent "crisis," like the deficit, maybe they won't notice that you aren't doing anything about a still too-high unemployment rate and a minimum wage that hasn't been raised in a decade.

The bottom line? Elected officials and candidates should not be allowed to get away with grandstanding on wedge issues, or constantly harping on non-issues, to the exclusion of pressing national problems.

We've all heard the expression "buyer beware." You are the political buyer. Beware of false prophets.

◊ SEVEN ◊

Your Money: The Economy

"It's the economy, stupid!" That was the rallying cry for the Clinton campaign in the 1992 presidential election. It could as well be resurrected today, with the U.S. economy suffering from the effects of a long and painful recession – making it one of the top concerns for women and men alike.

Just what the heck *is* the economy? For most people, *economics* is a word that either scares them or causes their eyes to glaze over.

Economists throw around such terms as *demand curves*, *elasticity*, and *marginal utility* that ordinary humans have no clue about. Because we seldom understand these terms and the economic theories they come from, we are left to sort out the rhetoric of experts (many self-appointed), candidates, and elected officials about what is "best for the economy."

The discussion here won't make it into any economics textbook, and economists would undoubtedly judge it too simplistic, but it will give you an idea of what the arguments are about when various proposals are put forward on how to produce a sound economy. And when you finish this chapter, you will have the background and details necessary to understand what's at stake for women every time decision makers take action to fix what ails the economy, or fail to do so.

The Personal (Economy) is Political

A simple dictionary definition of the economy is this: *the structure of economic life of a country.*

That's the dictionary definition. But for most people, the definition of the "economy" is very personal. If you and your family are doing well – you have a job at a decent wage that allows you to buy the things you need, save for retirement, and educate your kids without being terrified of the future – the economy is pretty good.

On the other hand if you are unemployed, in constant fear of being laid off, or have a job that does not pay enough, can't afford good health insurance, can't pay for gasoline and other basics, much less save any money – then the economy for you is pretty bad, regardless of what is happening on Wall Street.

Measuring How the Economy is Doing

The state of your personal economy depends on how the overall economy in the country is doing. If the national economy is *expanding*, it means there are enough jobs and more are being created, more goods and services are being produced, and people have the money to pay for them.

In an expanding economy, home ownership will be stable or on the upswing. Consumers can not only afford the basics, they will be able to buy extras such as a new television or a weekend vacation. This creates more jobs to produce these goods and services, resulting in more money circulating and continued economic growth.

Conversely, in a *shrinking* economy, job growth slows or employment actually declines, and layoffs will be on the rise. This results in less consumer spending as people tighten their belts in fear of, or in reaction to, job losses. As people buy less, demand goes down, so fewer goods and services are produced, which means lower business revenue and profit – leading to more layoffs and less personal and business investment.

The gross domestic product (GDP), a statistic issued by the Commerce Department, is the official measure of how well the economy is doing. The GDP totals up everything the economy has produced in the quarter, and tells how that figure has changed, on a percentage basis, from the previous quarter. A positive percentage change means the economy is expanding; a negative one means it's shrinking. An annual GDP growth rate of 3 percent or more is considered *robust*.

A *recession* is when there has been a decline in the GDP for two consecutive quarters. When there is a recession, or even talk of one, consumers may become more wary and stop spending – even if nothing has actually changed much in their personal situations. That in turn can contribute to decline.

The Eternal Debate – What Can Government Do? What Should the Government Do?

When the economy slips into a recession or near-recession as it did in early 2008, both political parties get nervous, and propose various "fixes" to get more money into circulation and stop the downward spiral. (It's unclear whether they're feeling the people's pain, or feeling the pain of trying to get elected in a downturn.)

As unemployment goes up and production goes down, there is usually not much disagreement that a stimulus is needed to spur more buying and restore confidence – but there are serious and fundamental disagreements about what kind of fix it should be.

Debate over how to produce a healthy economy goes to the very heart of the liberal/conservative philosophical divide. Conservatives put their faith in the business sector and the wealthy, while liberals and progressives believe government has a more direct role.

Trickle Down, or Trickle Up?

From the day he took office in 2001, President George W. Bush had one solution to virtually every economic problem – tax cuts primarily benefitting the wealthy. His philosophy was a simple-minded version of conservative arguments in general: if corporations and the wealthy individuals who fund them through investments pay lower taxes, they will invest those tax savings in ways that will create jobs, such as building new plants, acquiring new subsidiaries, or expanding product lines. Businesses will direct money to suppliers, contractors, and employees to accomplish these goals. Everyone will have more money to spend and the economy will grow.

This theory has been generally referred to as "trickle-down," or "supply side economics," meaning change made at the top of the wealth pile eventually makes its way to workers at the bottom. (The economist John Kenneth Galbraith noted that "trickle-down economics" had been tried before in the U.S. in the 1890s under the name 'horse and sparrow theory': "if you feed enough oats to the horse, some will pass through to feed the sparrows.") Corollaries are that private enterprise is always better than government spending, and the less government interferes in the "free market" through regulation, the better.

Trickle down sounds reasonable – if you believe the tax cuts for wealthy investors and corporations really will be spent on creating jobs instead of multimillion dollar bonuses for CEOs, fines and legal judgments for various abuses, or fatter dividends for stockholders. As for the expanding facilities and building new plants, that *could* work as advertised – unless the facilities are already in China and the new plants will be in India.

Liberals and progressives believe that putting money in the hands of those that actually need it to live on is a better plan to keep the economy going – because they spend more of what they have instead of just adding it to investment accounts. Low and moderate income people have to spend it all, every month, just to buy the basics.

Those subscribing to this school of thought would *not* replace the private sector, and in fact would agree that stimulating business in ways that actually create jobs is good (e.g. eliminating the tax incentives that cause businesses to move jobs overseas).

Progressives also believe that the government can have a positive influence on economic growth through spending tax dollars. They would create some jobs by repairing infrastructure such as roads and bridges, funding green energy research and development, hiring more teachers, police, and firefighters, and restoring government services that have been cut.

They hold the principle that in a recession, money should be injected into the economy as fast as possible. Even if the trickle down fantasy were to actually work, the "tax breaks for business and the wealthy" scenario would take too long to do any good (see chapter 8).

The Difference Interest Makes

Conservative rhetoric about "intrusive government intervention" notwithstanding, actions taken or not taken by the government have a great deal of influence over the economy.

One such action is controlling interest rates, or how much it costs to borrow money. This is done through the Federal Reserve Bank (generally called the Fed), which can be thought of as a "bank for bankers." To keep the money supply flowing smoothly, the Fed loans money to other banks at a certain interest rate for short-term loans.

This is the *rediscount rate,* often called simply the discount rate.

The discount rate that banks pay to the Fed influences the interest rate they charge their own customers. The discount rate is lowered from time-to-time to stimulate borrowing, or raised to dampen inflation.

As the discount rate goes up, banks have to pay more for money they borrow from the Fed, and in turn they have to charge more to businesses and consumers who borrow from them. That means interest rates on business debt, mortgages, car loans, and credit cards will go up.

When borrowers have to spend more on interest, they are less willing to borrow and buy on credit. So they have less to spend on goods and services. Conversely, if the cost of borrowing is cheap, purchases that are financed effectively cost less, so businesses and consumers are inclined to spend more.

Lower rates and a healthy economy can also increase banks' willingness to lend to businesses and households. This may increase spending, especially by smaller borrowers who have few sources of credit other than banks. In a shrinking economy, the idea behind lowering interest rates is to get both businesses and individuals to be more willing to borrow and spend, thus stimulating economic growth.

Lower interest rates enable businesses to borrow more to buy new equipment, open a new location, or upgrade their facilities. This creates new jobs, and if more people are working they have more money to spend. They in turn pay more taxes, so the government can function without incurring more debt. Lowering interest rates is also thought to instill confidence that "things are going to be all right," arresting downward slides that are triggered by fear or talk of recession.

On the consumer end, low interest rates may induce buyers to buy more goods or buy more expensive things, since the interest rate is a big determinant of the monthly payments on credit cards, mortgages, and car loans.

A quick example: suppose you can afford a $500 per month payment for a new car. With a 10 percent annual interest rate and a three-year loan, you can buy a car costing $18,000. But if interest is only 8 percent, you can go up to $18,500 and add some accessories for the same payment.

This is not necessarily bad, so long as interest rates remain stable. If you buy your car this year at the lower rate and the terms of your loan do not allow the rate to go up, then your rate is "locked in." If interest rates on new car loans go up next year, you won't be affected unless you want to buy another car.

But if interest rates on a loan you've already made are adjustable, and they are raised, the payments may now exceed the amount you budgeted. And you may be in trouble. That is exactly what happened in the case of the sub-prime mortgage crisis that is widely blamed for triggering the recession in 2008.

The Mortgage/Housing Crisis and the Recession – More Women Lost Their Homes

Subprime mortgages are high interest rate loans made to borrowers with low incomes or low credit scores – predominately women ("subprime" refers to the credit status of the borrower, not to the interest rate – which ends up very high). In the years leading up to the crisis and subsequent recession, some lenders marketed subprime loans very aggressively with initial "teaser" interest rates that were low enough for borrowers to afford, but structured to increase greatly after the first few months or first year. Huge mortgages were granted to people with incomes too low to sustain the payments, with assurances that they could refinance the loans or sell at a profit. First time borrowers, those with limited English, and borrowers who did not understand mortgages were often targeted. In many cases house payments *doubled*.

Very large numbers of borrowers could not make the payments, so they defaulted on the loans and lost their homes. Paving the way for the economy to fall into recession, the number of *mortgage defaults through fall 2007 were up 94 percent over the previous year*, with entire neighborhoods virtually abandoned.[117] This in turn affected local and state tax revenues, forcing cuts in public services.

The majority of subprime mortgages went to women. Even though their credit scores were, on average, roughly the same as those of men, they were 32 percent more likely than men to be channeled into high-interest subprime loans. Though this gender gap existed in every income and ethnic group, African-American women were hit especially hard.

Why? Part of the reason may be that women have less wealth than men, increasing the likelihood they were pushed to take these loans.[118] But plain old sex discrimination played a role too. Institutions that buy loans from mortgage companies estimate that up to 50 percent of the subprime loans went to borrowers whose credit was good enough for standard rate loans.[119]

The crisis triggered increased scrutiny by bank regulators, who are supposed to protect consumers from dishonest or predatory lending practices (like Rip Van Winkle, they had been asleep from 2001 to 2007). As scrutiny was stepped up, banks severely tightened their lending practices, not only to consumers but also to businesses, making it much harder for business to obtain loans for expansion and consumers to qualify for credit.[120]

News coverage of the crisis exploded, and people became more pessimistic and curbed spending, and "recession talk" in the media increased greatly. This prompted the Federal Reserve to lower interest rates drastically in January, 2008 to raise confidence and try to put a stop to the slide. But it was not enough to convince people – one month later 61 percent of the public said the economy was suffering through its first recession since 2001.[121]

Stimulus Packages - Women Win, Women Lose

When the economy falls into recession, or is about to, it is generally agreed that a stimulus is needed to stop the downward spiral. Congress, and belatedly the president, knew they had to act. In February, 2008, President George W. Bush signed a stimulus package (see below) in an unsuccessful attempt to arrest the slide.

The Bush Stimulus Package

The fight over the Bush stimulus was emblematic of the different economic priorities of the two major political parties. Democrats wanted to implement one-time tax rebates to working families, expanded unemployment benefits to those out of work, provide money to prevent home foreclosures, and give assistance to state and local governments to stop public service cuts.

Republicans at first insisted that making the Bush tax cuts for the wealthy permanent (they were slated to expire in 2010) was the only fix needed.[122] But as public pressure for a solution mounted, they agreed that a short term stimulus was warranted, and the Congress passed a relief package (the entire House and one-third of the Senate was facing re-election – Bush wasn't).

The House approved a $600 tax rebate check from the government ($1,200 for couples, plus $300 per child) for most workers, and for Social Security recipients who had income from a job or investments (but not those living solely on Social Security).

Workers making at least $3,000 who earned too little to pay personal income taxes would receive $300, plus $300 per child. Businesses got $45 billion in tax incentives, supposedly to invest in new plants and equipment.

The House bill included priorities of the Democrats (money directly to people who would spend it) and priorities of the Republicans (tax incentives for business). But the fundamental philosophical differences were more clearly evident in what the bill left out.

House Democrats wanted payments for poor seniors whose only income was Social Security (more likely to spend it than rich seniors living on investments), extension of unemployment benefits (again more likely to be spent immediately), and disabled veterans. House Republicans wanted to make everyone eligible for stimulus money – meaning write checks to the wealthy as well as middle income families and the poor – and make the 2003 Bush tax cuts permanent. Neither side got these additional provisions.

On the other side of Capitol Hill, Democrats in the Senate put up a fight to include the elderly poor and disabled veterans, an increase in monthly food stamp benefits, and an extension of unemployment benefits for those already out of work. They also wanted billions of dollars in energy tax credits and federally backed bonds for home construction.

Only the elderly poor and veteran provisions were added to the final House/Senate compromise. In exchange for those concessions, Republicans were allowed to insert language prohibiting undocumented aliens from receiving any benefits.[123]

Women were both winners and losers in the Bush stimulus package. The provisions adding benefits for the elderly who live solely on Social Security benefitted more women than men, because women are the majority of the elderly poor. Including low income workers with children who earn too little to pay taxes was also good for women, as this group is predominately composed of single mothers.

Where did women lose? While there was much talk about the sub-prime mortgage crisis and indeed it was the initial impetus for the stimulus package, nothing was done to help. In fact, it actually hurt. The package included a provision to temporarily permit federally chartered mortgage companies to divert money away from less expensive housing in favor of very large mortgages known as "jumbos." This meant less money for women with subprime loans, so many would continue to lose their homes in disproportionate numbers as the mortgage interest rates reset to levels they couldn't afford.

The failure to include an increase in food stamp benefits was also a loss for women. Nearly 70 percent of adult food stamp beneficiaries are female. According to the National Women's Law Center in Washington, D.C., more money for food stamps would have been a particularly effective way to target the poor and boost the economy.[124] Benefits could be quickly deposited on debit cards and used almost immediately at grocery stores, providing an economic jolt and aiding women in particular.

Women further lost out in Congress's failure to include an extension of unemployment benefits, but they didn't lose as much as men – because women already got less out of unemployment insurance. According to the U.S. Department of Labor, 37 percent of jobless men draw benefits, as compared to 33 percent of unemployed women.

That's because the system was designed during the Great Depression, when men dominated the labor market. Unemployment benefits were crafted as a safety net for those who worked full time, met a certain income threshold, and lost their jobs solely because of an employer's decision.

Though women are now a permanent part of the labor force, fewer women than men met these outdated criteria because they are more likely to work part time or hold lower-wage jobs, making them less likely to meet the system's earnings thresholds. And women are more likely to leave their jobs because of domestic violence, harassment or stalking, to follow a spouse, or to take care of their families. None of these reasons for job loss were covered by unemployment insurance.[125]

The Obama Stimulus Package

By the end of 2008, the housing crisis had worsened. More than 2.3 million homeowners coast-to-coast faced foreclosure proceedings, an 81 percent increase from 2007, which itself had been a record year. Unemployment was on the rise, and credit for consumers and businesses was very hard to get – even though major banks had received billions in bailout money from the Troubled Asset Relief Program (TARP - the bank bailout) at the end of the Bush administration.

The newly elected president and Congress knew another stimulus package was needed. Though very few Republicans supported the final legislation authorizing another stimulus, there was less wrangling in Congress because the Democrats now controlled both houses. President Obama signed The American Recovery and Reinvestment Act into law in February, 2009, less than a month after his inauguration.

This time there were a number of provisions that did benefit women, particularly low income women and those with children. Surprisingly little, however, was done to ease the mortgage crisis, still severe and still disproportionately affecting women. A one-time payment for low income Social Security beneficiaries (mainly female) similar to the Bush package was approved. Other provisions benefitting women:

- Expanded earned income tax credit, which provides money to low income workers, for families with at least three children. (Many such families are headed by single mothers.)

- $300 million for increased teacher salaries (jobs predominately held by women)

- $19.9 billion for the Food Stamp program (women are the majority of recipients)

- $86.6 billion for Medicaid and an increase in the number of those eligible(poor women and children are the majority of recipients)

- Expansion of the $1,000 child tax credit to cover more families, even those that do not make enough money to pay income taxes (again, many headed by single mothers).

- Expanded college credit to provide a $2,500 expanded tax credit for college tuition and related expenses for 2009 and 2010 (women have a harder time paying tuition than men, and more women finance tuition through credit cards)[126]

- Increased unemployment benefits for those out of work, and extended through December 31, 2009 (subsequently extended again, finally expiring in early 2014). More importantly, the flaws in the system noted above were fixed, for the first time since unemployment insurance was created in the 1930s. To claim its full share of the federal recovery funds, a state now has to show that it has already altered its unemployment insurance program along the right lines, or agree to adopt new rules that will grant benefits to hundreds of thousands of unemployed workers not previously covered by the system. What are the "right lines?"

- Benefits will now be provided to workers who must leave their jobs for compelling family reasons, such as caring for ill or disabled family members, relocating with a spouse whose job has moved to another area, or escaping domestic violence in which the abuser follows the woman to her workplace

- The earning test now makes it much easier for low-wage workers and new entrants to the work force (large numbers of women) to qualify for benefits

- Benefits are now available to workers seeking part-time work, which also includes many women.

These changes in the law represented a true "sea change" in unemployment benefits for women. However, they were part of a package that contained many provisions scheduled to disappear once the economy improves sufficiently. Women must now make sure that these new benefits are not taken away when the economy fully recovers.

On the downside, most of the jobs created by the Obama stimulus package were in construction, historically male dominated. The jobs targeted in fields dominated by women (child care, health-related) are notoriously low paid. Though an effort was made to require affirmative action for women in the "shovel-ready" construction projects so widely touted as the backbone of the package, that effort ultimately failed.

Nevertheless, this comparison of stimulus packages under two different presidents underscores the importance for women to act on their views and their self-interest. Just as economic slowdowns and recessions can be short-lived, they can also go on for many months and years, as we have seen since 2008.

Drinking Tea in 2010, and the Gridlock That Followed

Beginning with the 2010 elections, the country saw the rise of the "Tea Party" – which is not a political party at all, but a right-wing quasi-libertarian wing of the Republican Party (many "TP-ers" have expressed dissatisfaction with "traditional" Republicans). Tea-partiers held rallies all over the country against the government in general, the Affordable Care Act, taxes, the federal budget deficit, and the national debt. Though characterized as a grassroots populist movement, it drew large amounts of support from wealthy ultra-conservative Republicans such as the multi-billionaire Koch brothers,[127] and was a force in the turnover of the U.S. House from Democratic to Republican control.

With 60+ members in the House, the Tea Party caucus wielded enough power to shape the debate on a number of economic issues in 2011, most notably the fight over raising the debt ceiling. Until 2011, raising the maximum amount the U.S. is allowed to borrow had been a routine matter, with both Republicans and Democrats routinely voting for it with little or no debate.

In the summer of that year, the Tea Party caucus members insisted on tying the debt ceiling vote to deficit reduction, calling for many drastic cuts in government spending. At the same time they insisted that no taxes be raised, and that previous tax cuts for the wealthy not expire as scheduled. In the end, despite dire warnings from the White House and Wall Street alike, the differences between the parties were not resolved. Congress voted to raise the debt ceiling and to push the question of what to cut and what to tax to a congressional "super-committee."

But it was too late. They had prolonged the debate until the government was within hours of shutting down, and the Wall Street rating agencies were spooked. Standard & Poors downgraded the credit score of the U.S. government for the first time in history. The stock market tumbled and remained volatile for months. Months later, the super committee also failed to agree, so automatic cuts known as the "sequester" went into effect at the end of 2012. This resulted in choking off funding for many public sector jobs and slowing the recovery. This may have been a major factor in the 2012 elections, when only 48 Tea Party members were elected to the House, and no gains were made in the Senate (it had had no significant T-P presence prior to the 2012 election to begin with).[128]

Regardless, the gridlock in Congress can largely be laid at the feet of the Tea Party. Even though they are far from the majority, their caucus has enough votes to tie up the House and keep legislation from coming to the floor (with the collusion of the House Majority Leader John Boehner ®-OH)). In 2013 they forced a 16 day government shutdown because they again refused to raise the debt ceiling in an unsuccessful effort to defund Obamacare as the price of keeping the government open. The shutdown was extremely unpopular with the public, and weakened the Tea Party's influence. However, they have vowed to elect even more members in 2014, and are promising to replace more moderate Republicans with Tea Party candidates.[129]

Debt Ceiling Debate Fallout for Women

One big factor in both the rise of the Tea Party and the debates over the debt ceiling was an attack on public sector jobs and public sector unions. At the state level, these attacks were led by Wisconsin governor Scott Walker (a Koch protégé), whose "budget repair bill" was passed after a long fight. The bill cut funds to education and other public services, resulting in a 10 percent reduction in school money and the layoff of 354 teachers in Milwaukee alone.[130] Other states such as Ohio, Michigan, and New Jersey where the Tea Party is active have had similar proposals and initiatives.

In addition to the influence of the Tea Party, federal budget cuts and the lack of tax revenue in the states has contributed to the shrinking of public sector jobs. Because firefighters and police are often exempted from these layoffs, the axe has fallen mostly on women, who make up the majority of teachers, health workers, child care workers, and public welfare workers. An analysis by the Institute for Women's Policy Research (IWPR), in Washington, D.C. found that women employees lost 81 percent (473,000) of the 581,000 jobs lost in the public sector from December 2008 through July, 2011. By November of that year, of the 1.6 million jobs added to payrolls, 474,000 or 30 percent were filled by women and 1,126,000 or 70 percent were filled by men. In addition, more than 300,000 women dropped out of the workforce.[131]

These statistics, combined with job growth for women after the sequester ended in early 2014, illustrate the gender effects of debt ceiling fights and reductions in public spending. Two months after the sequester was partially lifted in a budget deal lasting until 2015, women's job growth had surpassed pre-recession levels for the first time since the recession began in 2008.

But the news was not all good, particularly for women of color. The long-term unemployment rate was still higher for black and Asian-American women as compared with both white women and of men. Hispanic women were about even with whites.[132] Even so, benefits for the long-term unemployed were cut off in early 2014.

For those women who found jobs, the outlook is still far from rosy. Between 2009 and 2013, 35 percent of women's job gains have been in low-wage sectors -- like retail, fast food and housekeeping -- while just 18 percent of men's jobs gains were in those fields. The trend has worsened a troubling disparity: women now make up 76 percent of the low-wage workforce, but only 47 percent of the workforce overall. And in those low-wage jobs there's a 9.6 point pay gap with men.[133]

Deficits and What Wars Cost You

> *Every gun that is made, every warship launched, every rocket fired signifies in the final sense, a theft from those who hunger and are not fed, those who are cold and are not clothed. This world in arms is not spending money alone. It is spending the sweat of its laborers, the genius of its scientists, the hopes of its children. This is not a way of life at all in any true sense.* (Dwight D. Eisenhower, former president and military commander)[134]

Besides the loss of life, the wars have been a major factor in the national budget deficit. President George W. Bush took office with a *surplus* of over $171 billion.[135] The budget *deficit* by 2009 was projected at $1,750 billion by the Congressional Budget Office. According to the Congressional Research Service, the estimated cost of the wars in Iraq and Afghanistan was scheduled to reach $1.41 *trillion* by the end of fiscal year 2012.[136] This cost was very close to President Obama's 2012 projected overall budget deficit of $1.6 trillion.

Even though war costs have been a big part of deficits (and the resulting national debt) for over a decade, there has been little mention of those costs in deficit-reduction plans and talks from either party. Most of the discussion has centered on cutting domestic programs such as Medicare, Medicaid, Social Security, and education, that will have a great effect on the well-being of U.S. women and children. Although some Defense Department cuts went into effect in 2013 as part of the sequester, none are directly tied to the wars.

While President Obama has not shown an inclination to drastically slash programs serving women and children in favor of the military (though he has level-funded many and eliminated a few, such as the Women's Educational Equity Act), there is no question that ongoing funding of military action impacts all other programs. Obama's 2012 budget request for Afghanistan was more than $100 billion, plus $13 billion to train Afghan forces and $5 billion a year on civilian assistance. Historically, domestic programs have been cut when war funding escalates.

Though there are some pro-war Democrats and a few anti-war Republicans, it's fair to say that the parties have opposite views on the need for continuing wars. Democrats in Congress wanted to end the war in Iraq long before a timetable for withdrawal was accomplished. Republicans stuck with the Bush/Cheney doctrine in voting to continue the wars with no timetable for withdrawal.

There was serious disagreement between legislators and parties about the need to continue the war in Afghanistan indefinitely, though the majority of the public says it was not worth fighting.[137] Republicans generally supported the 30,000-troop buildup announced by President Obama, though they opposed the announced late 2014 date for withdrawal. Democrats were divided, but most liberals opposed any buildup.

Just because there is no active war, it doesn't mean military spending will be cut. The impact of bloated military budgets, to the detriment of domestic programs that benefit women and children, puts much at stake in every election, because Congress has the last word on whether or not to fund military action or new weapons programs. Since 2010, when many deficit-cutting Tea Party members were elected to the House, we have seen ongoing "crisis" votes to keep the government operating, because they want to cut domestic spending – but not spending on the military.

The Big Argument for 2014

The economy promises to be one of the most contested issue in the 2014 elections, from congressional and gubernatorial races down to the local level. The fundamental differences between the parties, and liberal/conservative ideology, remain as entrenched as ever. If hard-core conservatives increase their control in Congress, gridlock and brinkmanship issues that affect the economy will continue. Spending cuts will continue to be put forth regularly as the solution to our fiscal problems, and women will pay the price.

According to the National Women' Law Center in Washington, D.C., cuts are unquestionably bad for women. Here are the points they make:[138]

- The most immediate deficit the nation faces is the lack of jobs – and further spending cuts make the deficit worse.
- Millionaires and billionaires don't need more tax cuts. The plan proposed by Senator Pat Toomey (R-PA), a super-committee member, would give

more large tax breaks to millionaires and billionaires.

- Cutting the Social Security cost-of-living adjustment (originally considered by the President as a bargaining chip) would especially hurt elderly women.
- Cutting Medicaid and Medicare would threaten women's health.
- All discretionary spending programs, including those specifically serving low-income women such as the Women Infants and Children's feeding program, Head Start, and Food Stamps are always on the list when cuts are discussed..
- With the budget fights settled until 2015, there is time for Congress to act responsibly.

Both short-term and long-term economic fixes are at stake in 2014 and beyond. Whether the economy improves in the short run or not, women must hold candidates and elected officials accountable for long-term solutions – solutions that recognize specific outcomes for women that can be far different than those for men.

Here are a few questions to help do that:

Did you, or would you have, voted for cutting off long-term unemployment benefits that passed in early 2014?

Did you, or would you have voted for the cut in food stamps that passed in early 2014?

What would you do to help the long-term unemployed, specifically women of color, to find jobs?

When the economy recovers, would you retain the new eligibility for unemployment benefits that include more women?

Even though the government spent billions to bail out banks and large corporations, they are now sitting on the money and not extending credit to small businesses and individuals. How would you fix that?

Now that the Iraq and Afghanistan wars are over, would you vote to cut military spending?

Have you, or would you, sign a pledge never to raise taxes on anyone for any reason?

If you would vote to give more tax cuts for the very wealthy, what programs, specifically, would you cut to pay for them?

Some women are still losing their homes as a result of the mortgage crisis, and the stimulus packages did almost nothing to help. How would you stop foreclosures and keep women in their homes?

◊ EIGHT ◊

Taxes

Taxes are a continuing part of the national dialogue, and they are part of the debate in every election for good reason. Everyone pays taxes of some kind, whether they are rich or poor. But various taxes affect people in different ways, depending on income.

If you have a very low income, you might pay no income taxes, and in fact could get money back from the government in the form of rhe Earned Income Tax Credit (EITC),a federal anti-poverty tax credit designed to supplement the earnings of low income workers by reducing or eliminating income taxes. When the EITC exceeds the amount of taxes owed, it results in a tax refund to those who claim and qualify for the credit. You would, however, still owe payroll taxes (Medicare and Social Security).

If you are wealthy and live on investments with no salary, you do pay income taxes (and capital gains taxes if you sell any investments at a profit) but incur no payroll taxes at all.

Since most people are neither very poor or very rich, they pay a combination of taxes, including payroll, income, sales, and property taxes (non-homeowners do not escape property taxes, as the costs are passed along by landlords as part of the rent). These taxes are assessed variously by the federal government as well as states, counties, cities, and school districts.

Individuals are not the only source of tax revenue; businesses also pay taxes. Taxes, of course, finance the various government operations, provide for government services such as police and fire protection, infrastructure such as roads and bridges, government benefits like unemployment compensation, Social Security – and wars.

Taxes affect everyone, but they can have differential effects for women. A *regressive* tax is one that takes proportionately more, percentage-wise, from those with less ability to pay. Conversely, it takes proportionately less from those with greater means. The sales tax, for instance, is a regressive tax. Since women in general make less than men, taxes that are regressive take a bigger bite out of women's incomes. Here's a simple example from Dr. Ralph Estes, a business professor at American University and scholar at the Institute for Policy Studies in Washington, D.C.

> Say your income is $20,000 a year, and you spend all of it on food, clothing, and other things subject to a 6 percent sales tax. So you pay $1200 in sales tax for the year. That amounts to 6 percent of your income.
>
> Now take a wealthy family with income of $500,000 a year. They don't need all that money to live on, so say they spend $100,000 on things subject to the sales tax. They would pay $6,000 in sales taxes. They would pay more in dollars, but remember they have a lot more dollars than you do.
>
> Now as a percentage of income, they are paying only 1.2 percent. And that's less than a fourth of the percentage you are paying. So the person with the lower income pays 6 percent of their income in sales tax, the person with 25 times as much income pays 1.2 percent. And that percentage continues to fall as income rises.
>
> That is exactly what we mean when we say a tax is regressive. It takes a bigger percentage bite out of the total income of those with a smaller ability to pay.[139]

A *progressive* tax is one that is more proportionate to ability to pay. The income tax is an example of a progressive tax. Those with greater wealth or income pay proportionately more, a higher percentage which results in a higher amount because they make more, while those with lesser means pay relatively less. A quick example using the numbers above:

> With no deductions, the family earning $20,000 a year would pay 10 percent, or $2000 in income taxes. The family earning $500,000 would pay 39.6 percent, or $198,000 in income taxes, assuming all of that income was from wages (capital gains and other types of income are taxed at much lower rates). So, not only is the wealthy family paying a higher percentage, it is paying a higher dollar amount because more dollars are being taxed. Thus, the income tax is a *progressive* tax structure. If $198,000 seems like a lot of money, it is. But that family still has $302,000 left to spend after taxes, whereas the low income family has only $18,000. In addition, the wealthy family is much more likely to have deductions for a home mortgage (and even a second home). They also do not owe payroll taxes on the portion of their income over $117,900, while the low income family owes payroll taxes on the full amount of their income.

Just about everyone who studies tax policy agrees that, to be fair and equitable, taxes should overall be progressive, not regressive.[140]

Historically, the total tax burden has been borne by both individuals and businesses in varying proportions. The corporate share is less than half of what it was 50 years ago. In 1955, corporate taxes accounted for nearly 30 percent of the total taxes collected, and individuals accounted for 58 percent. By 2013, individual payroll and income taxes accounted for 81 percent of total revenue, while corporate taxes had dropped to 10 percent.[141]

While we often hear that U.S. corporate tax rates are "the highest in the world," this is a highly misleading statement. The U.S. top corporate tax rate of 35 percent *is* one of the highest in the world, but the amount corporations actually end up forking over to the government is much lower–sometimes zero. This is due to a dizzying number of deductions, write-offs, and other accounting tricks that allow corporations to legally reduce their tax burden. A 2013 report from Citizens for Tax Justice a research organization in Washington, D.C., found that the 288 companies in the Fortune 500 that registered consistent profit every year from 2008 to 2012 paid an effective federal income tax rate of just 19.4 percent over the five-year period. One third paid an effective tax rate below 10 percent, and one in every 11 paid nothing.[142]

The top ten defense contractors saw their combined tax rate decline from 19.3 percent in 2008 to a mere 10.6 percent rate in 2010.[143] For ordinary individuals in 2014, the lowest percentage is 10 percent (before deductions) for incomes of $9,075 (single person) to $18,150 (joint return), while the highest percentage is 39.6 percent, for incomes over $457,600.

U.S. tax rates are actually lower than the average for developed countries.[144] While income taxes are still progressive, the rate on the highest income brackets is much lower than it has been in the past. The IRS reports that in 2008 (the latest year for which data are available), the 400 richest income tax filers paid just 18.1 percent of their adjusted gross income (AGI) in federal income taxes. That is down from 22.3 percent *just since 2000*, and is a only little over half of the top income tax rate of 35 percent that they are theoretically subject to. That's because more than half of the income reported by those 400 taxpayers consisted of capital gains and dividends subject to the preferential rates.[145]

When President George W. Bush took office in 2001, tax cuts were high on his agenda. In his first three years in office, taxes were cut in a number of areas – the most important cuts lowered income tax rates, lowered tax rates on investment income and on capital gains, and lowered the estate tax (it was actually zero for 2011-2012).

While the Bush tax cuts (President Obama signed a two year extension in 2010) provided modest benefits to low and middle-income families, they benefitted the rich disproportionately. The tax cuts are also a huge contributor to the budget deficits, which increases the national debt: A few quick facts:

- Rates were cut twice as much for households in the top 1 percent of earnings as for middle-income families. In 2011, the average Bush tax *cut* ($66,384) for a taxpayer in the richest one percent was greater than the average *income* of the other 99 percent ($58,506).[146]

- President Bush's tax cuts included the largest corporate tax alteration in two decades. The $143 billion bill had new tax breaks for oil and gas producers, corporate farmers, and companies with large overseas operations. Even Bush's Treasury Secretary John Snow criticized it as favoring foreign operations over domestic businesses.[147]

- According to the Congressional Budget Office, the tax cuts were the single largest contributor to the substantial budget deficits in recent years. "Cutting the deficit" was the reason House Republicans brought the country to the brink of default in 2011, and the reason many domestic programs were drastically cut under the sequester in 2013 (see Economy chapter).
- The cuts cost more than the Affordable Care Act.[148] And according to the Center for Defense Information, even with the spending for the wars in Iraq and Afghanistan, the federal budget would be in surplus now if the tax cuts for the wealthy and elite had not been enacted.[149]

In 2012, the tax cuts were made permanent for single people making less than $400,000 per year and couples making less than $450,000 per year, and eliminated for everyone else. Conservative politicians characterized letting the cuts expire as a "tax hike."

As an illustration of the effects of tax cuts for the very wealthy, consider these estimates from the Center on Budget and Policy Priorities in Washington, D.C. during the 2007 debate over making the Bush tax cuts permanent : "If the Bush tax cuts were extended without offsets, balancing the budget in 2012 would require cutting Social Security benefits by 28 percent, cutting defense by 38 percent, cutting Medicare by 44 percent, or cutting every other program other than Social Security, defense, Medicare, and homeland security (including education, medical research, border security, environmental protection, veterans' programs, and programs to assist the poor) by an average of almost one-fifth."[150] Women would have been disproportionately disadvantaged with cuts to the majority of those programs.

Tax Flim-Flam

Candidates and officeholders talk a lot about taxes and the role of taxes in our society. Explaining tax policy would take a separate book, but here are the basics.

In general, conservatives believe in "less government," and keeping taxes low is a way to achieve that. If the government has no money, it has to shrink and cut services. This is often called "starving the beast," meaning cutting the taxes that feed social spending.[151]

Conservatives also believe everyone earning a wage or salary should be taxed at the same rate regardless of income (regressive taxation). In addition, they maintain that income from investments should be taxed at a lower rate than income from performing a job.

Progressives and liberals generally believe taxes are necessary to achieve society's mutual goals and provide for the common welfare. They would quote Oliver Wendell Holmes, "Taxes are what we pay for civilized society." And they believe that those who are more fortunate should pay more, and progressive taxes are the fairest way to achieve this.

Red-hot tax rhetoric from candidates usually centers on "new" and "fair" tax plans. Some of these, such as flat taxes and value-added taxes, are radical departures from current tax policy. Others, such as eliminating estate taxes, are just drastic changes to tax programs or practices already in place. Here, briefly, is what each would likely mean for women.

Flat taxes: Under this scheme, everyone pays the same income tax rate, whether they make minimum wage or CEO-level megamillions. Flat taxes are by definition regressive.

Under various flat-tax proposals, the taxpayer can be an individual or business, most deductions (e.g. mortgage, child care, charitable contributions) would be eliminated, and fringe benefits would be counted as income. In some schemes, a progressive surtax could be applied to higher income levels.[152] Flat taxes, or "fair taxes," as some politicians have taken to calling them, are usually sold on the basis of simplifying tax returns and making the system more equitable.

For women, already the lowest earners, it means paying the same tax rate as Morgan Stanley CEO John Mack, who earned $41.4 million in 2007, the same year his company agreed to a $46 million dollar settlement for sex discrimination in pay. On top of that, women would most likely lose the few deductions they have, and any fringe benefits like health insurance would be taxable.

National sales tax or value-added tax: This tax is exactly what it sounds like. A federal sales tax would be instituted on top of the various state and local sales taxes. (Value added taxes amount to the same thing, though they are "hidden" because they are added at each stage of production before the consumer sees the bill.)

These taxes would replace the income tax. Again, they are highly regressive, as the rich pay much less in proportion to their income, because they spend proportionally less of their total income on goods and services which would be subject to the tax.

Sales taxes are often implemented with certain categories such as medicine and food exempted, only to be added back as people later get used to the tax and the state needs more money. These taxes also begin at low rates such as 3 percent – a major selling point of those pushing them – and inch up gradually.

Since all poor (majority female) and most middle income people spend all their money on necessities each month, virtually 100 percent of their incomes are already subject to sales taxes. But they may get some (minor) relief in the form of income tax credits or deductions and refunds, which would be eliminated under these schemes.

Eliminating "double taxation" on corporate dividends. Arguments for eliminating taxes on dividends are based on an argument that it is "double taxation." The idea is that corporations pay taxes, so when they distribute a dividend to stockholders, the money has already been taxed once and should not be taxed again.

But any taxpayer could make this same argument about sales taxes or property taxes. You've already paid income tax on the money you spend at the gas station, so paying a gasoline tax is "double taxation."

The problem with eliminating any tax is that the revenue has to be made up from other sources – meaning other taxpayers – or services have to be cut to cover the shortfall. These tax schemes overwhelmingly favor the rich. Women are overwhelmingly not the rich.

Abolishing the "death tax." "Death tax" is a term conservatives use to describe the estate tax or inheritance tax. The term refers to the federal tax on estates over $10.6 million for a married couple, or $5.3 million for an individual. But not the whole estate: taxes are due only on the portion of an estate's value that *exceeds* the exemption level. That means the estate tax is not a factor at all to over 99.7 percent of all U.S. estates.[153]

So repeal of the estate tax is of no benefit whatsoever to virtually all Americans, because they are never going to reach the threshold for the tax in the first place.

To the contrary, doing away with the tax for the few very rich who pay it will contribute to shortfalls for the majority – shortfalls that play out in such ways as cuts in Medicaid, cuts in the Women, Infants, and Children's food program, or children's health care appropriations, to name a few.

Positive Tax Changes for Women

Any plan that makes the tax system more progressive will benefit women, because women are the majority of the poor and the majority of minimum-wage and low wage workers. Even at higher levels of income, women make less than similarly situated men (see chapter 8).

But there are other ways the tax system disadvantages women, and these should be fixed. Here are a few suggestions from the Money column of *Ms* magazine.[154]

> **Get marital status out of the tax code**: The "household," which is the basic tax-paying unit in the U.S. system, is specifically defined to mean legally married couples (including same-sex couples) or single individuals. We should redefine the tax unit so that it does not depend on marital status.
>
> The easiest and fairest way to do this would be to follow the model used in almost all other industrialized nations, where every taxpayer is treated as an individual, regardless of the type of household. Such a change would permanently eliminate the "marriage bonus," where some couples pay less than two similarly situated individual taxpayers, and the "marriage penalty," where married couples pay more. This higher tax rate on earnings from a second worker has the practical effect of encouraging one spouse (usually the wife) not to work outside the home, which in turn lowers their lifetime earnings, endangers their job prospects in case of death or divorce, and lowers subsequent Social Security and retirement incomes.

Increase the Child Tax Credit, and apply it to all families with a payroll tax liability: Families can deduct $1,000 per child from their federal income taxes, no matter how many children they have. But working poor women get very little help from the Child Tax Credit, because it is deducted from the amount they pay in income tax, which is low because their incomes are so low. Yet many still have significant payroll tax bills (Social Security, Medicare).

More than 95 percent of Americans in the bottom 20 percent of the population pay more in payroll tax than in federal income tax, so expanding the credit so that it could be applied against payroll taxes would benefit low income women.

Institute paid family leave funded by unemployment taxes, with incentives for men to also take it: The United States is the only industrialized country on earth without some form of paid family leave. We should not only have a national system of paid leave, but go a step further and emulate Sweden's system. In order to get the full benefit, each parent must take a turn at caregiving – the benefit doubles if the father takes his turn.

This of course would not help single mothers, but for married couples it would go a long way toward getting men to do their fair share, leveling the playing field at home and at work.

Remove the caps earnings subject to Social Security taxes, and give a Social Security credit for caregiving: Social Security is the primary source of retirement income for women. The cries that Social Security is going broke (it's not), and the ever-present push to "reform" it through privatization, would lessen if more money was coming into the system.

For 2014 earnings above $117,000 are not subject to payroll taxes, meaning the rich once again escape their fair share. And just as income tax policies effectively punish second incomes through the "marriage penalty," thereby encouraging women to stay home and take care of kids or elderly parents, the Social Security system then punishes them by entering a big fat zero for each year spent at home. That means a more meager retirement.

As above, to get men to take their turn, the credit could be expanded if both spouses took caregiving time off.

Revoke favorable tax treatments for institutions that discriminate against women. Courts long ago ruled that religious schools that bar blacks are not entitled to tax exemptions. Yet churches that openly discriminate against women enjoy billions of dollars in tax savings through exemptions from income and property taxes, not to mention benefitting from the largesse of contributors who get to deduct their contributions from personal income taxes. In turn these funds are used to undermine women's rights.

Case in point: The Catholic church is perennially one of the largest contributors to anti-abortion referenda. The U.S. Conference of Catholic Bishops was widely credited with being instrumental in pressuring the House to pass the Stupak amendment in 2009, which effectively eliminated abortion coverage in both private and public health insurance.

The Bishops stepped up their attack on women in early 2012, campaigning hard to eliminate birth control coverage from insurance coverage at any institution remotely affiliated with a church (President Obama did not give in to the demands, but did allow churches themselves to opt out of providing birth control coverage). They later increased their demands to say any Catholic business owner should be exempt from providing the coverage. As of early 2014, the case was pending before the Supreme Court.

Tax rules also underwrite sex discrimination by allowing deductions for business expenses at places that discriminate against women. After a national controversy in 2003 over the exclusion of women at Augusta National Golf Club, where corporations spend millions entertaining clients at taxpayer's expense, Representative Carolyn Maloney (D-NY) introduced a bill in Congress to disallow such corporate writeoffs.

The bill (never passed) didn't say "private" clubs can't keep women out, or that corporations can't entertain at such places. They just can't expect taxpayers to foot the bill.

If some of the changes we need seem far-fetched or impossible, remember this: there was a time when the income tax itself was highly controversial. The suffragists used "No Taxation Without Representation," as a rallying cry. It's time women in the 21st century did the same thing..

Here are a few questions to get the discussion started:

Do you support a national sales tax? A VAT (value added tax)?

Do you support a "flat tax"?

Do you support a caregiver credit in Social Security?

Would you revoke corporate tax deductions for entertainment at places which discriminate on the basis or gender and race?

Would you increase the child tax credit, and would you apply it against payroll taxes as well as income taxes?

If you believe taxes should be lowered generally, what programs, specifically, would you cut or eliminate to pay for tax cuts?

◊ NINE ◊

Pay Equity
Show Me the Money!

The pay gap between working women and men in the U.S. continues to be one of the highest ranking concerns for women. It is also a priority for men, because when one earner in a family brings in less than she should, the family suffers overall.

Though "equal pay for equal work" has been the law since 1963, disparities in pay between men and women for full-time, year-round workers are not lessening substantially, and cannot be expected to go away naturally, as some conservatives claim (after all, it's already been 49 years).

According to U.S. Department of Labor figures for full-time, year-round workers, women's earnings in 2014 were on average 77 percent of men's. The gap has been the same for over a decade.

Earnings for women of color continue to be lower than those for white women, who earn 78 percent of men's wages overall. Asian American women make 79 percent. African American women come in at 64 percent of men's earnings, and for Native American women the percentage is 60 cents. Latinas are at the bottom with only 53 percent.[155]

Women face a pay gap in nearly every occupation. Here are a few other statistics:

- Nationwide, working families lose $200 billion in income annually due to the wage gap between men and women. That translates to between $700,000 and $2 million for individual women over the course of their work lives.[156]

- Women in non-traditional jobs, like the building trades that historically pay more, still get short-changed an average of $3,446 per year.[157]

- Women hold a disproportionate number of the minimum-wage jobs. In 2012, women made up approximately two-thirds of all minimum-wage workers.[158]

- Increasing the minimum wage to $10.10 would boost wages for about 15 million women and help close the wage gap.[159]

- Raising women's wages to that of men would mean adding $447.6 billion to gross domestic product, or GDP, and cutting the poverty rate among working women and their families in half, from 8.1 percent to 3.9 percent.[160]

- Men in traditionally female fields, such as child care, nursing, and teaching, make more than the women in these jobs.

- In 2012, the median weekly earnings for women in full-time management, professional, and related occupations was $951, compared to $1,328 for men.[161]

- Elderly women get over 22 percent less in Social Security benefits than men, largely due to lower lifetime earnings.[162]

But even these miserable facts don't tell the whole story. The pay gap gets worse for women over their work lives, including for college graduates in high paying fields. For example, men and women with professional degrees have similar earnings in their 20s. The earnings gap widens over time, so that by their late 30s, men earn over 50 percent more than women.[163]

The pay gap also widens greatly for women who drop out of the work force, even temporarily. According to a study by the Institute for Women's Policy Research, a woman who takes off for a single year will likely *never* catch up. She will earn less for up to 15 years after she returns to the workforce.[164]

What Causes the Pay Gap?

Many conservatives claim it is motherhood, not the fact of being female that causes the gender gap. But they do not say fatherhood causes lower pay, nor can they explain the pay gap for women who are childless or no longer raising children. It is obvious that the pay gap presents many problems for women, whether they are married or single, and whether they are mothers or not. And it can become like a self-fulfilling prophecy.

If someone has to take off work to take care of a child or elderly parent in a two-earner family, it makes economic sense for the lower earner to do it, because the family will lose less income that way. And because the lower earner is almost always the woman, she usually is the one to take time off.

This means she will fall behind others at her workplace, and may be seen as an unreliable or less serious worker, damaging her opportunities for promotion.

Women without children may still be seen by management as "potential mothers" and therefore devalued at promotion time. Single mothers, of course, are at the worst disadvantage, having no partner to take up the slack when caregiving calls.

There are several reasons for the pay gap, including job segregation – meaning some jobs are mostly held by men and others mostly by women. Women workers tend to be segregated into lower paying clerical and service jobs, while men dominate higher paying blue collar, management, and technical jobs.

"Women's jobs" have traditionally been seen by society as less valuable than "men's jobs," though the jobs may require the same level of skill, effort, responsibility and working conditions (e.g. shop foreman vs. clerical supervisor, or social worker vs. parole officer). But we've seen that even in job titles that are dominated by women, *men in those fields make more.*

Low minimum wages also contribute to the pay gap. Because adult women are the largest group earning the minimum wage, they are also the largest group to benefit when the minimum wage is raised. Fifty-nine percent of workers who received the last (2009) increase to the current rate of $7.25 were women. Over 1.25 million single parents (mostly women) with children under 18 benefitted.[165] The numbers would be even higher now (see above).

While the minimum wage increase helps, it is still not enough. At $7.25 per hour, a full time worker who takes no vacation will still earn only $15,080 per year before taxes. Even if a worker's wages are so low she doesn't owe income taxes, she still must pay payroll taxes. The minimum wage is not currently indexed to inflation, so women lose ground every year it is not raised. After adjusting for inflation, it is still less than the minimum wage through most of the period from 1961 to 1981.[166]

There have been many studies of the gender pay gap, with conservative groups claiming that women choose to make less because they don't want to work as much, drop out of the workforce, or want less risky or so-called "women's" jobs that pay less. But when all of these factors – and others such as education – are accounted for statistically, there is still a pay gap. *Experts agree that sex discrimination is the only logical explanation.*[167]

A compelling – and potentially damning – study in 2008 by University of Chicago sociologist Kristen Schilt and NYU economist Matthew Wiswall strongly indicates that gender counts. They looked at wage trajectories of people who underwent a sex change. The results: even when controlling for factors like education, men who transitioned to women earned, on average, 32 percent less after the surgery. Women who became men, on the other hand, earned 1.5 percent more.

Court Battles to Close the Gap

Court battles around pay discrimination at all levels have been ongoing since 1963, but the U.S. Supreme Court's most recent pay equity decisions – in 2007 and 2010 – demonstrated a bias in favor of corporations against women.

In a truly bizarre ruling (*Ledbetter v. Goodyear*), the Court said that a woman who believes she is being denied equal pay must file a complaint within 180 days after the first instance of discrimination occurs, even if it went on for years before she found out about it.

Prior to that ruling, the law had been interpreted to mean women had 180 days to bring action from the time they *learned about* the discrimination (e.g. they had been paid less than men doing the same work for years but didn't know it). The following letter excerpt from the plaintiff Lilly Ledbetter, says it all:

> I'm a former employee of Goodyear Tire and Rubber Company. For close to two decades, I was paid less

> than my male coworkers – even though I was doing the same work they were, and doing it well. The company kept the discrimination quiet and I didn't know about the pay gap until I got an anonymous note about it. Seeking to rectify this injustice, I brought Goodyear to court.
>
> A jury found that Goodyear had discriminated and awarded me more than $3 million in damages. But Goodyear appealed my case all the way to the Supreme Court and got a reversal of the jury verdict by one vote. The Court said I should have filed my complaint within six months of the original act of discrimination – even though at the time I didn't know the discrimination was happening, let alone have enough evidence to complain.
>
> My case set a new and dangerous precedent. According to the Court, if pay discrimination isn't challenged within six months, a company can pay a woman less than a man for the rest of the woman's career. I wonder what other forms of discrimination the Supreme Court will permit in the future.
>
> Sincerely,
> Lilly Ledbetter

The Ledbetter case galvanized organized women's groups and members of Congress to try and overcome the ruling. The Ledbetter Fair Pay Act, restoring the original intent of law as it had been interpreted for nearly 43 years, passed in 2009. Far from being an easy or quick fix, this was only possible after to two years of advocacy and lobbying, an increase in the Democratic majority in both houses of Congress, and a new president who supported its passage. While the statute will help women who learn they are being discriminated against in bringing legal action, it will do nothing to prevent wage discrimination in the first place – it just gets us back to where we were over 50 years ago.

In another landmark decision in 2010, the Roberts Supreme Court ruled in *Dukes v. Walmart* that although women in the company may have been denied pay and promotions because of their gender, they could not sue as a class. The Court ruled that giving discretion to individual store managers, which can result in discrimination, did not constitute a company-wide discrimination policy (even though discrimination was the clear outcome of such a policy). Only the company-wide written anti-discrimination policy counted. It further ruled that the claims were not sufficiently similar to qualify as a class, since they came from different parts of the country and different stores. The decision has already had wide-ranging consequences, with many class action suits being thrown out by lower courts, citing *Dukes,* even if the circumstances were not similar. *Dukes* has also had a dampening effect on attorneys' willingness to bring class actions, since they are often done on a contingency fee basis, and can cost hundreds of thousands of dollars before a decision is rendered.

Inability to sue as a class severely limits women's options for redress from workplace discrimination. Each woman must go it alone or with only a small group of co-workers, hiring a lawyer for many thousands of dollars (class action lawyers sometimes work *pro bono*, but lawyers handling small suits do not). Low-wage female workers cannot afford this, and without the protection of a group, individuals are much more likely to experience retaliation for complaining in the first place.

New Laws to Close the Pay Gap

A number of solutions to the gender pay gap have been proposed. One is to prohibit discrimination in jobs requiring the same levels of skill, effort, responsibility and working conditions, even if the job titles and duties are different. To avoid potential legal liability, employers would need to conduct internal surveys of their workplaces, evaluate them accordingly, and adjust wages for the job categories that are dominated by women (or dominated by men) that have been undervalued.

In a school district, this might translate to cafeteria servers (mostly women) being paid the same as custodians (mostly men). Even though the actual duties are quite different, the required skill level and effort are about the same.

This approach is known as *comparable worth*, and it has been used successfully in Ontario, Canada, as well as the state of Minnesota to narrow the gender wage gap. Conservatives charge that it would lead to "wage setting by the government," though there is nothing in the proposals that would require this, or even suggest it. Lowering wages for a given job category to make things equal would also be prohibited.

Comparable worth has been proposed by Senator Tom Harkin (D-IA) in his *Fair Pay Act* (a separate bill from the Ledbetter Fair Pay Act above). Another proposal in Harkin's bill is to require employers to report pay statistics by gender, race, and job category.

This disclosure concept was endorsed during the 2008 presidential primary campaign by Governor Bill Richardson of New Mexico. Richardson put it this way: "Much of the inequality would be eliminated if employers reported pay data by job classification, gender, and race. That way employees would know if they were being treated fairly, and employers could see if they had a problem that needed correcting. Not anyone's salary on a bulletin board, but meaningful statistics that would let people see how they are paid as a group." As governor, Richardson subsequently issued an Executive Order in

New Mexico requiring all state contractors to submit a gender pay equity report as a condition of contracting – the first and only such requirement in the nation.

There is another bill that has been pending on Capitol Hill since the mid '90s which many women's groups are supporting, called the *Paycheck Fairness Act*. It would beef up enforcement of existing laws, allow the Equal Employment Opportunity Commission to collect some pay data (not public) from employers, and provide training money for women to become better negotiators. Though some believe this bill has a chance of passing if conservatives do not dominate Congress, others are not sure it is the right path. It is considerably weaker than the Fair Pay Act. Once the Congress passes a major bill, action on that particular issue tends to be considered "done" for a least a dozen years or more. So passage of a weak bill would be much less valuable for women than holding out a little longer for one with real teeth.

Since legislation has not passed despite twenty years of effort by women's groups, a more "doable" strategy seems to be through the contracting process, following the New Mexico model. Contract dollars, whether federal, state, or local, are subject to a wide variety of requirements, including such things as providing health insurance to employees as a condition of contracting. The rationale for any requirement is accountability and transparency of how tax dollars are spent, and ensuring that contracts are not being given to companies that are unfair or abuse workers or the law. Adding pay equity reports to the list of requirements should be a priority. After all, companies already know who works for them, their job titles, and how much they are paid. (This solution does not, of course, affect companies who do not accept tax dollars. But it would affect many, many, employers, particularly those with thousands of employees and multimillion dollar contracts.)

Closing the Gap by Unionizing

The gender gap between what unionized male workers make and what unionized female workers make is just 9.4 cents, meaning that union women working full time make more than 90 percent of what union men do, according to an analysis by the National Women's Law Center.[168] While the overall national gender gap hasn't budged in a decade, it shrunk 2.6 cents between 2012 and 2013 among union workers.

The premium women see from joining a union is about $222 a week, and is equivalent to the increase in pay from a year of college. And when it comes to benefits, unionized women are far more likely to have health insurance and retirement plans – the effect is even greater than having a four-year degree.

The union path is not open to everyone, however. In many workplaces belonging to a union is not an option, and where employees have tried to unionize they often face retaliation, intimidation, and even firing. While women have become a larger share of the unionized workforce, now at more than 45 percent, the share of women workers who are in a union overall has declined.

One reason belonging to a union may have such an impact on the wage gap is that pay tends to be more transparent. Many workplaces prohibit employees from discussing wages, but union pay scales are often published or available for inspection. As stated above, when pay information is available, it discourages employers from discriminating and empowers employees.

The Last Word on Equal Pay

Even if new laws are passed, the fight won't be over. Conservatives and corporations can be counted on to challenge every pay statute, and keep doing so for years.

With the Supreme Court already having narrowed women's options in fighting pay discrimination, the choices in future elections and Court appointments become extremely important, both for passing stronger legislation and for safeguarding women from decisions that will further roll back the few remedies available.

Questions for legislators and candidates:

Do you support disclosure of pay statistics by gender, race, and job category? For all businesses? For businesses accepting taxpayer dollars?

Do you support the Harkin Fair Pay Act? Are you, or would you be, a co-sponsor of the bill?

Do you support new laws to ban discrimination in pay for jobs of equal skill, effort, responsibility and working conditions, even if the jobs are different?

Do you support raising the minimum wage, and indexing it for inflation?

How would you increase women's access to non--traditional jobs?

Would you support the nomination of a judge who was known for his support of corporations or opposition to workers in employment decisions?

◊ TEN ◊

Social Security: Will I Be Dependent on "The Kindness of Strangers" in My Old Age?

Social Security is one of the largest entitlement programs provided by the federal government. It is always an election year issue, because the money outlays are huge, because the population is aging, and also because some politicians like to use "the Social Security crisis" as a fear-mongering tactic or a way to promote schemes that will undermine the program. Their ultimate goal is to eliminate it altogether.

Before we get to a discussion of "fixes" candidates and lawmakers propose, a few quick facts about Social Security:

- Social Security does *not* face an immediate crisis, although there is a significant, but manageable, long-term financing problem.

- Social Security is in no danger of "running out of money." The Social Security Trust Fund is currently running a surplus. According to the Social Security Administration, with *no changes at all* Social Security can pay full benefits through 2033, and 75 percent of promised benefits after that.[169]

- Social Security is not draining the economy, and is not one of the causes of either the deficit or the national debt. The trust fund is 100 percent solvent with $2.6 trillion at the end of 2012, though the government does keep borrowing the money for other uses.

- Between 2012 and 2035 the baby boomers will cause a slight increase in Social Security outlays, after which costs will even out and resume a gradual and manageable growth rate.[170]

- Social Security is extremely popular among Americans, who overwhelmingly favor strengthening the program as opposed to cutting it. According to a recent survey, 84 percent of Americans believe the current benefit levels are not sufficient, 75 percent think we should raise benefits to provide a better retirement and 82 percent agree that preserving Social Security is necessary even if it means increasing taxes for all working Americans.[171]

Now let's take a quick look at a few facts about Social Security and its largest group of beneficiaries – women:

- Women represent 56 percent of all Social Security beneficiaries age 62 and older and approximately 68 percent of beneficiaries age 85 and older.[172] In addition to providing benefits to retired female workers, Social Security provides dependent benefits to spouses, divorced spouses, elderly widows, and widows with young children.
- For both women and men 65 and older, Social Security is the largest source of income compared with other sources including earnings, private pensions, and income from assets such as savings accounts.[173]
- Women rely on Social Security for a larger part of their retirement income than men because fewer

women have private pensions (29 percent of women have private pensions as opposed to 46 percent of men). Women who do have private pensions get on average, less than half of what men get.[174]

- The average annual Social Security income received by women 65 years and older is $12,188, compared to $15,795 for men – a gender gap of 23 percent.[175]
- Social Security is progressive – meaning it provides more generous benefits to lower lifetime earners for the amount of taxes paid in when compared to higher earners. Because women are still the lowest earners as a group, even when working full time and year round, they benefit from this distribution toward lower earners.
- Without Social Security, a large majority of women (58 percent) 75 and older would live in poverty, as compared to 41 percent of men in that age group. For those 65-74 the numbers are 41 percent and 32 percent respectively.[176]
- Social Security is particularly important for women of color. Twenty-six percent of black women on Social Security receive disability benefits, as opposed to 14 percent of all women.[177] Latinas have a higher life expectancy than the majority of the population, and tend to be concentrated in low wage jobs lacking private pension benefits.[178]

No one disputes that long-term financing for Social Security is something we must attend to as a nation, since it could eventually pay out more than it takes in unless some adjustments are made.

Politicians and parties propose various solutions, and present a variety of scare-tactic arguments about bankruptcy of the system – or even bankruptcy of the country – if nothing is done.

In fact, according to experts including the director of the Congressional Budget Office, threats to the economy from health care costs are far more significant than any impact from Social Security or retirement of the baby boomers.[179]

Fixing the Shortfall

Setting aside doomsday scenarios, both the government and a number of respected think tanks have put forth ways to close the gap between what Social Security takes in and what it will eventually have to pay out (called the "solvency target," or in plain English, the shortfall).

- For 2014 earnings subject to the Social Security payroll tax ("the cap") are $117,000 per worker per year. Anything over that is not taxed, meaning the very highest earners, including billionaires and CEOs garnering multimillion dollar salaries and even bigger bonuses, pay nothing on their incomes over $117,000. According to the government's own figures, eliminating the cap while leaving benefits as they are would actually create a long-term surplus.[180] And, it would make the Social Security tax much fairer. (Both Social Security and Medicare taxes are highly regressive – see chapter 8).

- Investing 15 percent of the Social Security Trust fund in stocks, instead of the Treasury Bills currently used, has also been suggested by experts and AARP as a way to close some of the shortfall. This is an approach used by many state pension funds. (Note: this is *not* the same thing as privatizing Social Security – see below.)

– Increasing the payroll tax by one percentage point each for employers and employee contributions would extend full funding of the trust fund until 2056.[181]

Obviously the first alternative is the easiest, and by far the fairest. Yet conservative think tanks and politicians repeatedly insist that the only way to "save" Social Security is by cutting benefits, privatizing the system, or both.

Privatizing Social Security means allowing individuals to divert part or all of the money they now put in Social Security into private accounts. The AARP and other experts have long agreed that privatization is not a solution, and would in fact make the projected shortfall in Social Security much worse.[182]

The privatization scheme is particularly dangerous for women for a number of reasons. Women live longer, and cannot outlive Social Security benefits, which are guaranteed for life. As we saw in the 2008 recession, stock market and other investments are risky and can be greatly diminished or wiped out completely in economic downturns. Even if such accounts should make money over the long term, women would have smaller amounts to invest, resulting in smaller payouts that might not last a lifetime. Brokers might not even want accept such small sums to manage.

Most importantly, Social Security provides benefits to widows and divorced spouses. There is no guarantee that a spouse would leave a private account to his or her widow, and it is almost certain such accounts would not be left to an ex-spouse. There is also no provision for division of private accounts in divorce.

Cutting benefits would also have a disproportionately negative impact on women, and benefit cuts are opposed by AARP as well as all of the major U.S. women's groups.[183]

Positive Social Security Changes for Women

In addition to strengthening the long-term outlook for Social Security, we need to be thinking of ways that the system can be strengthened and made more fair for women. (Social Security is intended to be gender neutral, meaning benefits of spouses, divorced individuals, and widows are available to both women and men on an equal basis. But since women are still by far the lower earners, these proposed improvements would have a proportionately greater benefit to women.)

In 1999, the largest coalition of women's advocacy groups in the country convened a meeting to talk about how to do this. They came up with a number of recommendations, all of which could be paid for through adjustments such as those above.[184]

> *Family service credit:* Currently those who drop out of the workforce to care for children or elderly parents get a zero in the their Social Security account for each year spent caregiving. This brings down the level of benefits at retirement, because those "zero years" of earnings are averaged in. A family service credit would mean caregivers would be given credit – at the level of minimum wage – for years out of the workforce when children are under the age of six, or providing for some "drop out" years when elderly parents need a full time caregiver.
>
> In 2013 a more detailed proposal for caregiving credit was put forward by the Older Women's

Economic Security Task Force of the National Council of Women's Organizations. It would provide the most benefits to lower earners and those who don't work at all while caregiving, but also provide some benefit to those who combine work and caregiving. Credits during caregiving years (which are now zero) would translate to higher Social Security benefits upon retirement, even if the credits were at a lower level than those for normal earnings.[185]

Improve eligibility for divorced spouses: Currently an ex-spouse can collect benefits based on a former spouse's higher earnings if they were married ten years. Improving the eligibility criteria would mean dropping this requirement to seven years, or a total of ten years of marriage and work history combined.

Improve widow(er)s benefit: Widows are the majority of the elderly poor, and their economic circumstances worsen as they age. Depending on their particular situation, widows currently collect half to two-thirds of the combined benefit when the primary earner dies. This benefit should be raised to 75 percent of the couple's joint benefit, to go no higher than the highest earner's maximum benefit.

After more than a decade, a few candidates and members of Congress are finally talking about changes like these, though many more are talking about cutting. They will need a push from women if any positive changes are to become reality.

Questions for officeholders and candidates:

Do you support diverting part or all of Social Security contributions to private accounts?

Would you remove the cap on earnings taxed for Social Security so that the very rich pay their fair share? If not, why not?

Does your plan for "strengthening" Social Security involve benefit cuts?

Do you think Social Security should be means tested?

Do you support benefit cuts in Social Security while maintaining tax cuts for the wealthy?

Does your plan help those with lower lifetime earnings, usually meaning women?

Do you think we should strengthen benefits for widows, lower earning spouses, and divorced spouses? How?

Do you support giving some Social Security credit for years spend caring for children or elderly parents?

◊ ELEVEN ◊

Health Care - Still Sick or Getting Better?

Without question, one of the most intense debates in the U.S. in the past few years has been over health care – who should provide it, who should benefit, how much it should cost, and whether it is a right or a privilege. There is no single "health care system" in the U.S. that provides insurance coverage for illness. There are several, depending on age, income, and job status.

By far the most common health care in the United States is privately purchased by employers and individuals from for-profit insurance companies (now regulated by the Affordable Care Act, also known as the ACA, Obamacare, or simply health care reform). Seniors are covered by Medicare, with the option of purchasing a supplemental policy sold by private companies to cover expenses not paid by Medicare. Medicaid is a federal insurance program administered by the states that covers very low income people. The Children's Health Insurance Program is a state-administered federal program for uninsured kids whose families cannot afford insurance but earn too much to qualify for Medicaid. There is also the federally administered Veteran's Administration Health Care, for current and former members of the Armed Forces. This chapter explains each of these systems in turn and their implications for women.

Private Insurance - The Affordable Care Act

The single largest change in American health care in the decades since Medicare was enacted in 1965 was passage of the Affordable Care Act in March of 2010. In the two years prior to ACA passage, citizens and elected officials alike expressed intense feelings and strong opinions about what should be done about the soaring costs of health care, insurance hassles and abuse, and how to cover an estimated 47 million uninsured. Major problems also include lack of technology for sharing information between hospitals, doctors, and other providers, use of emergency rooms for primary care by the uninsured, and not enough emphasis on prevention. By some estimates, chronic diseases (e.g. diabetes, hypertension, lung disease) costs the economy $2.8 trillion annually (75 percent of health care dollars), most of it for treatment instead of prevention.[186] Other budget busters are drug costs, overuse of expensive tests, not enough coordinated care, and over-reliance on specialists. Regardless, virtually no one on either side of the political spectrum denies that there are problems, which we must solve as a country.

However, there were (and are) basic differences in philosophy over solutions. Approaches to health care reform diverged widely in the debate. Advocates for and against an overhaul of the system took to the airwaves, town hall meetings – and in some cases the streets – to voice their opinions and do their best to influence the outcome. There were basic disagreements between the political parties.

In general, Democrats emphasized "universal coverage" – meaning everyone would have health insurance. Means of achieving the goal varied. A few advocated "Medicare for All," which would mean a single-payer system that would eliminate the control of for-profit insurance companies over our health care system. But that approach never got a serious hearing. Most systems under consideration mandated that people buy private health insurance or pay a fine, much like auto insurance.

Methods of paying the bill also varied, but virtually all Democratic schemes involved a partnership between employers, workers, and the government, with more help for people too poor to afford coverage.

Republicans generally argued that the medical system should be market based, rely on individual responsibility, and not involve the government at all. Many referred to *any* government involvement as "socialized medicine." (It is unclear whether they believe public schools are "socialized education," and if so, whether it's bad for the U.S. to have public education.) The schemes put forth that relied on the market involved further deregulation of the insurance industry, and leaving health care solutions up to the states instead of "relying on a one–size–fits–all, government–run system."[187]

When the ACA finally passed, it brought sweeping changes to the private insurance market which covers the vast majority of Americans. But it did not change the basic for-profit structure or in any way convert the system to a government-administered one. As before reform, employer provided plans come from private insurance companies, and most employers pay only part of the premiums; employees are responsible for a monthly payment as well. Employers may offer a choice of plans, or may be tied to a single plan that employees are required to join if they want insurance. Regardless, the great majority of private insurers still dictate the choice of doctors and hospitals that can be used. Prior to reform, the plans also dictated policy prices, co-pays, what was covered and at what level, and when a policy could be terminated or coverage capped.

Under ACA, those without employer-provided coverage who do not qualify for government plans because of age (Medicare) or income (Medicaid and other subsidies) must purchase a private plan on their own or pay a fine, and businesses that offer unaffordable plans or drop coverage altogether must pay fines as well. This is known as the "individual mandate." Prior to the ACA, these policies were extremely expensive, and carried very high deductibles. Denial or cancellation of coverage altogether was common, most often for "pre-existing conditions," which could be as basic as having had acne as a teenager. With passage of the ACA, low income people who do not qualify for Medicaid can get assistance in buying coverage, and such denials are outlawed.

Individual coverage not provided by employers is purchased through "insurance exchanges," meaning a marketplace of private insurance plans (subject to regulation as with other types of insurance) with different tiers, or levels of coverage, offered to individuals without health care or to small companies. The idea is that exchanges will, like any functioning regulated market, bring prices down so that personal and employer–provided insurance is both comprehensive (cannot legally skimp out on necessary care or otherwise abuse customers) and competitive (enough demand will force insurance companies to offer affordable policies in order to compete).

States may set up their own exchanges, or, if they opt not to do so, their residents can participate in exchanges set up by the federal government. As of early 2014, the majority of states had not set up their own exchanges. Most of those opting not to create state exchanges were headed by Republican governors or had Republican-controlled state legislatures. In order to discourage enrollment, fifteen states have gone so far as to establish strict rules to regulate the navigators – workers hired across the country trained to help people enroll in Obamacare.[188]

We will summarize additional provisions of the ACA (many still under heavy dispute and litigation and very much talked about by candidates) later in this chapter.

But to understand both the provisions and the dispute we first need to explore the landscape as it existed before the law was passed, especially for women.

Why Women Needed Health Care Reform

Health care was and still is a monumental concern for women. Before the ACA became law, almost half of women polled ranked it their highest priority, and 82 percent ranked it "very important," second only to the economy and jobs. In contrast, only 72 percent of men in 2008 said health care was very important – a 10 point gender gap. Sixty four percent of men and women alike told pollsters that health insurance companies refusing to pay for medical treatments, even when doctors said they were necessary, was a serious problem.[189] By 2012, after passage of the ACA, worries among women about health care had subsided somewhat. It ranked third in an open-ended question about the most important issue in the election.[190] More than twice as many women ranked abortion as most important, perhaps because opponents were successful in excluding insurance coverage of the procedure under the ACA.

Health care expenditures in the U.S. are 17.9 percent of the economy, well above the figure for any other industrialized country. Every year $2.6 *trillion* is spent in the U.S. on health care -– about $8,402 for every woman, man, and child in the country.[191] Even so, when we compare health outcomes –- measurements such as infant mortality or life expectancy–- the U.S. trails other nations.[192] Virtually every country in Europe has universal health care, as do Australia, Canada, and Japan.

Prior to passage of the ACA, the average cost of health insurance for an American family exceeded the entire yearly income of a minimum wage worker – and the majority of minimum wage workers are adult women.

That's probably a big reason why 47 million people in the U.S. had no health insurance, including almost one in five women. The numbers were terrible when broken down by race: 22 percent of African American women, 36 percent of Native American women, and a whopping 38 percent of Hispanic women were not covered.[193]

Over 15 percent of women had no first trimester pre-natal care,[194] and the vast majority of individual policies did not offer maternity benefits at any price.[195] Moreover, states could and did allow insurance companies to charge women more than they charged men for the same coverage (a practice known as "gender-rating") or to outright refuse coverage. According to a 2009 study by the National Women's Law Center, 95 percent of the companies practiced gender rating on individual plans, and 60 percent of those charged a 40-year-old woman who didn't smoke up to 63 percent more than a man who did smoke for the same coverage.

Drug prices were also a major health concern, particularly for women. Women between the ages of 15 and 44 spent 68 percent more on out–of–pocket health costs than did men, much of it on contraception. For young women, birth control was the single largest outlay, since insurance companies often refused to cover birth control pills (even though many covered Viagra-type drugs). There are also drug concerns for older women, discussed later in this chapter under Medicare.

Far too many children in our country were going without health insurance as well. According to the government's own figures, more than one in ten U.S. children were uninsured in 2009,[196] and one in twenty had no usual source of health care. About 1.8 million kids every year were unable to see a doctor because the family could not afford it, and 12 percent of those without coverage had not seen a doctor in over 2 years (some had *never* seen a doctor). Not surprisingly, children in single mother families are the most likely to be unable to get health care when they need it.[197]

While all of these problems did not instantly go away with passage of the ACA, the most discriminatory ones for women did. Gender rating was outlawed, coverage for birth control, maternity and pre-natal care was mandated, and subsidies for low income households became available. Despite the well-documented problems with malfunctioning computer systems when Obamacare was rolled out in late 2013, many other problems are disappearing as more families sign up for coverage and benefit from subsidies that make insurance affordable.

The Bottom Line – What Health Care Reform Does for Women (and Men)

The burden of not being able to afford care has had a greater impact on women than men. In one study, over 50 percent of women delayed seeking medical care because they couldn't afford it (compared to 39 percent of men); and a third faced difficult decisions to pay for needed care, such as giving up basic necessities.[198]

Individually purchased private plans had always been notorious for charging women more than they charged men for the same coverage (see above), and that was *not* because of maternity benefits. Most didn't offer maternity coverage at all. The rationale was that women are more likely to use health care services. This prompted Senator Barbara Mikulski (D-MD) to complain during the health care debate that insurance companies had long ago declared being female a pre-existing condition.

In addition to improvements to coverage in the programs mentioned above that disproportionately affect women, there are a number of additional provisions that will improve health care for women. The Affordable Care Act:

- Prohibits insurance companies from
  - denying women coverage due to a pre–existing condition (e.g., having a prior caesarian, being a victim of domestic violence)
  - excluding coverage of that condition
  - charging more because of gender or health status
- Requires coverage of preventive services, including mammograms and birth control, without deductibles or co-pays
- Requires insurance companies in the new insurance exchanges (virtually all) to offer maternity coverage
- Places a cap on what insurance companies can require people to pay in out–of–pocket expenses such as co–pays and deductibles
- Provides subsidies for those who cannot afford health insurance
- Prohibits all annual coverage limits in new plans and existing employer plans
- Requires coverage of basic pediatric services as well as dental and eye care services under all new health care plans

. . . And What the ACA Doesn't Do for Women

One place where women lost out in the ACA is abortion coverage. Though women in Congress put up an intense fight to mandate abortion coverage in the new insurance exchanges, they lost. The Affordable Care Act includes provisions that govern insurance coverage of abortion in state insurance exchanges. The 'Special Rules' (Section 1303) of the law and the related White House executive order issued by President Obama contain these new provisions:

- The law maintains current Hyde Amendment restrictions that govern abortion policy, which prohibit federal funds from being used for abortion services (except in cases of rape or incest, or when the life of the woman would be endangered), and extends those restrictions to the health insurance exchanges.

- The law also maintains federal "conscience" protections for health care providers who object to performing abortion or sterilization procedures that conflict with their beliefs. In addition, the law provides new protections that prohibit discrimination against health care facilities and providers who are unwilling to provide, pay for, provide coverage of, or refer women for abortions.

- The law allows states (through legislation) to prohibit abortion coverage in qualified health plans offered through an exchange. If insurance coverage for abortion is included in a plan in the exchange, a separate premium is required for this coverage paid for by the policyholder. In addition, President Obama's "Patient Protection and Affordable Care Act's Consistency with Longstanding Restrictions on the Use of Federal Funds for Abortion" executive order establishes an enforcement mechanism to ensure that federal funds are not used for abortion services, consistent with existing federal statute.

As of February, 2014, twenty-four states (Alabama, Arizona, Arkansas, Florida, Idaho, Indiana, Kansas, Kentucky, Louisiana, Michigan, Mississippi, Missouri, Nebraska, North Carolina, North Dakota, Ohio, Oklahoma, Pennsylvania, South Carolina, South Dakota, Tennessee, Utah,

Virginia, and Wisconsin) had laws prohibiting insurance coverage of abortion in state exchanges. Nine of those states – Idaho, Kansas, Kentucky, Michigan, Missouri, Nebraska, North Dakota, Oklahoma, and Utah – go even further and reach all plans in the state, banning insurance coverage of abortion in plans outside the exchange as well. This means that in those twenty-four states, a woman will not be allowed to purchase an exchange-based health plan that covers abortion services, and also may not be able to purchase a plan that provides insurance coverage for abortion from any source.[199]

- Because soaring drug prices can disproportionately affect women due to their lower incomes overall, an important issue is importing drugs from other countries such as Canada, where the same medications are cheaper. Prices for brand–name drugs in the U.S. are among the highest in the world, but it is currently illegal for private citizens to import them from other countries. Though overturning this prohibition was discussed in the ACA debate, it was kept intact in order to get the support of large drug companies.

The Big Arguments Continue in 2014 and Beyond

Repealing Obamacare has been a centerpiece for the party since it was enacted. Republican members of Congress and candidates attack it very frequently and promise if elected they will do away with it and leave health care to the "free market." As of early 2014, the House had voted 50 times to overturn the law, even though it has no chance to reach the Senate floor as long as the Democrats are in control.

The largest legal action against the law was filed almost immediately after it was signed. The Florida attorney general, later joined by 25 other states, charged that the individual mandate to purchase coverage is unconstitutional. (The reasoning is that the federal government cannot force individuals to buy something if they don't want it.) The states also said that since that linchpin provision is unconstitutional, the entire law should also be declared unconstitutional. After conflicting rulings by various lower courts, the Supreme Court ruled in 2012 that the individual mandate is constitutional and may be imposed under the ACA. (In a separate part of the ruling the Court altered the ACA rules on Medicaid – see the Medicaid section below.)

Another huge issue in ACA emerged in 2012 over coverage for birth control. The law exempts churches from covering birth control in their employee insurance plans if birth control is against their beliefs. But that was not good enough for the U.S. Conference of Catholic Bishops. They pressed the Obama Administration to also exempt any entity that was loosely affiliated with the church, whether or not the practice of religion is its primary activity. That would mean Catholic hospitals, universities, child care centers, and social service organizations could also deny birth control coverage to their employees.

After intense counter-lobbying on the part of women's groups, the Obama Administration ruled that the original exemption (for churches only) would stand. This unleashed a firestorm of protest from the bishops and also from every Republican candidate in the 2012 primary race for president. Charges of infringement on "religious freedom" filled the airwaves and pulpits. (Nobody talked about the religious freedom of non-Catholic employees who happened to need and want birth control.)

Three weeks later, the administration issued what it called an "accommodation." Religious institutions will still be required to cover contraception as part of any health care plan they offer to their employees, but they can opt out if they determine that the requirement violates their religious sensibilities. The burden would then fall on the insurance company to cover the cost. That insurance company would be required to inform the recipient of their benefits package in addition to paying for the contraception. Shortly after the accommodation was announced, some Catholic bishops refused to accept it and vowed to resist (though they didn't say they would flatly refuse to comply). They even insisted that not only should Catholic affiliated institutions be exempt, but any business owned by a catholic, period. Other Catholic organizations announced their acceptance of the ruling.

As of early 2014, several lawsuits challenging the birth control mandate were pending before the Supreme Court. Hobby Lobby, a for-profit business, contested the requirement on the grounds that it violates the religious freedom of the company's owners. If their argument prevails, presumably any employer could object to coverage of any medical procedure or drug on the grounds of corporate religious freedom. In a separate case, the Little Sisters of the Poor, a Catholic group of nuns employing 75 people, contended that even signing the papers authorizing the insurance company to pay for birth control violates their religious beliefs. The Supreme Court has exempted the nuns from the requirement pending appeal.

The Health Care System Under the Affordable Care Act - Rhetoric vs. Reality

If you are confused by the terminology, mischaracterizations, accusations, and doomsday scenarios accompanying the health care debate, you're not alone. But if voters are to be actively engaged in the ongoing dialogue with elected officials, candidates, and parties about health care, they need to know what the terms being bandied about actually mean, and not rely on rhetoric that is often times false or inaccurate. A few definitions:

> *Universal coverage* means just that – everyone has health insurance. Some have it through employers, some through individually purchased private plans, the very poor through government-subsidized programs, and some low income people through privately purchased plans that might be partially subsidized by the government.
>
> Universal coverage does *not* mean the government provides health care as a "welfare" or entitlement benefit to everyone regardless of income or employment status. Under the universal coverage schemes debated in Congress and ultimately passed in ACA, the for-profit insurance industry remains in place and plays a primary role in achieving universal coverage. Choice of doctors and hospitals under universal coverage is the same as it was before the ACA – controlled by the type of plan the individual is covered under, and in no small part dictated by insurance companies.
>
> *Single-payer* refers to a system of health care characterized by universal and comprehensive coverage, and the government would be the insurer issuing the payments. Everyone's health care would be paid for out of one publicly administered trust fund, funded by taxes on both individuals and business, which would replace our current multi–payer (i.e. insurance companies) system. Premiums to insurance companies would be eliminated.

While *single-payer would eliminate the role of insurance companies and the premiums paid to them*, the government would not be the primary *provider* of health care. It would just be the primary *payer*. There would still be freedom to choose doctors and other health care professionals, facilities, and services. Doctors would remain in private practice and be paid their fees from the government trust fund paid into by individuals and business. The government would not own or manage medical practices or medical facilities including clinics and hospitals, which would continue to be paid for their services.

Single-payer is what we have in place for seniors with traditional Medicare. Patients are free to use any doctor or hospital they choose, and Medicare pays the bill. Other countries with single-payer for everyone include Canada, Australia, and Japan. Despite the advocacy of this group and many others, and much discussion about a "public option"(which means single-payer), a universal single-payer system was never seriously debated by Congress in 2009 and is not part of ACA.

Proponents of single-payer systems, including many physicians and groups such as Physicians for a National Health Program (http://www.pnhp.org) cite huge savings from taking insurance companies out of the equation. These insurance companies, as the "middle man" in health coverage, spend billions on non-health care related expenses such as agent commissions, advertising, legions of employees to review claims (often searching for reasons deny coverage), and lobbying in Washington.

In January 2008, physicians in Massachusetts, where there was already a system that mandated universal coverage through the use of insurance companies (dubbed Romneycare in the 2012 election, after Republican candidate Mitt Romney who was governor when the system was adopted) issued an open letter to the country that reads in part:

> Although we wish that the current reform could secure health insurance for all, its failings reinforce our conviction that only a single-payer program can assure patients the care they need ... While patients, the state and safety net providers struggle, private insurers have prospered under the new law, and the costs of bureaucracy have risen ... All of the major insurers in our state continue to charge overhead costs five times higher than Medicare and eleven–fold higher than Canada's single-payer system ... A single-payer program could save Massachusetts more than $9 billion annually on health care bureaucracy, making universal coverage affordable.[200]

Socialized medicine is distinct and different from a single–payer system. In a socialized health care system, the government *owns* health facilities, and health personnel work for the government and draw their paychecks directly from the government. This is the model used in the U.S. Veterans Administration and the armed services, where the government owns the medical facilities and medical professionals are government employees.

International examples of socialized medicine can be found in Great Britain and Spain.[201] Red-hot rhetoric notwithstanding, *neither President Obama, anyone in Congress, nor either political party, presently advocates socialized medicine in the United States, nor did they do so during the debate over the Affordable Care Act.*

Traditional Medicare

While most health insurance in the U.S. is provided through private employer or personal funds, we have a few significant publicly-funded medical insurance programs that are important to women. The largest is Medicare, which is for people 65 and up and certain disabled people under 65. Though most of Medicare is paid for by the federal government, it requires a monthly premium from recipients.

Medicare is especially important to women, because they outlive men and will need health care coverage for a longer period of their lives. Women are also less likely to have private pensions that cover some medical needs like drugs, or provide supplemental coverage.

Medicare Part A covers only hospitalization or brief follow up care in a nursing facility. The vast majority of recipients meet eligibility requirements that do not require a payment for Part A.

But Part A does not cover doctor visits, diagnostic tests, medical equipment and the like. So most recipients also buy a second Medicare policy, Part B, to cover these shortfalls. A third, private, supplemental policy (generally dubbed Medigap) to cover everything the first two do not, such as deductibles, is also purchased by most Medicare recipients. By government regulation, Medigap policies are standardized across insurance companies. Benefits are clearly spelled out and do not vary from company to company, though the price of a given level of coverage may vary.

People insured under these traditional Medicare plans have complete control over their choice of doctors, hospitals, and specialists (although getting an appointment can be a challenge), though a very small percentage of facilities and doctors do not take Medicare. As noted above, Medicare is a single-payer system – and the government is that payer. That means people on Medicare do not have to file claims or hassle with insurance companies.

In 2014, Medicare Part B costs $104.90 per month (with a $147 deductible and high income recipients paying slightly more). A mid-priced supplemental Medigap policy (e.g one that would cover deductibles but not treatment in a foreign country) runs about $135 per month, depending on age and state of residence. Medicare premiums are rising rapidly, as are the costs of Medigap policies which must be purchased from private insurance companies. This is particularly relevant to older women, because their retirement incomes are lower than those of men, and women are less likely to get help with Medigap from former employers.

Drug coverage under Medicare (Part D) became operative in 2006. Though Part D plans are approved and regulated very loosely by the Medicare program, they are actually designed and administered by private health insurance companies, unlike Medicare Parts A and B.

Without question seniors needed some kind of drug coverage under Medicare, but Part D has come under much criticism from advocacy organizations, senior citizens, and members of Congress (though they're the ones that passed it). The biggest problem was a coverage gap, known as the"donut hole." Coverage was suspended each year when drug costs reached $2,930 and continued until they reached $4,700, even though seniors continued to pay Part D monthly premiums. This means many people paid 100 percent of their drug costs for part of the year, plus premiums. For the average senior, this was about 3½ months, over one quarter of the year.[202] Before Part D was passed by Congress, Senator Lautenberg (D-NJ) offered an amendment that would have required Medicare beneficiaries to sign a disclaimer that they understood, in plain English, the coverage gap in their plan before they could enroll in it. The amendment was defeated 43–56 with every single Republican in the Senate voting against it.

However, the problem will be solved with the ACA, albeit slowly. Obamacare closes the "donut hole" over time. Beginning in 2012, seniors got a 50 percent discount when buying brand name drugs and 14 percent discount on generic drugs covered by Medicare Part D. This reform gets stronger every year, increasing coverage and closing the donut hole until it disappears in 2020. From that point on, seniors will only pay usual drug co-pays.

Unfortunately, several other serious problems remain. One of the biggest is that *the federal government is prohibited from negotiating with drug companies for the lowest drug prices*. Congress prohibited such bargaining when it passed the Bush-era Medicare drug benefit in 2003, and the prohibition was kept in the Affordable Care Act in order to get large drug companies to support the legislation. Studies have shown that prices charged by Medicare Part D drug plans are 46 percent higher than those paid by the Veterans Administration, which does negotiate with the pharmaceutical companies.[203] The inability of the Medicare system to bargain with big pharmaceutical companies for better drug prices keeps prices high. For older women on fixed incomes, higher prices can cause cutbacks on needed drugs, or hard choices between medicine and food or heat.

Unlike Medicare supplemental plans, Part D plans are not standardized and are extremely confusing. Companies can change the drugs covered or drop drugs from coverage altogether, meaning people must shop all over again each year for a plan that covers the drugs they take. Plans can also raise the co-pays and premiums at will, and most have done so in great leaps.[204]

There are also problems for low income people who previously had their prescription costs paid by Medicaid. Part D replaced that coverage, and most of these recipients were automatically assigned to a Part D plan without any evaluation of their necessary prescriptions. Co-pays were instituted as well.

Medicare Advantage

A relatively new alternative to traditional Medicare is known as Medicare Advantage. Though HMO-type managed care programs have been available to enrollees under Medicare since 1997, they were greatly expanded in 2006 when the old plans were renamed Medicare Advantage, and incentives were created to induce for-profit HMOs run by insurance companies to participate.

Medicare Advantage plans are required to offer basic Medicare services and drug coverage under Part D. Beyond that, the government does not regulate them. That means that they can impose traditional managed care restrictions such as limiting choice of doctors and hospitals, and denying coverage for services or treatments (they also get to rule on any appeals you make when they deny coverage). Medicare sends the HMO a check every month on the patient's behalf, but the plans can set premiums and co-pays at any level they like.[205]

The non-partisan Medicare Payment Advisory Commission estimates that the federal government spends about 14 percent more on Medicare Advantage patients than on regular Medicare enrollees.[206] There have been many reported abuses in the selling of Medicare Advantage programs by insurance companies, including agents telling seniors they are "from Medicare," and the use of very high pressure sales tactics.

It has gotten so bad that state insurance commissioners want to prosecute the companies — but federal law does not allow states to pursue Medicare Advantage plans for fraud, as they can in other insurance markets.[207] Critics in Congress and such organizations as the American Medical Association and AARP say the plans are nothing more than a subsidy for private insurers – at a time when some others propose cutting physician fees for traditional Medicare enrollees.

During the ACA debate, President Obama consistently said Medicare Advantage programs should be reined in, because they are being unfairly subsidized at the expense of regular Medicare. By some estimates eliminating subsidies to Medicare Advantage programs would save the government more than $50 billion over five years, and $150 billion over ten years.[208] During the debate Republican critics charged that there would be "massive cuts to Medicare." This was not true. The ACA as passed cuts more than $200 billion in excess subsidies from the Medicare Advantage program ($136 billion directly and another $70 billion indirectly), phased in over time. Cuts to Medicare Advantage do not cut benefits under these programs (though the plans themselves may do so), The cuts do curb the excess subsidies to private insurers. The savings will be used to increase services under traditional Medicare, and to close the "donut hole" in drug coverage (see above). Though the American Health Insurance Plans (AHIP) and insurance lobbying organization predicted premiums would go up, this has not happened. Medicare Advantage premiums actually declined in both 2011 and 2012, while enrollment went up.[209]

Many candidates and elected officials will say Medicare is bankrupting the country, and we should cut back on it or make it available only to the poorest seniors. Others say the program should be turned into a voucher system, where recipients are given vouchers for a certain amount, and then must shop for a doctor or medical facility willing to provide treatment for the amount of the voucher. Both of these approaches would be bad for women. If Medicare is turned into a system for only the poorest citizens (the majority older women), it will then be mischaracterized as "welfare" instead of what it is – a program paid for by payroll taxes. Experience shows it is much easier to cut welfare programs than to cut items such as corporate subsidies and defense contracts. As for the other "solution," if Medicare is turned into a voucher system, there is nothing to prevent health care providers from requiring huge supplemental payments in addition to the voucher amount.

If Medicare is eliminated or even significantly curtailed, families will have to take up the slack and pay for health care for their parents and grandparents out of pocket. The program is very important for women, and female voters must ask the right questions before giving their support to any legislator or candidate.

Medicaid

Medicaid is a state administered health insurance program for the poor that is paid for in large part by the federal government through block grants (lump sum payments given to the states to spend under their state rules.)

Almost 60 percent of those enrolled in Medicaid are female.[210] Women have lower incomes overall and are also the most frequent custodial parents of children who are on Medicaid.

Even though states have leeway in crafting their Medicaid programs, they must comply with federal standards to get the federal government's money. Nevertheless states were generally free to set their own eligibility criteria for recipients until 2007, when the Bush administration imposed restrictions on the states' ability to expand Medicaid coverage to more low income families. The rationale was "to prevent coverage to families of modest incomes who may have access to private health insurance."[211] States had wanted to cover families of four making less than $60 thousand per year, up from $50 thousand.

With the economy in crisis in 2009 and many more people unemployed, the Obama administration increased Medicaid payments to the states. In order to qualify for the increases, states had to roll back any cuts that had been made after July 1, 2008.

The ACA expanded the pool of individuals eligible for Medicaid, which beginning in 2014 includes those below 133 percent of the poverty line (about $14,404 for a single adult or $29,327 for a family of four). Unlike previous Medicaid coverage, it now includes adults without dependent children (more men) and childless adults, greatly expanding the number of people covered. Initially the federal government planned to withhold existing funding if states didn't expand their programs.

Like almost every other provision of the ACA, expanding Medicaid was mightily resisted by those who opposed the law in the first place, and challenged in court as part of a lawsuit by attorneys general from several states. When the Supreme Court upheld the expansion in 2012, it included a critical caveat: The federal government may not threaten the states that don't comply with the loss of their existing funding. As a result, the Medicaid expansion is now optional for the states. As of February, 2014, 26 states had opted to expand their programs, two were considering it, and 21 had said no to expansion.[212] Failing to expand the Medicaid program appears to be a swipe at the Obama Administration on the part of states controlled by legislatures or governors that oppose Obamacare, since the federal government picks up 100 percent of the cost of expansion for the first three years, phasing down to 90 percent in 2020 and all subsequent years.

Children's Health Insurance Program (CHIP)

The Children's Health Insurance Program is a government funded program to provide health insurance for low-income children who are not covered under Medicaid. It was created in 1997 - passed by a Republican Congress and signed by a Democratic president. According to the Commonwealth Fund, a private foundation working for better health care, "the program represents a fine balance, designed to maintain equilibrium between states and the federal government, as well as between political conservatives and liberals."[213]

Like Medicaid, states have flexibility in designing benefits for CHIP, with the federal government paying an average of 70 percent of the cost and the states 30 percent. But also like Medicaid, the states must comply with federal requirements to get federal money.

In the original CHIP bill, children in families making up to 200 percent of the poverty line could be covered. The poverty line was then $21,200 for a family of four. When the program came up for reauthorization in 2007, Democrats in Congress tried to raise the level to 300 percent of poverty. President Bush vetoed the bill, saying it would be "an incremental step toward the goal of government–run health care." (His spokeswoman had charged the week before that it would be "socialized–type medicine.") Both statements were inaccurate, as the program is administered by private insurers and delivered by private nurses and doctors.[214] Congress was unable to override the veto, leaving the standard for eligibility at 1997 levels.

In early 2009, the Democratic Congress passed a new CHIP bill, which President Obama signed. It extended coverage to 11 million children (up from seven million) over a 4½ year period. Income restrictions were broadened and the states given more leeway in determining eligibility.

Under ACA, federal funding was extended from 2013 to 2015 and the federal match was increased for the years 2016-2019. ACA also prevents states from restricting CHIP eligibility standards, methodologies, or procedures from enactment until September 30, 2019.

Veteran's Administration Health Care

The Veterans Administration (VA), has traditionally provided VA care to all veterans, with copays for those veterans considered to be "non–poor"– generally those making $30,000 or more.

In January 2003, however, the Bush administration ordered a halt to the enrollment of "non–poor" veterans, citing not enough capacity. As a result, according to a Harvard Medical School study, millions of vets and their family members cannot afford health insurance and go without needed medical care. Others are unable to obtain VA care due to waiting lists at some VA facilities, unaffordable copayments for VA specialty care, or the lack of VA facilities in their communities.[215]

The Harvard research team estimates that 2,266 U.S. military veterans under the age of 65 died in 2008 because they lacked health insurance and thus had reduced access to care. That figure is more than 14 times the number of deaths suffered by U.S. troops in Afghanistan in the same year, and more than twice as many as had died since the war began in 2001. The researchers also noted the health reform legislation would not significantly affect this grim picture.[216]

In June, 2009, new regulations were put into effect by the VA. Income restrictions on enrollment for health benefits, while not eliminated, were relaxed. Consideration was also given to geographic area, recognizing that the cost of living in some parts of the country is higher than in others.

The ACA left veteran's health coverage essentially unchanged. Estimates of veterans without health coverage are now at almost 1.5 million. While women are a small percentage of veterans, they are especially vulnerable to cuts because of their lower incomes and longer lifetime needs for health care.

There is no doubt that we will continue to hear red-hot, red-meat rhetoric surrounding health care all the way until election day. Here are some questions for candidates:

The Affordable Care Act

Did you, or would you have, supported the Affordable Care Act?

Have you, or would you, vote to repeal the ACA?

Are you in favor of repealing the ACA, and if so, what would you replace it with? Please be specific.

If the ACA is repealed, we will lose protection from being dropped or excluded for pre-existing conditions, and once more face arbitrary caps and cessation of coverage by insurance companies. What would you do about that?

If the ACA is repealed, insurance companies will be allowed to continue to charge women more than men for the same individual policies. Do you think this is ok?

Do you think private insurance companies provide affordable service, and if not, how would you rein in rate increases?

Some people say the Affordable Care Act is socialized medicine, though the government does not own or control health care facilities, treatment, or medical professionals as would be the case in a socialized system. Do you think the ACA is socialized medicine, and if so why?

Our medical costs are far higher than those in other industrialized countries, and studies show our health outcomes are not as good. How, specifically, would you improve health care outcomes and affordability in the U.S.?

Do you think birth control and mammograms should be covered without co-pays or deductibles? What about Viagra-type drugs?

Knowing that abortion coverage is not part of health care reform, do you think businesses should be able to opt out of covering any other medical conditions or drugs because of "conscience clauses"?

Traditional Medicare/ Medicare Advantage

Do you support turning Medicare into a means-tested program? If so, do you still think workers should pay for it out of their monthly checks? How would such a Medicare program be funded?

Do you support turning Medicare into a voucher program. If so, how would you keep the vouchers

from becoming less valuable or worthless as health care providers raised prices?

Do you think cutting the extra subsidies to Medicare Advantage programs was the right thing to do, since those subsidies cost the government much more than traditional Medicare?

Do you think Part D drug programs should be better regulated? How?

Veterans Health Care

Do you think the Veterans Administration Health Care is adequately funded, given that some veterans can't get care because of enrollment restrictions?

Would you ease enrollment restrictions so that more veterans would be allowed into the program?

Would you expand veterans health care facilities so that geographic location is not such a hardship on veterans?

◊ TWELVE ◊

Reproductive Rights – The Perpetual Attack

Birth Control and Family Planning

Birth control has been under attack for much of U.S. history, with the legal assault beginning in the 19th century. After Charles Goodyear developed the vulcanization of rubber in 1839, rubber manufacturers started supplying not just condoms, but douching syringes and "womb veils" (or diaphragms and cervical caps), and what amounted to intrauterine devices (IUDs). By the 1870's, pharmacies were selling chemical suppositories, vaginal sponges and medicated tampons. All of these contraceptives were widely promoted in advertisements that were often detailed and graphic, giving us a disconcerting idea of some of the objects that women were encouraged to insert into their bodies.

Anthony Comstock, a onetime salesman in New York City and the philosophical father of anti-choice zealots today, believed birth control encouraged prostitution and fed the vice trade by separating sex from marriage and childbearing. He recruited others to his cause, and in 1873 they convinced Congress to pass a bill branding contraception obscene, and prohibiting its distribution across state lines or through the mails. Similar laws were passed in 24 states; they came to be known collectively as "Comstock Laws."

The Comstock laws did not do away with birth control – they merely led to it being marketed with the use of creative euphemisms describing "health devices" such as "married women's friends." Though courts and juries often looked the other way, the Comstock laws remained in effect until 1918, when the spread of venereal disease in the armed forces of World War I became a concern. A New York appeals court ruled that contraceptive devices were legal as instruments for the maintenance of health.[217]

After the decision, states repealed their Comstock laws, except for Connecticut. The staunchly Catholic Connecticut legislature repeatedly refused to roll back its statute. By the 1960s, it was the only state with such a law, although other states regulated the distribution of birth control devices or banned birth control advertising. The Planned Parenthood League of Connecticut had fought against Connecticut's prohibition for decades, and in 1965 they prevailed in the Supreme Court of the United States. The Court ruled in *Griswold v. Connecticut* that the right of married couples to use birth control is protected as part of a right to privacy under the Constitution.

The federal government began to take an active part in providing birth control in 1967, when 6 percent of the funds allotted to the Maternal and Child Health Act were set aside for family planning. In 1970, President Nixon signed the Family Planning Services and Population Act (known as Title X), which established separate funds for birth control. Title X clinics offer low income women voluntary contraceptive services, prenatal care, treatment for sexually transmitted diseases (STDs), and other services.

Medicaid, the nation's joint federal/state health insurance program for the poor, has specified family planning services as a mandatory benefit since the Nixon administration in 1972. According to the most recent data available, nearly 12 percent of all women of reproductive age rely on Medicaid for their health care, and the program provides just over six in ten public dollars spent on family planning across the country. It also was one of the very few services for which patient cost sharing was prohibited – until the Deficit Reduction Act of 2005, when states were allowed for the first time in more than 30 years to exclude family planning from the benefits offered to some groups of enrollees.

In addition, states could now charge fees for contraceptives or drugs used to treat sexually transmitted infections that are prescribed as part of a family planning visit. Another provision in the same bill caused brand name prescription prices for birth control pills dispensed by campus clinics to rise from about the $3 - $10 range per month to the $30 - $50 range, rendering contraceptives unaffordable for many college women.

The Guttmacher Institute, an organization researching reproductive health, says their data show that charging fees to poor women is a classic example of "penny wise and pound foolish." Many women cannot afford the co-pays, so will go without family planning services. To reduce both unintended pregnancies and abortions, programs should be expanded, not curtailed or eliminated.

California's experience is exemplary. The state's 2002 Medicaid family planning expansion prevented 213,000 unintended pregnancies, 45,000 of which would have been to teenagers. By preventing these pregnancies, the program helped women in California avoid a total of 82,000 abortions, 16,000 of which would have been to teenagers. And that's for just one year.[218]

President Obama proposed increasing access to family planning under Medicaid as part of the stimulus package passed in early 2009, but the provisions were removed before final passage after Republicans attacked the plan. Congress finally reversed the 2005 changes, sweeping away exorbitant birth control co-pays for Medicaid recipients and women on college campuses, when it passed the Affordable Birth Control Act in March of 2009.[219]

The influence of the U.S. on birth control and family planning policies and practices reaches far beyond our own shores. Maternal mortality remains high in many countries and more than 200 million women want, but cannot get access to, modern methods of family planning. We are a major influence in what happens worldwide, including funding for birth control, accessibility of reproductive health services, and control of information about family planning.

International family planning has in fact become a "political football" in the U.S., with conservative Republican administrations cutting or eliminating programs altogether, and Democratic ones lending some support (see a full discussion under Global Women's Issues). President Bush's Fiscal Year 2008 budget request to Congress included cuts of 25 percent, not only to the United Nations Population Fund (UNFPA), but also to all U.S. programs promoting family planning and reproductive health overseas. President Obama overturned the Bush era restrictions as one of his first acts after he was inaugurated in 2009.

Cutting Medicaid and the UNFPA are just two of the places where administrations differ, and where party control of Congress can make a difference. Other areas are the Title X family planning program (funded at below the inflation rate under George W. Bush and increased slightly under Obama), providing information about condom use and efficacy on government websites, access to over-the-counter emergency contraception (commonly referred to as Plan B), and information about birth control in sex education classes.

While Democrats have historically been much stronger supporters of family planning than Republicans, we should not believe that if Democrats are in control all the problems will be solved instantly. The anti-birth control forces are formidable, and they are able to influence politicians to vote against women's interests in this area, or at least to drag their feet or do nothing to overturn past harmful policies. The issues below are examples where nothing has been done, even with Democratic majorities.

Approval of over-the-counter emergency contraception was delayed until 2006, though the drug was approved by the FDA in 1998. It was approved without a prescription (but *behind the counter*) only for women 17 or older, who had to show a photo ID to the pharmacist. Sixteen-year-olds and under needed a prescription. This effectively prevented access, since getting a prescription usually takes longer than the 72 hour window in which the drug is effective, even if a younger teen has insurance to pay for seeing a doctor and the wherewithal to do it. The rule also limited availability to immigrant women who may not have a government photo ID. The FDA approved the sale of Plan B to younger teens in 2011, but the U.S. Department of Health and Human services under President Obama overruled the decision. The President claimed he had nothing to do with the ruling, but it was widely seen as political.[220]

In April of 2013, U.S. District Judge Edward Korman blasted that decision as putting politics ahead of science and ordered the FDA to allow unrestricted sales of emergency contraceptives. The Obama administration lost a round in the appeals court, too, and the Food and Drug Administration approved unrestricted sales of Plan B One-Step, lifting all age limits on the emergency contraceptive.[221]

Hospitals can (and some do) legally deny access to emergency contraception for rape victims. The Compassionate Assistance for Rape Emergencies Act would require hospitals receiving federal money to offer and provide emergency contraception to victims of sexual assault on request, but it has languished in Congress since first introduced in 2003.

Another birth control issue that has surfaced in the last few years is pharmacists refusing to fill birth control prescriptions if they are opposed to contraception. This so-called "conscience movement" is supported by such organizations as the U.S. Conference of Catholic Bishops and Pharmacists for Life International. Pharmacists who refuse say they have a "moral right" to refuse the prescriptions, and some go so far as to refuse to refer women to other pharmacies.[222] This obviously jeopardizes or eliminates the right of women to obtain drugs that are legally prescribed, not to mention allowing pharmacists to veto women's private choices. There is no question that refusal to fill emergency contraception pills leads to delays that can result in unwanted pregnancy.

The battle is being played out at the state level so far, with a few states having laws on the books that require the prescriptions to be filled, and another handful having laws that say pharmacists don't have to do so. No federal action has been taken yet. "Access to birth control" bills have been introduced in both the House and Senate, but have not gotten hearings. Since most of the activity on this issue is at the state level, it is particularly important that women ask any candidates running for state legislature where they stand on the issue. (And ask yourself: how much sense does it make for a person go to work for Colonel Sanders, then declare themselves a vegetarian and refuse to sell chicken – and still keep their job?)

One provision of the Affordable Care Act (ACA, or health care reform) is that birth control is covered without deductibles and co-pays in the new insurance exchanges. This has led to a firestorm of protest in 2012 from Catholic bishops and evangelicals, and many candidates are still running on promises to repeal the ACA.

Despite the general rule, the law exempts churches from covering birth control in their employee insurance plans if birth control is against their beliefs. But that is not good enough for the U.S. Conference of Catholic Bishops. They pressed the Obama Administration to also exempt any entity that was loosely affiliated with the church, whether or not the practice of religion is its primary activity. That would mean Catholic hospitals, universities, child care centers, and social service organizations could also deny birth control coverage to their employees.

After intense counter-lobbying on the part of women's groups, the Obama Administration ruled that the original exemption (for churches only) would stand. This unleashed a firestorm of protest from the bishops and also from every Republican candidate in the primary race for president in 2012. Charges of infringement on "religious freedom" filled the airwaves and pulpits. (Nobody talked about the religious freedom of non-catholic employees who happened to need and want birth control.)

Three weeks later, the administration issued what it called an "accommodation." Religious institutions are still required to cover contraception as part of any health care plan they offer to their employees, but they can opt out if they determine that the requirement violates their religious sensibilities. The burden then falls on the insurance company to cover the cost directly instead of as part of the institution's coverage. That insurance company would be required to inform the recipient of their benefits package in addition to paying for the contraception. Shortly after the accommodation was announced, some Catholic bishops refused to accept it and vowed to resist. They even insisted that not only should Catholic affiliated institutions be exempt, but also any business owned by a Catholic, period. Other Catholic organizations announced their acceptance of the accommodation. Litigation is pending seeking exemptions from the requirement for both religiously affiliated and private businesses whose owners object to birth control.

Conservative majorities and conservative leaders have shown in the past that they do not want to encourage birth control, and indeed in many cases would eliminate it altogether. And the future of domestic and international family planning programs, and therefore the fate of many women who may need birth control but cannot afford it, is still far from safe. Policies that influence women's choices and options are most definitely on the table in both state and federal elections.

Questions for candidates:

Do you believe in an individual's right to access to birth control without interference from the government?

Should hospitals receiving tax dollars be required to provide emergency contraception to rape victims if they are asked for it?

Do you support U.S. aid to international family planning programs?

Do you believe pharmacists should be able to refuse to fill legal prescriptions for any drug the pharmacy normally carries?

Do you think birth control and mammograms should be covered without co-pays or deductibles? What about Viagra type drugs?

Knowing that abortion coverage is not part of health care reform, do you think businesses should be able to opt out of covering any other medical conditions or drugs because of "conscience clauses"?

Abstinence-Only Sex Education

Abstinence-only-until-marriage sex education refers to a government-mandated method of teaching sex education to kids in schools that accept federal money. As a practical matter, this includes virtually all public schools and some private ones. While abstinence-only sex education is not supported by the Obama administration, it was strongly supported under George W. Bush and is still receiving $50 million per year in federal tax dollars. It is a stark illustration of how the path to misguided and downright harmful national policy can be very hard to change once it is begun, and because it is an excellent illustration of why majorities in Congress matter.

The mandate for abstinence-only sex education began way back in 1981 when Ronald Reagan was in the White House. The Adolescent Family Life Act was crafted by conservatives to prevent teen pregnancy – by promoting *only chastity and self discipline*. In those days, the programs also had a strong dose of religion, though specific religious references and providing classes in church sanctuaries were outlawed in 1993.

But federal money for abstinence-only continued to flow, and was increased dramatically in 1996, when $50 million per year was added by conservatives to President Clinton's high-priority welfare reform bill. Funding for abstinence-only burgeoned under the Bush Administration, going from $60 million a year to $176 million, and the 2006 budget noted that the request for abstinence-only programs would increase to a total of $270 million by 2008.[223] By 2008 Congress had lavished over $1.5 *billion* in state and federal dollars on this ideologically driven and unscientific "sex education."[224]

The law, a provision of the Maternal and Child Health Block Grant (under Title V of Social Security), was groundbreaking, both for its funding level and also for its unprecedented, eight-point definition of abstinence education. In a nutshell, Title V mandated that schools taking federal money teach *only* abstinence as a way to avoid pregnancy, disease, and psychological and social consequences of having sex, *to the exclusion of* other programs, such as information about birth control methods. It further directed that students must be taught that marriage is the only appropriate context for sexual activity, also required states to provide assurance that funded programs and curricula *not promote contraception and/or condom use.*[225] That's it – no birth control or protection against sexually transmitted disease, no medically accurate information about reproduction and child-bearing, and no acknowledgment that not everyone will marry and have children.

Several attempts to end or cut back funding for abstinence-only education by the Democrats in Congress failed during the Bush administration, because they did not have veto-proof majorities in the House and Senate. Though Democrats passed a bill in 2007 that ended Title V funding of the programs, the bill was vetoed by President Bush. A vote to override in the House failed by 2, demonstrating once again that the size of the majority matters.

After almost a decade of extravagant and ever-increasing money injections, the government's own long-term research by the Department of Health and Human Services has clearly shown that abstinence-only programs do not delay sexual initiation, nor do they reduce rates of either teen pregnancy or sexually transmitted diseases.[226] Moreover, the teenage pregnancy rate rose in 2006 for the first time since 1991, and the U.S. led the industrialized world in teen pregnancies. Government officials were "surprised" but had "no immediate explanation." At the same time, sexually transmitted disease rates, including syphilis, gonorrhea, and chlamydia, had been rising.[227]

These results, along with tightening program requirements that included a new directive to indoctrinate adults up to age 29 in community-based programs, contributed to a revolt in the states against abstinence-only sex education. The number of states that refused Title V abstinence-only funding grew from one (California) in the first year to 25 by mid-2009. Despite the mini-revolt, half of the states were still accepting the money, and by definition complying with the restrictive requirements for teaching sex education in public schools. But in one encouraging note, the teen pregnancy rate declined in 2008, perhaps as a result of half the states recognizing a failed policy.

In 2009, President Obama eliminated funding for abstinence only in his 2010 budget, instead allocating $164 million for teen-pregnancy prevention programs that have been proved "through rigorous evaluations" to delay sexual activity, increase contraceptive use (without increasing sexual activity), or reduce teen pregnancy. (An administration official said that no abstinence-only programs had met those standards.)[228]

Still, abstinence-only sex education is not dead, and like *Nightmare on Elm Street's* Freddy Krueger, keeps coming back to haunt schools, students, and parents. Twenty-five percent of the money for prevention is still open to abstinence-only programs, though they have to compete with other initiatives and prove they are effective. Senator Orrin Hatch of Utah added an amendment to the 2010 Affordable Care Act (health care reform) restoring $50 million per year in funding for abstinence only through 2015. Sapping even more tax dollars, the states must kick in $3 for every $4 the federal government provides for these failed programs.

Questions for Candidates:

Do you support comprehensive, age-appropriate sex education in the public schools?

How have you voted, or how would you vote, on providing public school money for abstinence-only sex education?

Do you think our (state, school district) should take federal money for sex education if it restricts that education to abstinence-only and nothing else?

Access to Abortion

> "For today, the women of this Nation still retain the liberty to control their destinies. But the signs are evident and very ominous, and a chill wind blows."
> —Justice Harry Blackmun, 1989 in the *Webster v. Reproductive Health Services* Supreme Court decision opening the way for state restrictions on abortion.

Some people believe that those who advocate for women's right to make their own reproductive choices are pushing "abortion on demand" on women. This is not the case. The so-called "abortion wars" are about a woman's right to control her own body and her medical privacy. Abortion rights advocates want women to be able to choose abortion, or choose to carry a pregnancy to term, without the interference of the government. They also believe that legal abortion should be available to women in other countries, because where abortion is outlawed, death rates from self-induced and illegal abortions are high – just as they once were in the United States. Contrary to rhetoric from the anti-choice right wing, abortion rights advocates do *not* endorse abortion as a method of birth control. While many women would never make the choice to have an abortion, the abortion rights movement is about preserving their rights as autonomous human beings as well.

Abortion was legal in the United States from the time the earliest settlers arrived. At the time the Constitution was adopted, abortions before "quickening" were openly advertised and commonly performed. States began to criminalize abortion in the 1800s, and by 1910 all but one state had criminalized abortion except where necessary, in a doctor's judgment, to save the woman's life.

The impetus for outlawing abortion was threefold. Some feared that newly arriving immigrants had birth rates higher than native-born white women, so outlawing abortion would up the birth rate of latter women and therefore stave off "race suicide." Anti-abortion legislation was also part of a backlash to the growing movements for suffrage and birth control -- an effort to control women and confine them to a traditional childbearing role.

Finally, the medical profession wanted more control over women's health.[229]

Abortion was often performed by "untrained" practitioners, including midwives, apothecaries, and homeopaths, thus competing with physicians for patient dollars. Physicians thus sought to eliminate one of the principle procedures that kept these competitors in business. Rather than openly admitting to such motivations, the newly formed American Medical Association (AMA) argued that abortion was both immoral and dangerous.[230]

Since very few abortions could be certified as necessary to save a woman's life, women were forced into the back alleys. Criminalizing the procedure did not reduce the numbers of women who sought abortions. Although accurate records were not kept, it is known that between the 1880s and 1973, many thousands of women were harmed as a result of illegal abortion. In the years before the Supreme Court legalized the procedure in 1973, the estimates of illegal abortions ranged as high as 1.2 million per year. Hospital emergency rooms treated thousands of women, many of whom died, and many suffered lasting health effects.[231]

Beginning in the 1960s with the women's liberation movement, one-third of the states liberalized or repealed their criminal abortion laws. The right to an abortion for all women in the U.S. was won in 1973, when the Supreme Court struck down the remaining restrictive state laws with its *Roe v. Wade* ruling. The ruling said that Americans' right to privacy included the right of a woman to decide whether to have children, and the right of a woman and her doctor to make that decision without interference from the state. It was not a ruling that granted wholesale "abortion on demand" to women. *Roe's* trimester-based analysis generally prohibits regulation of abortions in the first three months, allows regulation for protecting the health of the mother in the second three months, and allows complete abortion bans after six months, the approximate time a fetus becomes viable (able to survive on its own outside the womb).

Immediately after the ruling, the anti-choice forces mobilized, and they continue to work to prevent state funding for the procedure for poor women, to eliminate abortion counseling at home and in other countries through withholding U.S. family planning funds, and to mount campaigns and lawsuits to make abortion very difficult to obtain. Many also picket abortion clinics. Some clinics have been bombed or burned to the ground. Doctors are routinely targeted for harassment, and some have been murdered.

During President Bush's tenure, there were 3,291 violent incidents nationwide against abortion clinics. There were 86 outright blockades of clinics. Though such blockades are against federal law, only four incidents resulted in arrest. In 2010 after President Obama was elected there were 96 violent incidents including arson and assault at abortion clinics, and over 6,000 incidents of disruption, including bomb threats. As a possible indication that enforcement of the anti-blockade law has stepped up under the Obama administration, there was only one clinic blockade (no arrests).[232] Four federal indictments or sentences for clinic violence were handed down in 2011-2012.[233]

Violence, harassment, disruption, and blockades are actions that amount to domestic terrorism against the clinics, doctors, and the women who seek their services. The May 2009 murder of Dr. George Tiller, owner of one of the few remaining late-term abortion facilities in the country in Wichita, Kansas, brought national attention once again to anti-abortion violence. After several years the clinic reopened, but it is anybody's guess how long it will stay in business given the history of anti-abortion terrorism in Kansas. Anti-choice forces have also mounted concentrated legal attacks, passing restrictive state laws. Abortion law has become much narrower since *Roe*, including restricting pre-viability procedures, mandatory waiting periods, biased counseling, and parental involvement. Some legal entities, including the U.S. Justice Department under President Bush and the Kansas Attorney General, have tried to force hospitals to release women's private medical records, saying they are needed to determine if a crime has been committed.[234]

Two laws passed in Oklahoma in 2009 are examples of ongoing attacks on women's privacy. One bill, thrown out by the courts, said women had to undergo ultrasound using an invasive technique called a "vaginal transducer," and listen to doctor's explanation during the process before she could get an abortion.

The other measure required women seeking abortions to disclose information that would be put on a state-run website. That information includes previous pregnancies and live births; previous marriages; previous induced abortions; how the abortion was paid for; the reason for the abortion; and information about the mother's relationship with the baby's father, among other things. The law was declared unconstitutional and unenforceable in 2010, but anti-choice lawmakers vowed to rewrite both bills and resubmit them in future legislative sessions.[235] They tried to declare an embryo a person in 2012, but the Oklahoma Supreme Court struck it down as unconstitutional.

Even if state legislatures are not inclined to pass restrictive laws (and most are - see timeline at the end of this chapter), anti-choice activists have shown they will use state ballot initiatives to outlaw or restrict abortion. Ballot measures are proposed state laws that must be approved or rejected directly by voters within states. They can be placed on the ballot by legislatures, citizen petitions or other methods, and are most often held in conjunction with general elections.

In California, Colorado and South Dakota abortion-restriction ballot measures pushed by anti-choice forces were defeated by voters in 2008. Conversely, the women's rights movement was forced to use the initiative process in South Dakota in 2006 to repeal an abortion ban that had been passed by the legislature and signed by the governor, which included no exceptions for a victim of rape or incest or if a woman's health is endangered. Had the law not been repealed, proponents of the ban had envisioned it as a test case for outright repeal of *Roe* in subsequent court challenges.

It is daunting, to say the least, that the pro-choice movement will have to fight abortion bans state by state, year after year, if there are no federal protections. Anti-abortion activists are working in a number of states to get initiatives on the ballot that would extend constitutional protections to fertilized eggs by defining them as persons, even though similar initiatives in Colorado were rejected twice in 2008 and 2010, and in 2011 a Mississippi amendment was defeated at the polls. "Personhood for eggs" initiatives failed to make the ballot or clear legislative hurdles in roughly a dozen states in 2012, but at least three (Colorado, Ohio, and Nevada) are seeking to place initiatives on the ballot in 2014.

All of the "egg" initiatives would end a woman's right to choose, ban several of the most medically safe forms of birth control, restrict common fertility treatments, such as in vitro fertilization, and put an end to stem cell research. Perhaps most dangerous is the possibility that criminal investigations could be launched against women for their miscarriages.

A number of cases have been litigated all the way to the Supreme Court. The first outright federal abortion ban, prohibiting one type of procedure unless the life (but explicitly excluding the health) of the woman is at stake, was upheld in 2007. In the *Gonzales v. Carhart* and *Gonzales v. Planned Parenthood Federation of America* decision (known as Carhart II), the new Roberts Court upheld the federal abortion ban with a 5-4 vote, undermining a core principle of *Roe v. Wade*: that women's health must remain paramount. Writing for the majority, Justice Kennedy evoked antiquated notions of women's place in society and called into question their decision-making ability, said lawmakers could overrule a doctor's medical judgment, and that the "state's interest in promoting respect for human life at all stages in the pregnancy" could outweigh a woman's interest in protecting her health.[236]

The result of all of this harassment, both legal and otherwise, is that while abortion remains legal in the U.S., it is increasing harder to obtain. Not only are the above restrictions in place in many states, but clinics have shut down due to harassment. Eighty-eight percent of counties in the U.S. have no identifiable abortion provider, and the number rises to 97 percent in rural counties. That means one in four women have to travel over 50 miles, and 8 percent travel 100 miles or more.[237] With mandatory waiting periods and the inability of many women to miss work, this puts abortion out of reach.

It is uncertain whether *Roe v. Wade* will be overturned outright in the next few years, but it is looking increasingly likely with the new hard-core conservative majority against abortion rights. Those who think abortion will still be legal, only "just go back to the states," as many like to say, need to think again. As of December 2007, 43 states had laws on the books that will restrict the legal status of abortion or outlaw it altogether (commonly called trigger laws) when *Roe* is overturned.[238]

And don't fall for the line that these are "old" pre-*Roe* laws that will never be enforced – only 13 fall into that category, and there is certainly no guarantee that they won't stand up. In fact, anti-choice state legislators in many states can be expected to "stand guard" to see that these laws are not overturned. Chillingly, some states rushed to pass new trigger bans in 2007, in anticipation of a *Roe* overturn, right after the Carhart II decision (see Addendum).

The right to reproductive choice and medical privacy is the single biggest issue at stake for women's lives and health in the 2014 election and beyond. It is not only relevant to young women who may be faced with the abortion decision, but to all women who value their autonomy and privacy. Because it is both a federal and state issue and bans are looming at both levels, it is particularly important to confront candidates at both levels as to their views and intentions.

Questions for candidates:

Do you support a woman's right to abortion as embodied in *Roe. v. Wade*?

Do you oppose appointments to the Supreme Court of people who would overturn *Roe v. Wade* ?

Do you support any restrictions on the right to choose? If yes, which ones?

If *Roe v. Wade* is overturned, would you support a federal Freedom of Choice Act guaranteeing a woman's right to privacy in medical decisions, including whether or not to have an abortion?

Addendum
A Timeline on Reproductive Rights

1821: Connecticut passes the first law in the United States barring abortions after "quickening."

1860: Twenty states have laws limiting abortion.

1965: *Griswold v. Connecticut* Supreme Court decision strikes down a state law that prohibited giving married people information, instruction, or medical advice on contraception.

1967: Colorado is the first state to liberalize its abortion laws.

1970: Alaska, Hawaii, New York, and Washington liberalize abortion laws, making abortion available at the request of a woman and her doctor.

1972: *Eisenstadt v. Baird* Supreme Court decision establishes the right of unmarried people to use contraceptives.

1973: *Roe v. Wade* Supreme Court decision strikes down state laws that made abortion illegal.

1976: Congress adopts the first Hyde Amendment barring the use of federal Medicaid funds to provide abortions to low-income women.

1977: A revised Hyde Amendment is passed allowing states to deny Medicaid funding except in cases of rape, incest, or "severe and long-lasting" damage to the woman's physical health.

1991: *Rust v. Sullivan* upholds the constitutionality of the 1988 "gag rule" which prohibits doctors and counselors at clinics receiving federal funding from providing their patients with information about and referrals for abortion.

1992: *Planned Parenthood of Southeastern Pennsylvania v. Casey* reaffirms the "core" holdings of *Roe* that women have a right to abortion before fetal viability, but allows states to restrict abortion access so long as these restrictions do not impose an "undue burden" on women seeking abortions.

1994: Freedom of Access to Clinic Entrances (FACE) Act is passed by Congress with a large majority in response to the murder of Dr. David Gunn. The FACE Act forbids the use of "force, threat of force or physical obstruction" to prevent someone from providing or receiving reproductive health services. The law also provides for both criminal and civil penalties for those who break the law.

2000: *Stenberg v. Carhart* (Carhart I) rules that the Nebraska statute banning so-called "partial-birth abortion" is unconstitutional for two independent reasons: the statute lacks the necessary exception for preserving the health of the woman, and the definition of the targeted procedures is so broad as to prohibit abortions in the second trimester, thereby being an "undue burden" on women. This effectively invalidates 29 of 31 similar statewide bans.

2000: Food and Drug Administration approves mifepristone (RU-486) as an option in abortion care for very early pregnancy.

2003: A federal ban on abortion procedures is passed by Congress and signed into law by President Bush. The National Abortion Federation immediately challenges the law in court and is successful in blocking enforcement of the law for its members. Two other legal challenges (Carhart II, see below) were also mounted.

2004: *National Abortion Federation v. Gonzales*. NAF wins lawsuit against federal abortion ban. Bush Justice Department appeals rulings by three trial courts against ban to the U.S. Supreme Court. The case remains on hold pending the outcome of Carhart II.

2006: *Ayotte v. Planned Parenthood of Northern New England*, challenged New Hampshire's law requiring doctors to delay a teenager's abortion until 48 hours after a parent was notified, but lacking a medical emergency exception to protect a pregnant teenager's health. In a unanimous decision, the Court reiterated its long-standing principle that abortion restrictions must include protections for women's health.[239]

2007: *Gonzales v. Carhart* and *Gonzales v. Planned Parenthood Federation of America*, (Carhart II) In a 5-4 decision, the new Roberts Court upheld the federal abortion ban, undermining a core principle of *Roe v. Wade*: that women's health must remain paramount, and essentially overturning its decision in *Stenberg v. Carhart* (Carhart I), issued only seven years earlier. Writing for the majority, Justice Kennedy evoked antiquated notions of women's place in society and called into question their decision-making ability, said lawmakers could overrule a doctor's medical judgment, and that the "state's interest in promoting respect for human life at all stages in the pregnancy" could outweigh a woman's interest in protecting her health.[240]

2008 to 2011: The number of abortion providers nationally dropped 4 percent in a three year period. Nine states and D.C. saw an increase in providers, while 21 states saw declines. The remaining 20 saw no change.[241]

2011: According to the Guttmacher Institute, in the first quarter of 2011 916 measures related to reproductive health and rights had been introduced in 49 states (56 percent were laws restricting access). Fifteen had become law.

2011 to 2013: States enacted 205 abortion restrictions, more than had been enacted in the entire first decade of the 2000s.[242]

2013: The Supreme Court turned away an emergency application asking it to block a Texas law requiring doctors performing abortions to have admitting privileges at a nearby hospital. The Court ruled that the challengers to the law had not met a heavy procedural burden in asking the Supreme Court to alter an appeals court's provisional decision to let the law go into effect while it considers an appeal.[243]

2013: First city-level 20-week abortion ban in the nation defeated by voters in Albuquerque, New Mexico. The initiative was widely viewed as a test case for city bans nationwide.

2014: The Supreme Court issued a ruling saying the state of Arizona can't enforce its law to ban abortions after 20 weeks of pregnancy. The 9th U.S. Circuit Court of Appeals had ruled that the law violated U.S. Supreme Court rulings on abortion, including *Roe v. Wade*. Arizona appealed to the U.S. Supreme Court, asking the Court to reverse the appellate court ruling. The Supreme Court issued a brief order rejecting the appeal, giving no reason for their decision. The ruling does not affect similar laws passed in other states except the law in Idaho, which is also covered under the jurisdiction of the appeals court.[244]

◊ THIRTEEN ◊

Violence Against Women

Violence in U.S. society is a problem for both women and men. While men are more often victims of physical violence, certain types of violence disproportionately affect women and children – domestic violence, stalking, sexual assault, sex trafficking, and abortion clinic bombings and harassment.

Below are a few quick facts:

- Of female murder victims in 2010, 38 percent were killed by a husband or boyfriend.[245]

- Nearly 1 in 5 women (18.3 percent) and1 in 71 men (1.4 percent) in the United States have been raped at some time in their lives, meaning women are about 16 times more likely to have experienced rape.[246]

- Rape rates in the U.S. vary by race. Twenty-two percent of Black women have experienced rape at some point in their lives, White women 18.8 percent, Hispanic women 14.6 percent, American Indian or as Alaska Native women 26.9 percent, multiracial non-Hispanic women 33.5 percent.[247]

- One in 6 women have been stalked during their lifetime, compared to 1 in 19 men.[248]

- One in 4 women have been the victim of severe physical violence by an intimate partner, while 1 in 7 men have experienced the same.[249]

- Domestic violence remains prevalent at every level of American society, despite strengthened laws and penalties. The need for services clearly outstrips resources. The National Census of Domestic Violence Services documented 10,471 unmet requests for services in one 24-hour period in 2012.[250]

These few facts do not begin to describe the scope of the problem. There are many other equally shocking statistics on violence involving women and children. The reader is referred to the American Bar Association for information on statistics and other aspects of the issue, including details on the Violence Against Women Act. http://www.americanbar.org/groups/domestic_violence.html

Stopping Violence – What We Have

The first comprehensive federal legislation responding to violence against women was introduced in 1990. The Violence Against Women Act (VAWA) took four years to pass, and was signed by President Clinton in 1994.

It established a number of discretionary grant programs for state, local, and Indian tribal governments, including grants to aid law enforcement officers and prosecutors, encourage arrest policies, stem domestic violence and child abuse, establish and operate training programs for victim advocates and counselors, and train probation and parole officers who work with released sex offenders.

VAWA also funded battered women's shelters, rape prevention and education, reduction of sexual abuse of runaway and homeless street youth, and community programs on domestic violence. In addition, it mandated several studies of violent crimes against women.

The Violence Against Women Act made a number of changes in federal criminal law. Penalties were created for stalking or domestic abuse in cases where an abuser crosses a state line to injure or harass another, or forces a victim to cross a state line and then physically harms the victim in the course of a violent crime.

The law strengthened penalties for repeat sex offenders, required restitution to victims in federal sex offense cases, and allowed evidence of prior sex offenses to be used in some subsequent trials regarding federal sex crimes.

VAWA set new rules of evidence specifying that a victim's past sexual behavior generally was not admissible in federal civil or criminal cases regarding sexual misconduct, and that rape victims be allowed to demand that their alleged assailants be tested for HIV.

VAWA was reauthorized in 2000, 2006 and again in 2013, retaining most of the original programs and creating new ones to prevent sexual assaults on campuses, assist victims of violence with civil legal concerns, create transitional housing for victims of domestic abuse, and enhance protections for elderly and disabled victims of domestic violence. The 2006 version also created a pilot program for safe custody exchange for families of domestic violence, and included changes in the federal criminal law relating to interstate stalking and immigration. The stimulus package President Obama signed into law in early

2009 contained $225 million in increased funding for the Violence Against Women office at the Department of Justice. In 2013 additional protections were added for Native American women living on reservations, granting tribal jurisdiction over domestic violence.

The federal Debbie Smith Act is a grant program designed to eliminate the "rape kit" backlog, by preventing states from diverting the funds for other kinds of DNA backlogs. The kits contain DNA evidence collected in rape cases, and could lead to the apprehension of rapists. Nationwide, advocates say there are up to 180,000 untested kits sitting on shelves in police departments, some as long as 10 years.[251] The Sexual Assault Forensic Evidence Registry (SAFER) Act, passed by Congress as part of the 2013 reauthorization of the Violence Against Women Act, re-focuses the Debbie Smith grant program on ending the backlog. State and local grantees must now use a greater percentage of Debbie Smith funds—up to 75 percent from 40 percent—directly on analyzing untested DNA evidence, or enhancing the capacity of labs to do so. Previously, the greater portion of funds went to initiatives like training, education programs and equipment for law enforcement.

To aid in the process, the SAFER Act provides state and local governments with funding to conduct one-year audits of the untested rape kits in their possession and upload data on every individual kit into a national web-based registry . The registry has the potential to enhance efforts to end the backlog, though it is a voluntary program.

Stopping Violence – What We Need

Despite the fact that almost all of the money from VAWA goes to local resources and supports the National Domestic Violence Hotline located in Texas (where Laura Bush is reported to have been a donor at one time), conservatives continue to claim it is a handout for "national feminist groups." Some want to do away with VAWA altogether.

Women's advocates must constantly defend VAWA and the national statistics on violence that are its underpinnings. Even though most of the statistics come from the federal government, conservative advocacy groups actively try to "debunk" the numbers. As a result, funding for VAWA is under incessant attack.

One gap in VAWA is in legal assistance to victims of domestic violence, which the law does not address. Studies estimate that fewer than one in five low-income survivors of domestic violence ever even see a lawyer. Yet legal advice is key for these women as they seek help from the police or court system.

Often, stopping the violence hinges on the ability to obtain effective protection orders, initiate separation proceedings, or design safe child custody arrangements. Without legal knowledge, these options are not accessible.

In 2008, then-Senator Joe Biden introduced The National Domestic Violence Volunteer Attorney Network Act that would meet this demand for legal assistance by mobilizing 100,000 volunteer attorneys willing to work on behalf of survivors of abuse. The bill did not receive hearings. If such a measure should become law it the future, it would give the National Domestic Violence Hotline funds to provide legal referrals to victims who call in requesting help.[252]

Human Rights Watch recommends that the Department of Justice authorize comprehensive studies that more accurately track sexual and domestic violence in the U.S., especially among individuals who are least likely to be surveyed by the National Crime Victimization Survey that is conducted every two years.

Questions for legislators and candidates:

- # Do you support (or did you vote for) continued full funding for the Violence Against Women Act?
- # Do you support The National Domestic Violence Volunteer Attorney Network Act that would provide volunteer attorneys for low income domestic violence victims?
- # Do you think the federal government should collect more statistics on violence against women?

◊ FOURTEEN ◊

Our (Sick) System of Sick Leave, Maternity Leave, and Family Leave

Paid Sick Leave

There are no federal or state laws guaranteeing sick leave for employees in the United States. Whether sick leave is granted is entirely up to employers, except in Philadelphia (public agencies and contractors only), Connecticut, San Francisco, Washington, D.C., Seattle, Jersey City, N.J., New York City, and Portland, Ore., where paid sick leave laws are in place. Measures in the last three were passed in 2013. Grassroots groups in states including Arizona, Minnesota, Illinois and North Carolina are working to put paid sick leave laws before their legislatures in 2014.

Because there is no requirement for paid sick leave, nearly half of Americans have no benefit for self-care or to care for a family member. For the lowest earning families (bottom quartile), 71 percent have no paid sick leave. For families in the middle (next 2 quartiles), 36 and 25 percent, respectively, lack such leave. Even for families in the top fourth of the income bracket, 16 percent do without paid sick leave.[253] Frighteningly, during the H1N1 flu pandemic of 2009, some 77 percent of food service workers had no paid sick leave, undoubtedly resulting in many of them reporting to work with the virus.[254]

This puts us in stark contrast to much of the world – 145 countries provide paid sick days for short or long-term illness, and more than 79 give 26 weeks of time off for illness, or provide leave until the worker recovers.[255]

For those workers lucky enough to have paid sick leave, the benefit is limited in how it can be used. A very high percentage of plans are limited to personal illness; employees can't use it to care for ill family members.

State laws are not much help. Only a few states require employers that do offer the leave to broaden it to give workers greater leeway in using their sick days (e.g. caring for sick kids).

Maine was the first state to pass such a flexibility law in 2002; California, Connecticut, Hawaii, Minnesota, Washington and Wisconsin have since adopted similar measures.[256] While these laws help, they apply only to employers choosing to offer sick leave in the first place – there is no requirement that companies have to provide the benefit.

And there is a growing backlash from business interests. Ten states have passed paid sick leave bans in the past three years, seven of them in 2013, according to research by the Economic Policy Institute (EPI), a think tank that focuses on issues concerning low- and middle-income workers.[257] Similar bans are under consideration in 14 other states, along with efforts to weaken or eliminate current laws that mandate paid sick days for private businesses.

A bill called the Healthy Families Act has been introduced in Congress in every session since 2004. If it ever passes, it will require companies with 15 or more employees to provide minimum paid sick leave and employment benefits of: (1) seven days annually for those who work at least 30 hours per week; and (2) a prorated annual amount for part-timers working 20-29 hours a week (or who work between 1,000 and 1,500 hours per year). The new law would not affect workplaces that already have more generous sick leave policies. As of the beginning of 2014, only a little over one fourth of the members of the Congress had signed on to the bill, which was languishing in committee with no hearings scheduled.

Pregnancy Leave

Like sick leave, there is no federal mandate that companies grant paid pregnancy leave. Still, there is a little more legal protection for pregnancy compared to sickness.

The Pregnancy Discrimination Act (passed in 1978) says if a woman is temporarily unable to perform her job due to pregnancy, the employer must treat her the same as any other temporarily disabled employee (e.g. someone who is injured or has had a heart attack).

So if the guys in the executive suites get leave time to recover from a coronary, the girls in the word processing department must be treated equally when it comes to pregnancy, since both conditions would be considered a temporary disability. But if employers opt not to provide any paid time off for temporary disability, both workers are out of luck.

By way of comparison, out of 167 nations cited in a United Nations 2010 report, 162 had some form of paid maternity leave, leaving the United States in the company of Lesotho, Papua New Guinea and Swaziland.[258]

If the U.S. ever gets paid family leave, it will go a long way toward relieving some of the family and job stress associated with pregnancy and childbirth.

Family Leave

The United States has had *unpaid* family leave since 1993, when President Clinton signed the Family and Medical Leave Act (FMLA). It was the first major bill signed into law by the newly sworn-in president, after a long and bumpy ride to the Oval office. FMLA was the result of eight years of Congressional debate, thirteen separate votes, and two vetoes by President George H. W. Bush.[259]

Basically, the FMLA grants 12 weeks of unpaid leave for workers (on the job at least a year) who work for a company with 50 or more employees and can satisfy other requirements concerning hours and earnings. This means less than a fifth of new mothers and only about half of the U.S. workforce overall qualify, and many of those who do can't afford to take the leave. It is not ordinary sick leave – it can only be used for *serious* health conditions of the employee, care of a *seriously* ill spouse, child, or parent, or for care, birth, or adoption of a child.

But the key word here is *unpaid*. Even for those whose workplaces are mandated to grant the benefit, many employees cannot afford to take it.

Once again, the U.S. lags behind other countries. Ninety-eight of the 167 other countries that have guaranteed paid maternity leave offer 14 or more weeks off with pay, 66 provide paid paternal leave, and 37 ensure paid leave for illness of a child.[260] In Sweden, parents share 480 days of paid parental leave per child, and the benefits amount to 80 percent of the stay-at-home parent's salary. There are extra incentives to encourage men to take their share.[261]

Nevertheless, U.S. business groups (and the lawmakers and candidates they support) generally oppose such legislation. They say it would cost employers too much. No one asks how much lack of paid leave costs families.

There is some relief from states and cities, but not much. On January 1, 2014, Rhode Island joined California and New Jersey in offering workers paid family leave. New York and Massachusetts have paid-leave bills pending, and Connecticut, Vermont and New Hampshire have formed task forces to study the issue. Several other states, including North Carolina, Colorado and Oregon, have considered it and may move bills again. (Though a bill passed in Washington state in 2008, it has not been implemented.) While it's good that states and cities are moving on the issue, a piecemeal approach is not the answer. Access to family leave should not depend on where one lives. We need comprehensive federal legislation.

Women are now half the workforce and in it to stay, and it is in the national interest to craft a system whereby both women and men can take care of children and elderly parents when an emergency arises – without losing their jobs or suffering setbacks at work.

Because women are still the primary caretakers in society and still make less than men overall, lack of paid leave can mean giving up a job altogether. And while an increasing number of men are also taking on caregiving obligations, men who ask for leave time are often denied or penalized because of stereotypes that caregiving is only "women's work."[262]

Since 1993, when FMLA was signed by President Clinton, there's been little action in Congress. That has changed recently, with the introduction of the Family Medical Insurance Leave Act by Kirsten Gillibrand (D-NY). It would create a system of paid family leave financed by a payroll tax evenly split between employers and employees. Both would pay into a giant insurance pool – much like Social Security – and the wage replacement would come from that pool when needed. A good idea – but for now, passage seems a long way off. Gillibrand's bill has just a single co-sponsor (where are the other 98 members of the Senate?), and companion legislation has not been introduced in the House.

Both women and men support better family leave policies, according to national polls. A 2010 survey of registered voters found that 76 percent wanted paid leave laws for family care and childbirth, 69 percent endorsed paid sick day laws, and 82 percent said they would support legislators who worked for stronger laws against discrimination and unfair treatment at work. Sixty-four percent overall supported policies to give workers the right to ask for a flexible schedule (70 percent of women, and 71 percent of parents).[263] An election night poll in November 2012 found strong support along party lines, with 73 percent of Republicans, 87 percent of independents, and 96 percent of Democrats saying the issue was important.[264]

The problems of work-family balance are not going to go away. Some lawmakers have recognized that by introducing legislation to help solve the problems, and candidates need to address them too. It is up to women to pose the hard questions and determine whether a candidate supports family-friendly workplaces or not.

Questions for legislators and candidates:

Do you support paid sick leave for employees? Have you, or would you, co-sponsor one of the bills now in Congress to provide it?

Do you support both maternity and paternity leave for birth or adoption of a child?

Do you support *paid* family and medical leave? Have you, or would you, co-sponsor a bill to provide it?

Do you support a comprehensive national plan for paid sick days and paid family leave that does not depend on the state where an employee lives?

◊ FIFTEEN ◊

Child Care

In the 1970s, feminists used to say "the personal is political." They meant that problems we often interpret as personal – to be solved on our own without society's involvement – are actually reflections of the political will of the country and its leaders. Some examples back then were lack of equal access to universities, employers legally refusing to hire women or firing them for being pregnant, and domestic violence – to name just a few. Thanks to the women's movement, consciousness was raised, and people came to see these as systemic problems that society as whole should deal with. New laws were passed and programs created to address these issues and others.

One place the message still hasn't gotten through is child care. Most families have been taught by the culture to believe that when it comes to child care the "personal is personal," meaning families are on their own and there's little that can be done about it. Except for a few children's advocacy groups, there is no organized lobby for a national child care system.

In terms of national policy, the U.S. government and families alike tend to view child care as a family problem, not a public responsibility. This is the opposite view from countries in other parts of the world that provide public child care. Whether child care *should* be a public responsibility is controversial in the U.S. (at one time public schools were also controversial with the education of children viewed as a "family matter").

Conservatives believe women (not men) should stay home with their children, unless they are poor single mothers, who should definitely go to work. Liberals give lip service to child care as being in the public interest, but do little to make it a reality.

As more and more women enter the work force and families cannot afford for one parent, or the only parent, to stay home, the need for quality, affordable child care increases. The overall labor force participation rate of mothers with children under 18 was 70.5 percent in 2012 despite the economic downturn.[265] Nearly one-fourth (24 percent) of the 75 million children under age 18 live in a single-mother family.[266]

Availability and Cost

The availability of affordable childcare can have a large impact on women's choices about work. Childcare is often prohibitively expensive: the Organisation for Economic Co-operation and Development estimates that the cost of center-based care for two children in the U.S. could amount to as much as 37 percent of a single parent's income – a considerably larger portion than almost all other countries.[267]

Child care tends to be the first or second-largest household expenditure, running from $5,574 to $16,430 per child per year. By contrast, the average annual cost for an infant in center-based care is higher than a year's tuition and fees at a four-year public college in every region of the U.S.[268]

While child care and pre-kindergarten are not the same thing, expansion of pre-k programs would help ease the child care crunch. Pre-k programs are administered by the states, and they vary widely, both in availability and funding.

According to The National Institute for Early Education Research at Rutgers University, only nine states plus the District of Columbia currently make pre-k available to all four-year-olds, and most have no state-funded pre-k program for three-year-olds. Overall, state-funded pre-k programs in the U.S. currently serve only 28 percent of four-year-olds and a paltry 4 percent of three- year-olds. Ten states have no state-funded pre-k program at all.[269]

According to the *New York Times* using 2007 figures, the U.S. could have a year's worth of universal pre-school (half day for all three-year-olds, full day for all four-year-olds) for the cost of two months of the war.[270] Updating the estimate to reflect 2011 war expenditures for Afghanistan and Iraq,[271] universal pre-school for a year could be provided for a about five month's war cost.

Child care is one of the most challenging problems facing families today, whether they are two-parent families or single mother families. U.S. parents pay almost all of their child care costs without state or federal assistance, amounting to a large portion of household income (over 25 percent for families below poverty level).[272] This is undoubtedly the main reason why enrollment in child care and early childhood education is lower in the U.S. than in other industrialized countries.

Most families struggle with child care, regardless of whether their incomes are low, medium or high.

That's because we have a hodge-podge of arrangements, and the availability of good care depends as much on where one lives as on income.

Of course the higher one's income, the greater their ability to pay – if there is a decent program to pay *for*. Private in-home care by a nanny is almost exclusively limited to high income families, but even that does not guarantee the availability of a trustworthy and competent caregiver.

Wages for child care providers, whether in homes or in child care centers, are notoriously low – the median wage is $9.38 per hour.[273] Benefits are also minimal. This can add up to standards being compromised to get workers, and there is a great deal of turnover. Ninety-seven percent of these low-paid, low-benefit jobs are held by women.[274] Not surprisingly, the few men in the field earn more than the women.

Child Care Programs in the United States: A Brief History

Beginning in the 1930s, the U.S. government provided a modicum of public support for child care by offering some "back door" child care assistance through public programs meant to allow women to stay home with their children in the absence of another breadwinner.

In the Social Security system, this was (and still is) in the form of survivor's benefits. If a mother with small children became widowed, survivor's benefits assured she could stay home and care for the children herself (though initially based on the father-provider-mother-caretaker model of the 1930s, the benefit is now available to either widowed parent).

In 1935, divorced or never-married mothers who were not widows were given entitlement to far less generous payments through the Aid to Families With Dependent Children (AFDC) program that came to be known as "welfare." It was assumed that with these payments, poor mothers would also stay home and take care of their own children.[275]

Government policy changed briefly during World War II, when women were needed in the work force. The government provided child care centers, some even open at night to accommodate shift workers. But at the end of the war, the centers were abruptly closed; female factory workers fired, and the jobs turned over to men.[276]

A modest federal tax break was enacted in 1954 for working parents with child care expenses. Programs that were viewed as educational or developmental gained support in the 1960s, when the Head Start pre-school development program (usually half-day) was implemented for children from deprived backgrounds.

In 1971 Congress passed a federal child care bill, but it was vetoed by President Nixon who called it the "Sovietization of American children." President Ford vetoed another one in 1974.

Over the years, welfare programs changed to an emphasis on getting single mothers *into* the workforce, with some support for outside child care that continues to the present day. Child Care Development Block Grants to the states were created in 1990 to help low-income families and those receiving or transitioning from public assistance with child care.

Has Anything Changed?

Virtually nothing has changed in the 21st century. We still do not have a national child care program, or even a national plan. No programs (just a few modest tax breaks) exist for non-poor families.

The programs we have for low-income parents are meager. Public child care funding in the U.S. goes mostly to poor families, but even if these children are eligible for federal assistance, the great majority do not *actually receive* it. According to the U.S. Department of Health and Human Services, only 18 percent of federally eligible children receive child care assistance.[277]

According to the U.S. Department of Health and Human Services, funding levels for the Child Care and Development Block Grant provided for only one out of 10 eligible children even before the recession.[278] Thanks to the American Recovery and Reinvestment Act (stimulus funding) and President Obama's request for increased money for child care, in 2011 both Head Start and the Child Care & Development Block Grant received boosts of $340 million and $100 million respectively, on top of 2010 funding levels.[279] While this was good news, child care funds were cut anyway as the recession continued. By the end of 2011 the money had all but dried up, and states were cutting back by as much as 30 percent.[280] With the political attacks on public sector workers that reached a groundswell in 2011, there were widespread reports of child care workers being laid off as well.

Under the across-the-board spending cuts known as "sequestration" in 2013, the number of children participating in Head Start/Early Head Start once again took a hit, declining by 57,000. But in fiscal year 2014, 90,000 children were added, including 40,000 in Early Head Start, an increase of more than one-third. The Child Care and Development Block Grant program was funded at $2.36 billion, up $154 million from the sequestration levels, and said to allow 22,000 additional children to participate. Unlike many other domestic programs, child care spending is now higher than it was in fiscal year 2010.[281]

The situation in the U.S. differs markedly from other countries, where child care and/or early childhood education is viewed as a public responsibility. Many countries in Europe have some form of national child care. For example, almost 100 percent of French three-, four-, and five-year-olds are enrolled in the full-day, free *écoles maternelles*; all are part of the same national system, with the same curriculum, staffed by teachers paid good wages by one national ministry.[282]

While the U.S. is a long way from such a system, advocates argue that we should be thinking about one where most if not all children in the country can be served, even if it is not through a universal and standard model like the one in France.

Despite the rising cost of child care, the government's child and dependent care tax credit has remained unchanged since 2003—and, adjusting for inflation, has actually fallen over the same period. In most cases, middle and high-income families receive a 20 percent tax credit on child care expenses up to $3,000 for one child and a maximum of $6,000 for two or more children, resulting in a maximum benefit of $600 or $1,200. In theory, lower-income families can claim 35 percent of their expenses on the same costs, but in practice few low-income families owe enough tax to benefit from the credit.[283]

Advocates say a simple change in tax law would allow middle-class families to get a bigger tax break to cover the rising cost and necessity of child care. Having a single 35 percent tax credit rate for all families would eliminate the disparities in the tax credit and nearly double the maximum allowable credit from $1,200 to $2,100 to help account for the increased cost for child care.[284]

Opponents of any kind of government help with child care say countries with child care have higher taxes, and taxes would surely go up in the U.S. if we followed suit. That is probably true. But if we view what families are paying now as a "tax" that is not shared by everyone, a modest tax hike for a better system that all families could benefit from does not look so bad. There is strong support among parents to provide increased funding to improve the quality of child care by paying $10 more in taxes each year (73 percent of all parents, 78 percent of parents with children under age 5).[285]

The economists Suzanne Helbrun and Barbara Bergmann did a cost analysis in 2002 for a medium level system that would provide affordable care of improved quality to families, including those in the middle class. Starting with national average fees for care of children aged 0-12, they estimated the annual cost of a mid-level program with affordable co-pays, including how much additional money would be needed over costs of low-income programs now in place.[286]

Using the best available data from the Consumer Price Index, and estimates of government spending on low income programs in 2010, the current cost of their plan would be about $74 billion per year, with a new money portion of $51 billion.[287]

The additional money is about the same amount the Bush and Obama administrations spent to bail out General Motors, [288] and less than a fourth of the cost of the bank bailouts.[289] For the price of the defense spending for *one year* (2010)[290], the child care plan could operate for over 16 years – the span of an entire childhood.

Questions for candidates:

What would you do to help working families with child care expenses?

What would you do to increase the availability and affordability of child care?

Do you support public funding for universal pre-kindergarten for four-year-olds? For three-year-olds?

Have you, or would you, sponsor any bills that would help working families with child care? What kind of bills specifically?

What is the next step you will take to move toward universal pre-kindergarten?

◊ SIXTEEN ◊

Long Term Care

In the U.S., long-term care has historically been treated as a private problem, unless you are among the poorest. Even then, there are few government resources. Medicare, the nation's medical insurance system for those over 65, does not pay for personal or custodial services or long-term care. Medicaid, which provides health insurance for those with very low incomes and few if any savings or assets, will pay for nursing home or home-based care. But services and benefits depend on the state where you live, and generally assets must be "spent down" in order to qualify. The Department of Veterans Affairs (VA) *may* provide long-term care for service-related disabilities or for certain eligible veterans (e.g. low income).[291]

Long-term Care in Other Countries

The U.S. is far behind other developed nations in long-term care policy and practice. Long-term and elder care varies in other countries, but many provide some assistance regardless of income.

According to an article by Martin Tolchin in the *New York Times*, "In Canada, 8 of the 10 provinces now provide some form of long-term care coverage for all citizens. The Netherlands provides long-term nursing home care for the entire population. Japan offers two kinds of long-term care. There are geriatric hospitals that resemble American nursing homes, for those who need skilled medical care, and for which the Government pays the entire bill for those 70 years old and above.[292]

A Woman's Issue

Since the U.S. comes up short not only on national policies but on programs as well, long-term care is an issue that most families must solve on their own. And it is very much a women's issue.

The long-term care problem hits women "coming and going," so to speak. Women live longer and therefore need long-term care more than men, and women are still the overwhelming majority of caregivers, whether paid or unpaid. The MetLife Mature Market Institute projects that half of U.S. adults will eventually need some kind of long-term care. Seventy-two percent of nursing home residents are female, and 90 percent of paid direct-care workers and 61 percent of family caregivers are women.

Nationally, staff turnover in nursing homes averages 70 percent per year for aides and 50 percent for nurses, meaning patient care is uneven and unreliable.[293] Two thirds of U.S. nursing homes are owned by for-profit companies,[294] many of them corporate chains paying notoriously low wages, which are undoubtedly a major contributor to this turnover.

Unlike workers in care facilities, home care aides have historically not even qualified for the minimum wage. A labor department rule dating back to 1975 had been used to classify these workers as "companions," a class of workers that did not qualify for the minimum or for overtime. Overturning the decades-old exemption, the U.S. Department of Labor under President Obama extended minimum wage and overtime benefits to the mostly female and minority workforce of nearly two million home health-care workers, effective January 1, 2015.[295]

Purchasing Long-term Care

Private long-term care insurance must be purchased on the open market from insurance companies, generally while the individual is still healthy – and preferably young – in order to be affordable. These expenses can approach $100,000 per year in some parts of the country. Obviously most families find this far out of reach.[296] As a result, most long-term care services are either provided by unpaid caregivers (mostly female), or paid out-of-pocket.

Caregivers, particularly women and members of low-income families, are faced with tremendous stress. Many get caught in a difficult spiral. They are forced to take time off from work, forgo promotions, and maybe even drop out of the workforce altogether to care for elderly relatives. Consequently, they work less and earn less, which reduces the Social Security and pension benefits they receive. And women, who generally live longer than men, must stretch their meager resources much further.

Needed: Changes in Public Policy

Long-term care insurance was part of the Affordable Care Act (health care reform) passed in 2010. Known as the Community Living Assistance Services (CLASS) Act, the program was intended to be purely voluntary, paid for by insurance premiums, and open to all working Americans. It would have provided a basic lifetime benefit of a least $50 a day in the event of illness or disability, to be used to pay for even non-medical needs, such as making a house wheelchair-accessible or hiring a home caregiver to assist with basic tasks. However, the Obama administration determined that the plan was unworkable, and dropped plans for implementation in October, 2011.

Even though those plans were scrapped, some provisions of the ACA may apply to long-term care purchased on the private market. Some companies announced plans in 2014 to use "gender rating" for policies, meaning charging women more than men for the same coverage. Gender rating is outlawed for policies subject to the ACA. The National Women's Law Center has filed a lawsuit against several insurers, reasoning that because they offer long-term care policies through Medicaid partnership programs in several states, they receive federal assistance, meaning they cannot discriminate on the basis of sex under the ACA. Litigation could take several years, meaning women may be out of luck until the issue is settled by the courts.[297]

While we clearly do not have the long-term care supports that we need, the need for long-term care could be reduced with other changes in public policy. According to AARP, most older people and those with disabilities want to remain independent and get the assistance they need at home or in their communities, not in nursing homes. Providing care at home or in an assisted living facility can improve quality of life and provide better value for the dollars spent.

Many of the services elders need to stay in their own homes are not medical. Transportation, help with bill-paying, and help with shopping or daily self-care are all needed services for which there is at present little or no support.

Providing support for these services, even funding volunteer networks, could go a long way toward keeping elders in their own homes longer, at the same time providing a higher quality of life than nursing home care that is expensive and oftentimes below par.

Questions for candidates:

Are you satisfied with the fact that the U.S. lags far behind other developed nations when it comes to long-term care for the elderly?

What would you do to ease the financial burden of long-term care on families?

Do you think a federal or state program to provide affordable long-term care insurance is needed?

Do you think Medicare should be expanded to include long-term care?

How would you improve transportation options for seniors who can no longer drive?

Should Medicaid and Medicare support non-medical services to keep seniors out of nursing homes longer?

What would you do to improve the standards for nursing homes and insure that patients are cared for adequately?

Do you think the government should support pilot projects in liveable communities, with services that keep seniors in their own homes longer, to see what works best? How would you do this?

◊ SEVENTEEN ◊

Education and Title IX - Back to "Separate But (Un)equal"

> "No person in the United States shall, on the basis of sex, be excluded from participation in, be denied the benefits of, or be subjected to discrimination under any educational program or activity receiving federal financial assistance." – Title IX of the Education Amendments of 1972

With these few words added to our national body of laws, sex discrimination in educational institutions that receive federal funds became illegal. Because many private schools accept some federal money, the law covered them as well as public schools at all levels – from kindergarten through graduate school. Title IX was needed because sex discrimination (overwhelmingly against girls and women) was rampant in many areas of education. Most people did not realize this, because in those days sex discrimination was viewed as "normal." It was "normal" that girls could not have school sports teams; it was "normal" that girls could not be crossing guards; it was "normal" that girls were barred from auto mechanics and boys were barred from cosmetology; it was "normal" that medical, engineering, and law schools could refuse to admit women or limit female enrollment with strict quotas. It was also normal for girls to be expelled for becoming pregnant, and pregnant teachers to be fired when they began to "show." And a little sexual harassment was normal too – after all, "boys will be boys."

Title IX has been an unqualified success. The numbers bear this out:

- In 1971, women were 40 percent of undergraduates overall, but could still be barred from college altogether or required to score higher on admissions tests to gain entrance.[298] By 2013 women were projected to make up 57 percent of undergraduate enrollments.[299] (Gender gaps are higher than average between Black and Hispanic women and men, and there are still more Asian men enrolled than Asian women.)[300]

- In 1971 women were awarded fewer than 10 percent of medical and law degrees and 14 percent of doctorates. Females are now approaching 50 percent in all of those areas, though they still lag significantly in engineering and computer science.[301]

- In 1971, females were 1 percent of dental school graduates. By 2011 they were over 46 percent of graduates.[302]

- In 1971, only 294,015 girls participated in high school athletics. According to the U.S. Department of Education. Today, over 2.7 million girls participate in high school athletics, an 847 percent increase. This has not taken away opportunities for males, who are still the majority of high school and college athletes.[303] By 2010 girls participated in greater numbers than in the beginning of the decade; however, girls' share of total athletic opportunities decreased across the decade as compared to boys' share.[304]

– The Supreme Court has ruled that sexual harassment in the schools, either by peers or school personnel, is illegal under Title IX. Before, victims of harassment – including boys – had no clear way to stop it or seek justice after it happened.

Despite its obvious success, Title IX has been under constant attack since it was passed in 1972. Though the word "sports" does not appear in the law, Title IX has become closely linked in the public mind with increased opportunities for girls in athletics. Conservatives have brought lawsuits, calling it a "quota system" and charging that it is detrimental to men, particularly in sports programs.

Nothing in Title IX requires schools to eliminate men's teams. Research shows that the biggest reason minor men's sports are dropped at the college level is the football budget - which takes the lion's share of athletic dollars.

In 1984 during the Reagan years, the Supreme Court issued a ruling that severely limited the scope of the law for four years – until Congress restored it with the Civil Rights Restoration Act of 1987. The speaker of the House of Representatives during President George W. Bush's first term, Dennis Hastert ®-IL), was an ardent opponent of Title IX. An ex wrestling coach, Hastert called Title IX a "gender-based quota system," and said that if the Supreme Court upheld a Title IX decision against Brown University, it would "set a dangerous precedent." (The Supreme Court did uphold the complaint.)

In 2005 the Bush Department of Education issued a Title IX "clarification," which allowed schools to refuse to create additional sports opportunities for women (but not men) based solely on email interest surveys. According to the new interpretation, failure of a female student to answer an email survey could be counted by the college as a lack of interest in participating in sports. At the insistence of the Senate Appropriations Committee, the Department of Education conducted a study on the effects of the new rule in 2006, and confirmed that it had weakened the law. But the Department also refused to make any changes in the "clarification."[305] The rule remained in effect until April of 2010, when the Obama Administration rescinded it.

During the first 35 years of Title IX, single-sex classes and extracurricular activities were largely limited to physical education classes that included contact sports and to sex education, because gender segregated classrooms and schools before the law was passed had been a hindrance to equal opportunity for girls. Prior to Title IX, girls were seldom sent to flagship math and science acceleration programs or special "star" schools for high achieving students. These spots were tacitly (or sometimes openly) reserved for boys. The only single gender girl's schools tended to be those for pregnant students – with far fewer resources than even the regular classrooms afforded.

But on January 8, 2002, President Bush signed into law the No Child Left Behind Act (NCLB), a bipartisan bill which had passed both houses of Congress with large majorities. Through a little-noticed provision, NCLB called on the Department of Education to promote single-sex schools. In response, new Title IX guidelines were issued in 2006, allowing gender segregated schools and classrooms for the first time since 1972. These changes were not made by Congress, but by the Bush administration's appointees at the Department of Education, underscoring once again the importance of which party is in power. School districts can now set up single-sex options as long as the other sex is offered something "substantially" equal. "Substantially" is not defined, and unlike the punitive evaluation requirements for progress under NCLB generally (see below) the method for measuring success of single-sex education is undefined.

Since the weakened the guidelines of Title IX were issued, there has been a proliferation of sex segregated schools and classrooms, though there is no consistent evidence to indicate that kids learn better in these classrooms than they would in mixed gender schools with the same resources.[306] In other words, if mixed classrooms had the same low teacher-to-pupil ratios, increased funding, and individual student attention afforded in the new segregated ones, it is likely that all the students would benefit. Indeed there is evidence that socioeconomic status, school size, selectivity, and school resources are bigger factors than gender in the success of graduates of all-female or all-male colleges. The trick is not to separate students by gender, but to give all students the best educational experience possible.[307]

Proponents of single-gender schools and classrooms often cite a "boy crisis," setting up an artificial school battleground between boys and girls. While boys are now behind girls in achievement, it is because girls have improved more rapidly, not because boys' achievement levels have fallen.[308]

The movement has also brought a proliferation of sex-role stereotypes back into the schools. In 2006, Livingston Parish, Louisiana announced a plan to compel gender segregation in all classes in a formerly co-ed school. In their plan, they cited an "expert" with no education credentials who contends that "boys need to practice pursuing and killing prey, while girls need to practice taking care of babies." The plan was dropped after the American Civil Liberties Union filed suit on behalf of a girl who resisted the forced segregation.

These stereotypes can hurt boys as well. In a California experiment with dual academies, boys were seen as "bad" and taught in a more regimented way, while girls were seen as "good" and taught in more nurturing, cooperative, and open environments.[309]

But just because a few schools have dropped their gender-stereotyped plan under threat of litigation does not mean that single gender education is dead – far from it. A comprehensive 2012 study by the Feminist Majority Foundation in Washington, D.C. found that single sex schools and classrooms have been instituted in all but a handful of states (though not statewide anywhere), and further that most are in violation of Title IX, which still requires extensive documentation as to how such segregation contributes to the elimination of discrimination even under the relaxed rules.[310]

Parents who now support or are considering single gender schools and classrooms should study the conservative positions on Title IX and single sex education, as they generally promote sex-role stereotyping and lesser treatment for girls as students. Parents should also ask themselves what the term "substantially equal" means in the Bush-era regulations. Would it be "substantially" equal to offer one gender smaller class sizes and more teachers than the other sex? What about offering the two genders different content in their classes, perhaps based on unscientific stereotypes about boys and girls?

In February of 2012 the Dallas Independent School District made national news when it excluded girls from a field trip to see the movie "Red Tails," about the Tuskegee airmen in World War II. The trip for the boys cost $57,000. The girls were left behind, and "some" were shown a 6-year-old movie "Akeelah and the Bee." The justification provided by the district was that theatre space was limited, and school officials thought the boys would enjoy the "Red Tails" outing more than the girls. They added that gender specific events are often held. The reader can decide if this situation is "substantially equal."

While the Obama Justice Department has filed an amicus brief in one lawsuit stating that there should be a specific appropriate justification for each sex segregated class, they have done nothing to enforce the existing law (Title IX) which governs whether the sex segregated classes and schools meet the required criteria for non-discrimination. Advocates believe the relaxed standards should be specifically overturned, since they are regulatory and not mandated by law, and in fact weaken the law.

The Women's Sports Foundation has published these recommendations from researchers:

- The Office for Civil Rights should strengthen its enforcement of Title IX in secondary schools to ensure that girls receive equal opportunities to reap the many valuable benefits of playing sports.

- Federal policymakers should require high schools to publicly disclose gender equity data about their athletics programs.

- Urban schools, in particular, should redouble their efforts to increase the numbers of athletic opportunities that they provide to girls.

- All schools should have Title IX coordinators and should regularly conduct Title IX self-evaluations to ensure that they are complying with the law.

Questions for candidates:

Do you believe the Bush-era Department of Education regulations that weakened Title IX and once again allow single gender schools and classrooms should be overturned?

Do you believe schools planning single gender classes should be required to thoroughly

justify such classes as to their effects in overcoming discrimination, as required by law?

Do you think the U.S. Department of Education should step up enforcement of Title IX, particularly in light of the proliferation of single gender classes?

Do you think high schools should be required to publicly disclose gender equity data about their athletic programs, including funding, facilities, and sports opportunities?

◊ EIGHTEEN ◊

Affirmative Action is Our Business (and Education Too)

Though many people don't know exactly what the term "affirmative action" means, it makes them nervous anyway. They think it means a preference for hiring unqualified people (usually Black or female) over more qualified applicants (usually white men), merely because of race or gender. They also believe it means that there are "quotas" for unqualified applicants that must be filled.

The term "affirmative action" actually describes a number of policies that actively seek to overcome discrimination in hiring and promotion, in government contracting, and in education. Affirmative action can also refer to the process by which the under-representation of certain groups, including women, in a given work force is corrected. It has nothing to do with quotas (they are in fact outlawed), nor does it mandate preferences.

The rationale for affirmative action rests on the fact that white males have historically been hired and promoted in greater numbers than women and male members of minority groups, and further that women and minorities are channeled or segregated into certain job categories which often pay less and offer fewer opportunities for promotion. Looking at it this way, one could say that affirmative action is meant to overcome a system of preferences (unwritten of course) that has been in place for much of our history.

Affirmative action is a part of the anti-discrimination fabric of U.S. law. Discrimination in employment on the basis of race, religion, color, national origin, or sex is illegal under Title VII of the Civil Rights Act of 1964. But while Title VII prohibits discrimination, it does nothing to change the systems that foster discrimination in the workplace and education in the first place.

Because of this shortcoming, in 1965 President Johnson signed Executive Order 11246, prohibiting discrimination by the federal government and private employers and universities holding federal contracts on the basis of race, color, religion, and national origin, *and* requiring them to establish affirmative action plans for hiring and equal treatment on the job. Sex was added in an amendment to the Executive Order in 1967.

The requirement for affirmative action plans at the federal level *only* applies to the government itself, and to businesses and educational institutions holding federal contracts. The idea is that our tax dollars should not be used to underwrite discriminatory policies on the part of businesses or schools benefitting from those tax dollars. *Affirmative action does not apply to private business in general*, though many companies not receiving federal contracts have developed affirmative action plans because they value diversity and believe it is good for business.

Affirmative action was designed to break down the "old boy network" by encouraging personnel and procurement decision-makers to look beyond personal acquaintances, golf partners, and other insider networks. This is very important not only to job-seekers but to women- and minority-owned businesses, since there are affirmative action requirements for spreading federal contracting dollars fairly (see Chapter 15).

Conservatives have always attacked affirmative action programs as "quotas," and have also called them "reverse discrimination" against whites, usually white males. As stated above, affirmative action does not require quotas – quotas are specifically prohibited. (It is interesting to note that unwritten "quotas" have been in place for women and minority men for decades. Those "quotas" enforce the norm of granting these groups only a small share of jobs at the top, promotions, and leadership opportunities – and they gave rise to affirmative action in the first place.)

An affirmative action employment plan seeks to insure that a company work force is representative of the population of available qualified workers in the surrounding area; in other words, a plan that produces the same work force that would result if there were no discrimination.

In addition to general hiring goals a good affirmative action plan also includes goals for specific jobs. That's because it's possible to have a work force that technically represents the surrounding pool of workers, but is segregated by job category. An example would be a work force where the total is 50 percent male and 50 percent female, but 98 percent of the managers are male and 98 percent of the clerical workers are female.

For most jobs, affirmative action does not mean the workforce must reflect the total population of minority or female workers in a given area, since all of them are not qualified for every job. The number of women and minorities in a given position need only reflect the number of *qualified, available workers in the general pool of workers from which a company is drawing.*

For example, if women constitute 45 percent of the available workers in a city, an affirmative action plan for hiring unskilled workers could reasonably have a goal of 45 percent women in unskilled positions, since all women in the general labor market are presumably qualified for unskilled positions.

For skilled positions, only the number of qualified women in the surrounding labor market would be used as a basis for hiring goals. If it is known that 22 percent of the graduates of area engineering programs are women, then a reasonable affirmative action goal is 22 percent women for entry level hiring, and a mid-level engineering work force that is 22 percent female in a few years.

A plan for reaching female and minority applicants to let them know about job openings is normally included in affirmative action, since word-of-mouth advertising of openings in predominantly white male companies yields predominantly white male applicants.

Civil Rights or Civil Wrongs?

While support for affirmative action is strongest among blacks (93 percent – no gender breakdown available), support among white women and men is also quite solid. Even so, we see a gender gap: white men strongly favor affirmative action programs (65 percent) but white women are even more supportive (71 percent). Over all groups, support grew by 12 points from 1995-2007.[311] In mid-2009, even as a controversial affirmative action ruling took center stage during the confirmation hearings for Supreme Count Justice Sotomayor, public support was still very high, with affirmative action programs for women drawing the strongest support (63 percent).[312] By 2013, support was down when the question was asked only in the context of racial discrimination, with 53 percent saying affirmative action is still needed, 37 percent saying it should be phased out, and 10 percent unsure. No data was reported by gender, and gender was not included in the question.[313]

Federal affirmative action programs were reaffirmed by the Supreme Count in 1995.[314] Since then conservative attacks have shifted to the states. Many states have affirmative action goals of their own for state employment, state contracts with private firms, and admission to state universities. (It is ironic that white females have been used as plaintiffs in some high profile lawsuits seeking to outlaw affirmative action programs in education, though white women have historically benefitted greatly from affirmative action programs – not only in education, but also employment and government contracting.)

Attacks on affirmative action at the state level are mostly in the form of ballot initiatives to outlaw the programs. The highest-profile attack was Proposition 209, passed in California in 1996 with consequences still reverberating today.

Called the "California Civil Rights Initiative" on the ballot, Proposition 209 amended the California constitution to outlaw state affirmative action programs in public education, public employment, and state contracting. Although the constitutionality of the initiative was legally challenged, the U.S. Supreme Court denied further appeal in 1997 and let Proposition 209 stand.

Since the California initiative, five more state anti-affirmative action initiatives have been successful: in Washington State in 1998, Michigan in 2006, and Nebraska in 2008, Arizona in 2010, and Oklahoma in 2012. A 2008 initiative in Colorado was narrowly defeated.

The initiatives are led by one man, Ward Connerly, an African American who is very closely affiliated with contractor groups that contribute most of the money to his organization.[315] In addition to his outright victories, Connerly's threat of an anti-affirmative-action initiative in Florida in 1999 prompted then-Governor Jeb Bush to ban "racial preferences" at public colleges and universities as a preemptive measure. Racial affirmative action has also been discontinued at individual institutions, such as the University of Georgia and Texas A&M.

Only one affirmative action case has reached the Supreme Court in recent years, and the verdict was indecisive. Abigail Fisher, a white woman, claimed that the University of Texas-Austin unconstitutionally discriminated against her after the state's flagship university rejected her application in 2008 under its race-conscious admissions program. In 2013 the Court issued a mixed opinion. It did endorse prior Supreme Court decisions establishing affirmative action as constitutional to further states' compelling interest in fostering a diverse student body. But the majority maintained that the U.S. Court of Appeals for the 5th Circuit did not give a hard enough look at UT-Austin's race-conscious admissions program, sending the case back to an appeals court for further review, which could take a year or more.[316]

These so-called civil rights initiatives are dishonestly named, as they are *anti-* civil rights initiatives. Most voters see the titles and mistakenly believe they will increase opportunities for minorities and women, not do away with them. When the City of Houston changed the ballot description of a Connerly-backed city initiative to make it clear that the measure would overturn affirmative action, it was soundly defeated.

Publicity usually centers around "unfair" university admission policies, though the true target is believed to be government contracting. In one sense it doesn't matter – once the initiatives pass, they apply to schools, jobs, and contracts equally. And they apply to white women as well as minority women and men, and the results are stark:

- In the first year after Washington state's initiative passed, the freshman class at the state university had 40 percent fewer blacks and 30 percent fewer Hispanics than the previous freshman class. And Washington has seen business drop dramatically for firms owned by minorities and women that previously qualified for set-asides.[317]

- Faculty at the University of Michigan warned, shortly before the initiative passed, that likely effects would be elimination of programs to increase female enrollment in pre-college summer recruitment programs for science, math, and vocational programs, as well as a drop in the number of females receiving scholarships in Michigan.[318]

- The percentage of women employed in the construction industry dropped 33 percent following the passage of Proposition 209, despite an increase in the number of people employed in the construction industry overall.[319]

- In the first six years after Proposition 209, contracts to women-and-minority-owned firms were cut in half, resulting in an estimated loss of $1.4 billion. Many have struggled to stay in business, shrinking drastically in the number of jobs they are able to provide .[320]

- The effect of 209 was evident in the first year in which it affected admissions; at UC Berkeley Law School: admissions of Black students dropped by 80 percent and Hispanic students by 50 percent.[321]

- By 2006, ten years after Proposition 209 passed, only 100 African-American students (20 of those were recruited athletes), women and men, enrolled at UCLA – 2 percent of the 4,802 total, the lowest in more than thirty years. This occurred even though the percentage of African-American applicants meeting admission requirements for the University of California system has risen steadily since 1996. Critics have labeled this "race-based exclusion."[322] The situation has gotten worse with time. By 2010, UC Berkeley, the California system's flagship school, was one of the lowest in the nation among its peer institutions, with only 17 percent minority enrollment – despite the fact that it is located in a highly diverse area. Four years later, in the Fall of 2013, underrepresented minority enrollment had dropped to 15 percent.[323] The Director of Undergraduate Admissions blamed Proposition 209 directly.[324]

- The University of California has also noted a significant decline in the number of female faculty since Proposition 209 was implemented.[325]

The situation in California after Proposition 209 is so bad there is now an effort to repair some of the damage through the California Affirmative Action in Education Amendment, which may be on the November, 2014 ballot as a legislatively-referred constitutional amendment. It would delete some provisions in Proposition 209 and allow preferential treatment in public education for individuals or groups based on race, sex, color, ethnicity, or national origin.[326]

There is no question that affirmative action is still needed. The pay gap between women and men begins right after college and grows in succeeding years.[327]

Job segregation remains the norm, with women concentrated in teaching, nursing, clerical and sales – relatively low paid positions when compared to "men's jobs" like technical, management, and skilled trades.

According to the research group Catalyst there are a mere 23 women heading Fortune 500 companies in the U.S. – just 4.6 percent (and that was touted in the press as a record high!). In 2013, women held 16.9 percent of Fortune 500 board seats, women of color held only 3.2 percent, and 10 percent of the companies had *no* women on their boards.[328] Minority women are also hardest hit by cuts in admissions to professional schools and also by loss of job opportunities.

Women-Owned Businesses Don't Get the Business

Women in business have much at stake in the elections, particularly those who want to contract with the federal government. The United States government spends over $500 billion per year contracting with private business for goods and services. It is the largest purchasing organization in the world. The bulk of these contracts go to large corporations such as KBR and Halliburton.

Even though the number of women business owners is growing at twice the rate of other businesses, a large gap still exists in the share of federal dollars going to contracts with women-owned businesses. In the fiscal year ending September, 2013, federal contracting went down for women-owned businesses as a share of all contracts, and continued to fall short of the government's goal, resulting in a several billion dollar shortfall. [329]

For many years women were not included in programs setting aside procurement dollars for small disadvantaged businesses, unless they were members of racial or ethnic minority groups. To remedy the situation, Congress passed a law in 1994 mandating a 5 percent set-aside for women-owned businesses. The law -- the Equity in Contracting for Women Act -- was created to improve the track record of the federal government in awarding a fair share of annual procurement spending to women-owned businesses.

Six years later the goal had not been met, so in 2000 Congress ordered the Small Business Administration (SBA) to write new rules to ensure that women-owned businesses got the targeted amount. It took the Bush administration seven years after that to actually develop and publish the rules, finally coming out with them in December, 2007. It might not have happened at all had the United States Women's Chamber of Commerce not sued the SBA in 2004 to force the agency to follow the Congressional mandate.

When the rules did come out, female business owners were outraged. Even though the SBA's own data revealed that women got a disproportionately low number of contracts in three fourths of the 140 industries in which the agency does business, it listed only four where women-owned businesses could be preferred. One of those was furniture manufacturing – primarily done offshore.

In addition, the rules limited broad eligibility to small businesses owned or controlled by economically disadvantaged women. Contracts awarded under the program were tiny – held to $5 million or less for manufacturing and $3 million or less for other areas.[330]

In 2008, new numbers revealed that despite the lawsuit filed by the Women's Chamber, federal contracting continued to short women-owned businesses by over 22 percent of the goal, resulting in a $12 billion loss.[331] By 2010, federal contracting continued to short women-owned businesses by 18 percent of the government's 5 percent goal, again resulting in a several billion dollar shortfall.[332]

In contrast, the six top recipients of federal contracts are Lockheed Martin, Boeing, Northrop Grumman, Raytheon, General Dynamics, and BAE Systems. Collectively, they scoop up close to a quarter of all federal procurement spending, totaling almost $400 billion in the period between October 2006 and November 2011 alone.[333]

In October 2010, the 5 percent regulation that established a federal procurement program for women-owned small businesses at last was finalized. The program became effective in February 2011, and contracting officers at federal agencies were able to start setting aside contracts for women owned businesses in early 2011. In May of 2013 the Small Business Administration announced the removal of caps on the contract award size for which women owned concerns had been able to compete.[334]

Though progress is finally being made, it is likely to take years for women to catch up – and a lot depends on who's in charge at the top. The last two decades have shown that much depends on the administration in power, and its willingness to enforce (or impede) the law. Recently there are signs of improvement (as well as more work to be done), according to a report by the National Women's Business Council.[335]

- Since 2000, the number of federal agencies meeting the 5 percent goal has generally increased, although there are more agencies meeting the contracting goal than the dollar goal.
- Since 2000, Women Owned Small Businesses (WOSBs) have received an increasing share of contracts and awards, not only within the 83 designated industries but in other industries as well. WOSBs are generally meeting the contract threshold within the 83 underrepresented industries, but they remain underrepresented in terms of awards share.
- In 2012, WOSBs were awarded 182,791 contracts worth $11.5 billion. That amounts to 11.5 percent of all contracts and 5.3 percent of all award dollars.

Although it is clear that WOSBs have made substantial progress in the federal marketplace, there are still areas for improvement. Some findings from the report may be useful for WOSBs in the procurement arena, most notably that:

- There is a high rate of turnover among WOSB vendors. Almost half the total received contracts only in a single fiscal year. Vendors receiving contracts in multiple fiscal years were able to secure a larger portion of contracts through the use of the set-asides. Thus, it is important for women business owners to stay involved in procurement.

- Award dollars are concentrated among a small number of vendors. For example, in 2012, 20 percent of awards (amounting to $2.3 billion) went to 44 vendors. The other 80 percent of awards ($9.2 billion) went to 17,648 vendors.

The National Association of Small Business Contractors has called on the Obama Administration to enforce fines and legal consequences for large businesses that misrepresent their use of small business sub-contractors or erroneously represent themselves as "small," "women-owned," or "minority-owned."[336]

Questions for candidates:

Do you support or oppose affirmative action in education, employment, and contracting?

How would you prevent the drastic drop in university admissions for minority students that has been shown to happen when affirmative action programs are eliminated?

What would you do to eliminate the "glass ceiling" in earnings and employment opportunities for women, particularly as they try to move up the ladder?

Do you believe in set-asides in government contracting for women-owned businesses?

Would you limit these set-asides to disadvantaged women?

How would you be sure the Small Business Administration complies with the mandate from Congress that women-owned businesses get 5 percent of contracting dollars?

Would you raise the amount of dollars the government sets aside for these contracts? How?

◊ NINETEEN ◊

More than a Few Good Women – in the Military

Almost one in seven members of the military serving on active duty – some 200,000 – are women, including 69 generals and admirals. Overall, they make up 14.5 percent of our armed forces, with a nearly identical percentage in National Guard and reserve units. More than 280,000 women were deployed to Iraq or Afghanistan, and about 150 died.[337]

Traditionally, military women have faced a number of obstacles to full equality, including denial of combat jobs, rape and sexual assault, access to abortion, and equal treatment as veterans. This chapter outlines each of the problem areas, with information on what has – and has not – been done about them.

Denial of Jobs

Although females have served in the U.S. military since 1901, until very recently they were the only American women whose professional advancement was artificially curtailed by government laws and policies. In the last decade, laws banning women from serving on military aircraft with combat missions and aboard combat ships were repealed. But under the combat exclusion rule dating back to 1994, women were still barred from serving aboard submarines, in infantry, armor, and most artillery units, or in special forces units, even though military leaders themselves said these bans were increasingly artificial and meaningless given today's combat realities.[338] According to a 2011 report to Congress from the Military Leadership Diversity Commission, lack of the ability to gain combat experience (a major criterion for promotion), is the main reason only 16 percent of military officers are female. Their primary recommendation was opening combat jobs to women.[339] The public also supports – by a 75 percent majority – opening combat jobs to women.[340]

Despite the combat exclusion rule, women were in fact put in combat roles in Afghanistan and Iraq, through being "attached" to combat units. But they were sometimes dropped into those units without proper training, and they got no official credit for the combat experience – which is required for advancing up the ranks.[341]

After many years of campaigning by advocacy groups and women in the military themselves, the rules are finally changing. In November of 2012, four women who served in Afghanistan or Iraq filed a federal lawsuit to end the ban on combat roles for women. The suit maintained that despite the fact that changes had been announced earlier in the year that opened more than 14,000 positions to women, females were still barred from 280,000 military jobs.[342]

In June of 2013, the Pentagon announced that women will now be permitted to serve in the Navy SEALs, the Army Rangers, and the Marine infantry. (These, of course, are the units where even the majority of men are likely to fail.) However, if the women succeed in completing the Marine training, they will not become infantry officers because the program is "experimental." Still, the Pentagon now says the emphasis is on inclusion. Service branches have until January 2016 to decide which combat positions will be open to women. If a branch of the service decides that a specific job should still be off limits, that branch will have to ask the defense secretary for an exclusion. It's anybody's guess how many such exclusions will be granted.

Rape and Sexual Assault

Rapes and sexual assaults against women in the U.S. military – by other soldiers, contractor personnel, and training officers – have long been identified as serious problems . Air Force general William Begert, who investigated sexual assault in the military way back in 2004, uncovered scores of rape accusations, a rising trend of reported abuses, and the most basic shortcomings in tracking the crime and attending to its victims.[343]

By 2012, a damning report by the Pentagon revealed that sexual assault in the U.S. Army had increased 64 percent since 2006, with 3,191 reports. But in announcing new initiatives to bring down the numbers, then-Secretary of Defense Leon Panetta said that, realistically, the estimate for assaults "actually is closer to 19,000." A new Pentagon study a year later, in 2013, put the number at 26,000, a 37 percent increase over the same period only the year before.

While women comprise 14 percent of the Army ranks, they account for 95 percent of all sex crime victims.[344] The Air Force reports that it's own survey finds one in five women have been sexually assaulted.[345] However, sexual assaults at military academies are down slightly. The Defense Department's annual report for academic year 2012-2013 found that such assaults had decreased to 53, down from 58 in the prior academic year.[346]

Women working for war contractors in Iraq have also been raped, with contracting companies such as Halliburton/KBR ignoring or covering up the allegations. These women have no access to the military justice system, and the companies have required them to sign pre-employment arbitration agreements cutting off their access to the U.S. criminal justice system.[347] An amendment to the Department of Defense appropriations bill in 2009 guaranteed such women a day in court by withholding contracts from companies that require binding arbitration in cases of sexual assault (30 senators voted against it). However, the provision must be reviewed annually and the DOD can exempt contractors from complying in the name of "national security."

Attention on sexual assault and rape in the military has recently drawn intensified scrutiny from Congress, particularly women in the Senate. It has long been known that the main reason women are reluctant to report sex crimes against them is the structure of the reporting system. Women must report rapes and assaults to their commanding officers, who are more often than not also the commanding officers of the perpetrators.

Commanding officers have near-total authority over whether a case is prosecuted and in selection of jurors. In the small fraction of reported cases that are prosecuted, they can overturn convictions without explanation. Commanders also decide whether or not assaults go on the record, and (emulating the Catholic church on pedophilia) can transfer perpetrators to other assignments without noting past history.

In 2013 the House passed a defense bill stripping commanders of their authority to dismiss findings by court-martial, establish minimum sentences for sexual assault convictions, permit victims to apply for permanent transfers, and ensure that convicted offenders leave the military. These provisions have not passed the Senate.

In 2014 Senator Kirsten Gillibrand (D-NY) put up a fight in the Senate with a bill to remove decision-making on prosecuting sexual crimes from the chain of command, putting it instead in the hands of military prosecutors. Her bill, opposed by Secretary of Defense Chuck Hagel, was defeated. A different measure, championed by Senator Claire McCaskill (D-MO), passed. That bill leaves the chain of command intact, but eliminates the "good soldier" defense that takes irrelevant factors such as the service record of the accused into account. It also requires that in every decision on promotion in the military, the commander's record on the handling of sexual-assault cases must be taken into account. It is unclear whether any of these provisions will pass the House. Until there is agreement between the two chambers and a bill is signed into law, the current system that greatly disadvantages victims will remain in place.

Access to Abortion

Despite the alarming rate of sexual assault in the military which obviously can result in pregnancy, until 2013 U.S. military women could not obtain abortions in military facilities unless their lives were endangered (no rape/incest exception), even if they paid for the procedure with their own money. Nor could military insurance cover abortions except for life endangerment. That means military women did not have the same coverage provided to civilian women who work for the federal government, to women on Medicaid, and those serving time in federal prisons.[348]

The restrictions were eased by a small amount with the military budget bill signed by President Obama in early 2013. Servicewomen and members of families covered by military insurance can now obtain abortions for rape and incest in addition to life endangerment. If an abortion is needed or wanted for any other reason, it cannot be obtained at a military facility, and it cannot be paid for by military insurance, even if performed at a private hospital.

When deployed overseas, this extremely restrictive abortion policy creates major hardships – women must resort to unsafe local facilities, or petition for leave to travel to a safe hospital or clinic in another country. In many foreign countries, abortion is illegal, meaning nonmilitary facilities are not available, whether safe or not.[349] Obviously this situation is a danger to the health and well being of military women and female members of military families covered by military insurance. While bills to overturn military abortion restrictions have been introduced in Congress, none have had committee hearings, nor have they attracted a critical mass of co-sponsors in the House or the Senate.

Veteran's Services

The Department of Veterans Affairs (VA) projects that by 2040, 18 percent of veterans will be female.[350] Yet the VA seems ill-equipped to serve the needs of women. As military women return from fighting in Iraq and Afghanistan, they are finding that veterans' services aren't meeting their needs.

According to the latest figures available from the VA, homelessness among female veterans of the Iraq and Afghanistan wars has increased over tenfold in a six year period —from 150 in 2006 to 1,700 in 2011. They are the fastest growing segment of the homeless, some of whom suffer from mental illness.[351] Sexual trauma is a common thread in the stories of women who become homeless after returning from service. A study from UCLA Medical Center and the VA of Greater Los Angeles estimated that just over half of homeless women veterans were victims.[352]

Divorces in the Army have doubled since September 11, 2001, with one in five couples separating within two years of one spouse's deployment. Women in every military branch are twice as likely to get divorced as men.[353]

Critics charge that Congress has failed to appropriate adequate money for counseling and support services to help keep families together after the deployment has ended.

Additionally, there have been too many horror stories of women and men going away to combat, only to return and discover they have lost custody of children. This has happened because state family court judges have ruled that state family law takes precedence over the Servicemembers Civil Relief Act, the federal law that protects members of the military from such events as property foreclosures while they are away, but does not safeguard them against loss of their children.

Though the law was completely overhauled in 2003, it did not clearly spell out custody rights for service members deployed overseas. During the 2008 primary season, some Democratic candidates supported amending and clarifying the federal law to specify that it does apply in custody cases, and that a parent's absence due to a deployment cannot be used to justify permanent changes in custody or visitation.

Advocates want to ensure that jurisdiction rests with the state where the child resided before the soldier deployed, to prevent non-custodial parents from moving children to more "sympathetic" states when seeking changes in custody orders. Though a bill to this effect was introduced in 2009, it never became law.

Clearly the United States must do better by its women in the active military, and female veterans. Here are some questions for those in a position to make those improvements.

Questions for candidates:

Do you support allowing women to hold all military assignments for which they are qualified?

If not, are you willing to change your mind on combat restrictions for women if you see solid evidence that such restrictions are not militarily justified?

Did you, or would you have, voted for the Gillibrand bill removing jurisdiction over military sexual assault from the chain of command?

What would you do to stop the epidemic of sexual harassment, rape, and sexual assault that military women are experiencing from other soldiers and contractors?

Do you think women who work for contractors who are raped should have access to the U.S. criminal justice system? The military justice system? Did you vote for, or would you have voted for, the Franken amendment guaranteeing such women their day in court?

Do you support widening the availability of abortion services for women in the military beyond rape, incest, and life endangerment at military medical facilities? Have you, or would you, sponsor any bills to that effect?

How would you help returning veterans with family problems of divorce and family violence that seem to be associated with deployments?

How would you protect military personnel from losing legal custody of their children while on deployment?

◊ TWENTY ◊

Lesbian and Gay Civil Rights

Sixty-three percent of Americans say they have a close friend or close relative who is gay or lesbian. Yet discrimination against lesbian women, gay men, bisexual and transgendered (LGBT) individuals continues in the workplace and in public policies and programs.

Polls since 2004 have consistently shown that most American voters favor legal recognition of gay and lesbian couples, through either domestic partnership laws or marriage. Approval for legalizing same-sex marriage jumped by 11 percentage points from 2010-2013, with 58 percent of Americans supporting it.[354] Gay adoption has also gained more acceptance, with 56 percent of women and half of men in favor.[355]

After decades of advocacy and legal campaigning, the last few years have brought significant strides in lesbian and gay civil rights. Progress has been made in the military, in civil and federal protections, and in the right to marry. It has not been easy or quick.

The 11-year battle over amending the law to protect LGBT people from violent hate crimes is a perfect example of why *elected* majorities matter. Though wide majorities of *citizens* have favored protecting LGBT people from violence by including them in the legal definition of hate crimes, it took over a decade to get a law in place. Hate crimes expansion was first proposed in 1998, the year Matthew Shepard, a gay college student, died after he was beaten and tied to a fence in Wyoming. The Senate passed a Hate Crimes Prevention Act (HCPA) 65 to 33 in 2004. The House passed it by 223 to 199 in 2005. But the Republican-controlled Congress squashed the bill in negotiations. The House passed the bill *again* in 2007 with 55 percent (including 25 Republicans) voting for it, but it was not enough to overcome a threatened Bush veto.[356]

After the 2008 election that brought Democratic control to both the House and the Senate and put President Obama in the White House, the Matthew Shepard and James Byrd, Jr. Hate Crimes Prevention Act, which added gender, gender identity, and sexual orientation to the definition of hate crimes, was passed by Congress and signed into law by President Obama on October 28, 2009.

In late 2010 President Obama signed a law repealing the Clinton-era "Don't Ask, Don't Tell (DADT)" policy, which had prevented lesbians and gays from serving openly in the military. This was particularly important for women, because though women comprised between 14 percent and 15 percent of U.S. military personnel, they comprised more than twice that proportion (30 percent) among those discharged under DADT from 1997 through 2009, when female discharges reached a high of 39 percent.[357]

American voters favored repeal of the policy (56 percent to 37 percent), including those with family in the military (50 percent to 43 percent).[358] Nearly three in four (73 percent) members of the military say they are personally comfortable in the presence of gays and lesbians.[359] In addition to the repeal of DADT, equal treatment in military employment also has very high support, with 80 percent of Americans saying gay men and lesbians should have equal job rights.[360]

Proponents of gay and lesbian rights won another significant victory in 2013, when in *United States v. Windsor*, the Supreme Court struck down a provision of the 17-year-old Defense of Marriage Act (DOMA) that denied federal benefits -- like Social Security benefits or the ability to file joint tax returns -- to legally married same-sex couples. Striking down that part of DOMA impacted around 1,100 federal laws, including veterans' benefits, family medical leave, and tax laws. There were about 130,000 married same-sex couples in the United States who up to that point had been treated as unmarried in the eyes of federal law.[361] Since *Windsor*, bans on same-sex marriage have been found unconstitutional in New Jersey, New Mexico, Oklahoma, Utah and Virginia. (The Virginia, Utah, and Oklahoma decisions are stayed, pending the outcome of appeals.)

As noted in chapter 6, there is nowhere near enough support to pass a federal constitutional amendment banning gay marriage that some Republicans in Congress want. Anti-gay ballot initiatives and rhetoric reached unprecedented decibel levels in the 2004, when voters passed them in 13 states, but has cooled in subsequent elections as public opinion has changed. Four anti-gay marriage state ballot measures were approved in 2008, including the hotly contested Proposition 8 in California, which rescinded an existing constitutional right to gay marriage (the recission was invalidated by a federal appeals court in February 2012). All were heavily bankrolled by religious groups.[362] The single initiative on the ballot in 2009 was in Maine, where voters overturned the marriage equality law passed earlier in the year. There were no new ballot initiatives in 2010, and the only one in 2012, in Minnesota, was defeated.

The Minnesota experience is illustrative of a national trend on the issue. The ballot measure to ban same sex marriage in the state constitution was not only defeated, but turnout against the initiative helped change both houses of the state government from Republican majorities to Democratic ones. That led to passage of a bill to legalize gay marriage, signed into law in 2013.[363]

Support for Gay, Lesbian Partner and Spouse Rights

Do you think there should or should not be -- [RANDOM ORDER]?

	Yes, should	No, should not	No opinion
	%	%	%
Inheritance rights for gay and lesbian domestic partners or spouses			
Nov 26-29, 2012	78	18	4
May 7-10 2009	73	24	4
Health insurance and other employee benefits for gay and lesbian domestic partners or spouses			
Nov 26-29, 2012	77	20	3
May 7-10, 2009	67	30	2
Adoption rights for gays and lesbians so they can legally adopt children			
Nov 26-29, 2012	61	36	3
May 7-10, 2009	54	44	2

GALLUP

Public opinion has changed rapidly in the last few years. Here are results from Gallup polling from 2009-2012:[364]

Though the landscape is changing rapidly with legal victories and new litigation almost every month, as of February, 2014, 33 states still ban same-sex marriage (3 struck down and under appeal), most by constitutional amendment. Same-sex marriage is legal in 17 states.[365]

Despite the turnaround in public opinion and significant progress for lesbian and gay couples, there is still work to be done. Though some LGBT workers have had limited success in challenging employment discrimination under Title VII of the 1964 Civil Rights Act (which bars sex discrimination), there is no federal law specifically prohibiting sexual orientation or gender identity discrimination. At the state level, only 21 states have laws barring employment discrimination based on sexual orientation, and only 17 also include gender identity in those laws.[366] Legal recognition of sexual orientation in employment laws would protect individuals from discrimination in the workplace.

A very large majority of Americans now believes that gays should be protected from discrimination at work. Support for equal employment opportunity has reached near-universal levels, with over 90 percent answering "yes" to the question: "In general, do you think homosexuals should or should not have equal rights in terms of job opportunities?"

Questions for those that represent you (and those who aspire to do so):

Do you support or oppose a constitutional amendment to outlaw same-sex marriage?

Do you believe the *U.S. v. Windsor* Supreme Court decision was rightly decided, granting legal recognition for married same-sex couples for federal benefits?

Do you support including sexual orientation in laws that prohibit workplace discrimination? Have you, or would you, sponsor a bill to do that?

Did you support or would you have supported overturning the "Don't Ask, Don't Tell" policy banning gay men and lesbian women from serving openly in the U.S. military?

Did you, or would you have voted for the bill that expanded hate crimes laws to cover sexual orientation?

◊ TWENTY-ONE ◊

Global Women's Issues

In the every election, candidates and voters have the opportunity to spur the United States toward greater global leadership in improving the lives of women worldwide, especially in poverty stricken regions, conflict areas, and emerging democracies. Our government has sometimes exercised leadership in bettering the situation for women around the world, but often the efforts have stalled, or in some areas gone steadily backward.

Reproductive Health and Family Planning

One of the longest-running and contentious areas of U.S. influence regarding women internationally has been international family planning. The United States began its involvement during the Nixon administration. Since then, it has become highly politicized.

The history of the United Nations Population Fund (UNFPA) is instructive as to how family planning has become the proverbial "political football." The UNFPA was created to support family planning and reproductive health services, including maternal and child health care, in low-income countries. The United States was UNFPA's largest contributor, and we matched all other contributions in the first several years of the program's existence.

Funding cuts began in the early Reagan years, and money was cut off entirely from 1986 through the end of George H.W. Bush's term in 1992. The justification was that the program did not comply with restrictions that had been passed by Congress in 1985, which bar U.S. funding for any international organization that the *president determines* "supports or participates in the management of a program of coercive abortion or sterilization." This prohibition has been dubbed the "global gag rule."

President Clinton restored funding to UNFPA in 1995. That year, representatives from 179 nations met at the U.N. International Conference on Population and Development in Cairo, to develop a landmark plan linking economic and social development with women's reproductive rights. They set a goal of universal access to reproductive health services by 2015, with UNFPA as the lead agency, and pledged to invest $17 billion in population programs annually by 2000.

The U.S. Congress appropriated $50 million for UNFPA, but then withheld $10 million of it, stipulating that no U.S. funds could be spent in China because of its birth limitation policies.

On his first business day in office, President George W. Bush reinstated the Reagan-era "global gag rule," which prohibits the granting of U.S. funds to any overseas health clinic unless it agrees not to use its *own, private, non-U.S. funds* for any abortion-related services.

Since the main work of many of these clinics is birth control information (thereby reducing the need for abortion), women in poor countries have suffered.

Lack of funds has caused many clinics to close altogether.[367]

Despite repeated appropriations from Congress – and several reports from government agencies concluding that there is no evidence that UNFPA has knowingly supported or participated in a program of coercive abortion or involuntary sterilization in China – President George W. Bush used this argument to withhold funds. By 2006, the total amount allocated by Congress but denied by President Bush came to $160 million.

In keeping with the trend since UNFPA was put in place, President Obama overturned the gag rule as one of his first acts after he was inaugurated in 2009. The memorandum rescinding it also allowed the U.S. Agency for International Development to once again provide millions of dollars to programs offering medical services, birth control, HIV prevention and other care.

In May of 2011 the Republican-controlled House of Representatives voted to completely cut off federal family planning funds to Planned Parenthood (a major provider of reproductive health services in underserved countries), because the organization also provides abortion services, though not with federal money. The bill was defeated in the Senate, but only because a threatened filibuster by Democrats made passage contingent on 60 votes. Underscoring the point that majorities matter, the bill drew 47 votes, all Republican.

Another bill to defund Planned Parenthood's global activities was introduced in the House in January of 2013, but it had not come up for a vote as of February, 2014.

Women in Conflict Areas

Afghanistan

As we all know, for over a decade the United States was engaged in two wars. The war in Afghanistan began in 2001, in retaliation for the September 11 attacks on New York and Washington by Al Qaeda terrorists. Afghanistan was known to have sheltered the group and its leader, Osama bin Laden.

At the time the Afghanistan conflict started, women and girls were being persecuted by the Taliban, the militia then ruling the country. They were denied basic human rights: not allowed to work or go to school, forced to wear head-to-toe burquas with even the eyes covered by mesh, and confined to their houses unless accompanied by a male relative. Women were stoned to death in stadiums filled to capacity for infractions such as sex outside marriage.

President George W. Bush promised to liberate women from this tyranny, and some progress was made in the initial stages of the war. But over the years, as the Taliban gained back much of the strength they lost immediately after the start of the war, women and girls have been persecuted once more. Girls' schools were routinely burned to the ground (by one estimate, one per day), female teachers killed for "going against Islam,"[368] and in 2009 President Hamid Karzai signed a law that legalized marital rape, which included clauses allowing men to deny their wives food if they refused to have sex.[369] Though President Obama verbally condemned the law, the United States did not make overturning it a condition of continued military or humanitarian assistance. In late 2011, Karzai publicly approved a decision by the Afghan government to pardon a woman who had been imprisoned for adultery after she had been raped – but only if she agreed to marry the rapist.[370]

Since the announcement of the U.S. pullout planned for 2014, violence against women has escalated, and women are back in the burqua in fear of their lives. According to international press reports, assassinations of female leaders, public stonings, bombing of girls' schools, and oppression by the Taliban are steadily rising. A report issued by the United Nations in December, 2013, found that women's seats in parliament had been reduced from 25 percent to 20 percent, and prosecutions for violence against women still represented a small percentage of reported incidents.[371] It is clear that there are intensifying fears that the withdrawal of international money and staff members and the 2014 western troop pullout will leave women particularly vulnerable.

Iraq

Even though there was no evidence that Iraq was connected to Al Qaeda in Afghanistan, once the Iraq war began in 2003 the country became a haven for terrorists from other countries. As husbands disappeared or were killed in the fighting, women lost much of their freedom to move about and hold jobs. Many turned to prostitution to support themselves and their children.[372]

President Obama completed the process of withdrawing American combat troops from Iraq in

December, 2011. In his 2011 withdrawal speech and ceremony, he did not mention Iraqi women or women's rights.

Since that time, the situation for Iraqi women has markedly deteriorated. The United Nati on's Women in Iraq Factsheet (2013) states:

> *Years of repression, economic sanctions, and armed conflicts have led to deterioration in the lives of women in Iraq and an associated loss to the country since women are marginalized and unable to contribute economically, socially, and politically. Iraqi women today suffer from a lack of educational opportunities, a lack of health care and limited access to the labour market as well as high levels of violence and inequality. These conditions are often exacerbated by misconceptions of traditions, cultural and social values, false perceptions, and a lack of awareness of women's rights and potential, as well as institutional and legal barriers.*[373]

In February, 2014, Human Rights Watch reported that Iraq authorities are illegally detaining thousands of women, including many subjected to torture, the threat of sexual abuse and other ill-treatment, despite promises of reform.[374]

Other Arab and Middle Eastern Countries

Women were greatly involved in the "Arab Spring" uprisings that started in Tunisia in the spring of 2011 and spread to Egypt, Libya, Yemen, Syria, and across the Persian Gulf. Since then, Arab women have relished the promise of a change -- but it is still unclear whether change that translates to true equality with men can be realized.

In March 2011, the military in Egypt forcibly expelled protesters from Tahrir Square -- the epicenter of pro-democracy protests. Female protesters were arrested along with the men, and forced to undergo "virginity tests" while in captivity. Sexual assaults and beatings of women continue. In Egypt's first parliamentary elections after the dictator Hosni Mubarak was overthrown – largely seen as the nation's first free and fair vote -- only nine of the newly elected 498 parliamentarians were women. Twelve women reached parliament in 2012, 2 percent of the total.[375]

The ongoing civil war in Syria has been especially hard on women. Before the war Syrian women had some level of independence in society compared with their counterparts in the Arab world. Though the government boasted reduced penalties for honor killings targeting females and women had to get permission from a male relative to travel abroad, there was participation in public life through schools and working outside the home. Since the conflict began, women have been forced back into burquas, are not allowed in public without a male relative escort, and in some areas of the country are prohibited from working outside the home and getting an outside education.[376]

In Libya, dozens of nongovernmental organizations led by women have popped up since Arab Spring. Thirty three women were elected to parliament in 2012 after women's groups lobbied hard for an election law that facilitated women's political participation.[377] Despite this, very few women take part in any type of civic activity to express their views on social and political issues, and 57 percent say that they feel completely (37 percent) or somewhat (20 percent) restricted in leaving their houses without permission.[378]

Though it is not a conflict area and is considered friendly to the U.S., Saudi Arabia remains one of the most oppressive countries for women, who cannot drive and must obtain permission from a male guardian to work, travel, study, or marry.

Women across the region worry about the disconnect between women's participation on the streets and their stark absence from the formal political process. And women's rights advocates around the world are concerned that the ascension of Islamist parties, some who want to institute Sharia law which is extremely oppressive of women, will not only fail to liberate women in these countries, but set them back.

Sub-Saharan Africa[379]

Civilians in Africa's conflict zones – particularly women and children, but also men – are often vulnerable to sexual violence, including rape, mutilation, and sexual slavery. This violence is carried out by government security forces and non-state actors, including, rebel groups, militias, U.N. peacekeepers, and criminal organizations. Some abuses appear to be opportunistic, or the product of a larger breakdown in the rule of law and social order that may occur amid conflict. Other incidents appear to be carried out systematically by combatants as a strategic tool to intimidate and humiliate civilian populations seen as sympathetic to opposing factions.

While such abuses are by no means limited to Africa, weak institutions in many African states can mean that victims have little redress; in addition to health and psychological consequences, survivors are also often shunned by their families and communities. The Democratic Republic of Congo (DRC), where security forces, rebel organizations, militias, and other armed groups have inflicted sexual violence upon the civilian population on a massive scale is a case in point, though such activities are prevalent in other areas of the continent.

Congress has repeatedly expressed interest in bringing attention to the issue and support for programs to address it through legislation and hearings. Most recently, the "conflict minerals" amendment to the Dodd-Frank Wall Street Reform and Consumer Protection Act, signed into law in 2010, references reported links between illicit mining activities and high levels of sexual and gender-based violence in DRC.

Former Secretary of State Hillary Clinton took the lead on the Obama Administration's initiative to address sexual violence through speeches, official travel, public remarks, writings, and actions at the United Nations. Despite the efforts of Clinton and numerous congresses over the years, the issue of sexual violence in conflict is complex, and seemingly intractable. It has implications for international programs and policies related to health, humanitarian relief, global women's issues, the justice sector, the security sector, and multilateral activities. Potential issues for Congress include the authorization and appropriation of targeted assistance programs, oversight of programs already in place, and urging of allies to participate.

In September of 2013 Secretary of State John Kerry announced $10 million in funding for a new

U.S. initiative to prevent and respond to gender-based violence in humanitarian emergencies worldwide. Secretary Kerry emphasized that in the face of conflict and disaster, we should strive to protect women and girls from sexual assault and other violence. As of this writing, it is too early to gauge how much aid will go to Africa, or how the money will be applied.

International Treaties

The Women's Human Rights Treaty: CEDAW

The major worldwide treaty guaranteeing the rights of women worldwide is known as CEDAW, which stands for Convention on the Elimination of all Forms of Discrimination Against Women. To shortcut the unwieldy name, it is often simply called the women's human rights treaty.

CEDAW is the most authoritative U.N. human rights instrument protecting women from discrimination. It is the first international treaty to comprehensively address fundamental rights for women in politics, health care, education, economics, employment, law, property, and marriage and family relations. The United States is the only industrialized country in the world that has not ratified CEDAW. By not ratifying, the U.S. is in the company of countries like Iran, Sudan, and Somalia.

The CEDAW treaty was actually signed by President Carter in 1980, and sent to the U.S. Senate for ratification. To be ratified after the president signs it, a treaty must be reported out of the Senate Foreign

Relations Committee and scheduled for a vote on the Senate floor. Once on the floor, it must pass by a two-thirds majority.

This is another case where committee control is important (see chapter 2), because the committee chair can schedule hearings and committee votes to send legislation to the floor, or bottle it up without a hearing for many years.

Both Democrats and Republicans have at various times been in control of the White House and the Senate since President Carter signed the treaty. But the Senate Foreign Relations Committee has failed to act under both parties. Hearings were not held until 1990, a full ten years after Carter signed the treaty. In 1993, sixty-eight senators signed a letter asking President Clinton to support ratification of CEDAW. After a 13-5 favorable vote by the Foreign Relations Committee in 1994, a group of conservative senators then blocked a Senate floor vote.

Eight years later, in June 2002, the Senate Foreign Relations Committee held another hearing, and the Committee voted 12-7 in favor of sending CEDAW to the full Senate for ratification. Time ran out on the congressional session before a floor vote could be scheduled, meaning the process would have to be repeated by a new Foreign Relations Committee. Another hearing was finally held in late 2010, but the treaty did not come up for a vote in the Senate. No hearings have been held since.

Conservatives do not want the U.S. to ratify CEDAW. They say that it is a "global Equal Rights Amendment," and that it would "do away with Mother's Day." Progressives, human rights, and women's rights groups urge that it be ratified, arguing that the

U.S. cannot occupy the moral high ground in global women's rights until our country signs the treaty. If the U.S. does not sign, it encourages other nations to ignore the provisions of the treaty, and thus slow or stop the progress of women worldwide.

The treaty has been used as a basis to advance women in the countries that have signed it, in areas such as providing education for girls, access to health care, political equality, the right to inherit property, and spousal rights in property ownership. All of these have helped in alleviating global poverty for women.[380]

Other Treaties Affecting Women

The 1995 United Nations Fourth World Conference on Women adopted what is known as the Beijing Platform for Action for Women. One provision is the recognition that women and children are particularly affected by the indiscriminate use of land mines, and the Platform urges ratification of international treaties that would prohibit them.

In December 1997, the treaty banning the use, production, trade and stockpiling of antipersonnel mines was signed in Ottawa, Canada by 122 nations. Seventeen years later in 2014, more than 80 percent of the world's states had ratified the treaty, including most members of NATO. Thirty-five countries worldwide have not yet joined – including the only two in the western hemisphere, the United States and Cuba.[381]

The Convention on the Rights of the Child is the most widely accepted human rights treaty. Adopted by the United Nations in November 1989, it spells out the basic human rights to which children everywhere are entitled: the right to survival; to develop to their fullest; to protection from harmful influences, abuse and exploitation; and to participate fully in family, cultural and social life.

The four core principles are non-discrimination, devotion to the best interests of the child, respect for the views of the child, and the right to life, survival and development.

The treaty protects children's rights by setting standards in health care, education, and legal, civil and social services. The Convention on the Rights of the Child has been ratified by *all* governments except two: the richest, the United States of America, and one of the poorest, Somalia.[382] Although signed by the Clinton Administration, the treaty has never been submitted to the U.S. Senate for consideration. The Obama Administration has said that it intends to submit the treaty to the Senate, but with no firm timeline.[383]

Questions for candidates:

Do you support U.S. aid to international family planning programs? Have you, or would you, vote to fund these programs in full?

Would you support repeal of the "global gag rule" on organizations that provide legal abortion services overseas?

Would you vote to continue full funding to the United Nations Population Fund and

remove the president's discretion in withholding funds?

Would you be in favor of withholding military or humanitarian aid from any country that does not grant full rights to women?

Women are being persecuted in both Iraq and Afghanistan, and not allowed basic human rights by the religious police. What would you recommend the U.S. do now to help women in those countries?

Would you make adherence to international human rights principles for women in Iraq and Afghanistan a condition for those countries receiving continued U.S. monetary and military assistance?

What can the U.S. do to ensure the rights of women as new governments are formed in the Middle East?

Do you think the U.S. is doing enough to protect women in African conflict areas from sexual violence?

Do you support the ratification of CEDAW by the United States? What would you do to see that the treaty comes up for a vote?

Do you support the anti-land mine treaty, and the international treaty on the rights of the child?

◊ TWENTY-TWO ◊

The Last Word – Equal Constitutional Rights

Much of this book is about threats to the rights granted to women under various laws, such as Title IX (prohibition of discrimination in educational programs) and Title VII (barring discrimination in pay and employment), and the continuous assault on such laws by conservatives.

One reason that women must be constantly vigilant about protecting their rights under statutes and regulations is that women do not have *fundamental equal rights with men* in the U.S. – meaning equal rights under our Constitution.

Although polls show that most people believe otherwise (see chapter 5), women are *not* explicitly guaranteed equal rights with men under the United States Constitution. Without having equal rights constitutionally protected, women must rely on a patchwork of laws (e.g. Equal Credit Act, Pregnancy Discrimination Act, Equal Pay Act) that can be repealed or weakened at any time by acts of Congress, or in some cases by regulations and presidential executive orders.

Additionally, courts can and have narrowed protections originally guaranteed by statute, resulting in women having to wage long campaigns with new bills in Congress to restore what's been taken away or weakened.

Title IX is a case in point. The law was passed in 1972. It prohibited discrimination against women and girls in educational institutions receiving federal funds. The law was challenged, and the *Grove City v. Bell* decision in 1984 declared that only *individual programs* receiving federal funds were subject to the law, not institutions as a whole. (So, for example, if the medical school got federal funds but other programs didn't, discrimination was barred only in the medical school.) Women's groups had to mount a four-year fight to pass legislation overturning *Grove City* and restoring the original intent.

More recently, in 2007, the Supreme Court reversed 40 years of precedent by negating a major portion of Title VII of the Civil Rights Act which had protected women from pay discrimination (see chapter 9). It took intense lobbying and a change in party control of Congress and the White House, from Republican to Democratic in the 2008 elections, to pass the Lilly Ledbetter Fair Pay Act in 2009 restoring the law to its original interpretation.

Without a constitutional amendment guaranteeing equal rights for women, these types of battles are likely to continue as Congress and the courts become more polarized.

Because equal rights are not explicitly protected in the federal Constitution, the rights of women also often depend on the state in which they live. For example, until it was outlawed by the Affordable Care Act, women paid higher rates than similarly situated men for the same health coverage in all but a handful of states. It is still legal (and very common) in the great majority of states to charge women more for other types of insurance.

Similarly, state courts have ruled that state Equal Rights Amendments protect women's rights to reproductive services under Medicaid, but women whose states do not have ERAs are not so protected.

The proposed Equal Rights Amendment is not complicated. The entire text is only 52 words:

> Section 1. Equality of rights under the law shall not be denied or abridged by the United States or by any state on account of sex.
>
> Section 2. The Congress shall have the power to enforce, by appropriate legislation, the provisions of this article.
>
> Section 3. This amendment shall take effect two years after the date of ratification.

The Equal Rights Amendment embodies a simple concept that had the blessing of both political parties until the Republicans struck it from their platform in 1980; they have never restored support. The Democrats followed suit in 2004, but restored platform support for the ERA in 2008. (See the latest platforms in Appendix).

For an amendment to become part of the Constitution, it must be passed by a two-thirds majority in each chamber of Congress, and then sent to the states for ratification. Each state votes on ratification separately, and an amendment cannot become part of the Constitution unless it is ratified by three-fourths of the states.

The Equal Rights Amendment was first introduced in Congress in 1923, on the heels of ratification of the 19th Amendment (1920) giving women the right to vote. The ERA was finally passed out of Congress and sent to the states in 1972, with a seven year deadline for ratification (later extended three years).

The ratification drive succeeded in 35 states, but 38 were needed for it to become part of the Constitution. The ERA has been reintroduced in every Congress since, but has never again been put to a vote. (The deadline was not in the amendment, but in the preamble, causing some scholars to make the argument that the time limit is non-binding, meaning that even today, only three more states would be needed for it to be ratified.)

The Equal Rights Amendment has been introduced by its chief sponsor, Representative Carolyn Maloney (D-NY). Though it has a high number of co-sponsors, it has not been scheduled for committee hearings which could lead to floor votes in Congress.

Conservatives argue that equal constitutional rights will result in "abortion on demand" and "unisex toilets," though the amendment mentions neither. When they're not raising the specter of unisex toilets (guess they've never been on an airplane), conservatives also argue that a new amendment isn't needed because the "equal protection under the law" clause of the Fourteenth Amendment already guarantees equal rights for women.

That is not true. The Fourteenth Amendment was passed to protect African-American men from discrimination. Courts have consistently failed to find sex discrimination as serious (what lawyers call *level of scrutiny*) as race discrimination under the Fourteenth Amendment.[384]

The result has been that many discriminatory practices – barring women from certain military jobs, establishing boys-only public classrooms and schools, and openly discriminating against women in insurance programs to name a few – are still legal.

Women in the U.S. lag far behind women in the rest of the world when it comes to constitutional equality. Most individual countries in Europe have formalized equal rights for women in their constitutions, and equal rights are included in the Treaty of Lisbon, which amounts to a European constitution. Women have had equal constitutional rights in Japan since 1946, and the constitutions of many other countries worldwide declare women as legal equals to men.

Since the 1990s, new constitutions in countries like Mozambique, Namibia, Ethiopia, Malawi, Uganda, South Africa, Rwanda, Burundi, and Swaziland have included non-discrimination or equality provisions, prohibiting customary practices if they undermine undermined the dignity, welfare or status of women.

With one of our two major parties not having equal constitutional rights for women in their platform, it is especially important to confront candidates in every election as to their intentions regarding the Equal Rights Amendment.

Questions for candidates:

Do you support the Women's Equality Amendment to the U.S. Constitution?

Have you, or would you, co-sponsor the amendment in Congress?

Would you push for hearings and a congressional vote on equal rights for women?

Do you think equal rights for women should be a part of your party's platform?

Until equal rights for women are in the Constitution, will you pledge to work to eliminate unequal treatment of women in all forms, all domains, and all legislation?

The Political Parties and Their Platforms

Party platforms are revisited in presidential election years, and voted on at the national party conventions. They remain in effect until the next presidential election. While there are some changes every four years, general philosophy is highly consistent from one election to the next, and the wording is often nearly identical to the previous platform.

Platforms serve as "blueprints" for the parties, articulating their political philosophies as well as specific promises and plans for what the party will accomplish if it has control. Platforms can be dozens of pages long; we have included only those topics and points most relevant to women and discussed in this book. Issues (our captions) are in alphabetical order, with platform page numbers noted in parentheses. Categories and captions between the two platforms are not a perfect match, since platforms differ slightly on issues they address.

All quotes below are verbatim, and are presented without comment. In a very few cases, words in square brackets [ ] have been added for clarity. Administrative actions and bills most relevant to women promised in the platforms, that have been signed into law since the platforms were adopted in 2012, are noted in curly brackets { }. We have tried not to burden the reader with platform content that is pure rhetoric, pronouncements against the other party, or self-congratulation for past accomplishments. We include only what the parties clearly state they stand for, and what they plan to do.

We encourage readers to review the platform statements that follow carefully, and use them to hold elected officials and candidates alike accountable. Have they adhered to their promises and positions? If not, why not? If not yet, when? What have they done specifically to advance a particular position or promise?

Moving America Forward
2012 Democratic National Platform

Abortion, Family Planning, and Sex Education:

The Democratic Party strongly and unequivocally supports *Roe v. Wade* and a woman's right to make decisions regarding her pregnancy, including a safe and legal abortion, regardless of ability to pay. We oppose any and all efforts to weaken or undermine that right. We strongly and unequivocally support a woman's decision to have a child by providing affordable health care and ensuring the availability of and access to programs that help women during pregnancy and after the birth of a child, including caring adoption programs. (18)

The President and the Democratic Party believe that women have a right to control their reproductive choices. Democrats support access to affordable family planning services, and President Obama and Democrats will continue to stand up to Republican efforts to defund Planned Parenthood health centers.

Democrats support evidence-based and age-appropriate sex education. (18)

President Obama and the Democratic Party are committed to supporting family planning around the globe to help women care for their families, support their communities, and lead their countries to be healthier and more productive. (31)

Children/Education:

We are committed to ensuring that every child in America has access to a world-class public education so we can out-educate the world and make sure America has the world's highest proportion of college graduates by 2020. It means we must close the achievement gap in America's schools and ensure that in every neighborhood in the country, children can benefit from high-quality educational opportunities. (5)

We will continue to strengthen all our schools and work to expand public school options for low-income youth, including magnet schools, charter schools, teacher-led schools, and career academies. (5)

Homeland Security is prioritizing the deportation of criminals who endanger our communities over the deportation of immigrants who do not pose a threat, such as children who came here through no fault of their own and are pursuing an education. (13)

We support expanding the Child and Dependent Care Tax Credit. We must protect our most vulnerable children by supporting our foster care system, adoption programs for all caring parents, grandparents, and caregivers, and protecting children from violence and neglect. (14)

We support expanding the Child and Dependent Care Tax Credit. (14)

The President and the Democratic Party will fiercely oppose harsh cuts in Medicaid that would [diminish or eliminate] health care for millions of Americans with disabilities, workers with disabilities, and families raising children with autism, Down Syndrome, and other serious disabilities. (15)

Equal Rights

At the core of the Democratic Party is the principle that no one should face discrimination on the basis of race, ethnicity, national origin, language, religion, gender, sexual orientation, gender identity, or disability status. Democrats support our civil rights statutes. We are committed to protecting all communities from violence. We are committed to ending racial, ethnic, and religious profiling and requiring federal, state, and local enforcement agencies to take steps to eliminate the practice, and we continue to support enforcement of Title VI. (17)

We are committed to equal opportunity for all Americans and to making sure that every American is treated equally under the law. We are committed to ensuring full equality for women: we reaffirm our support for the Equal Rights Amendment, recommit to enforcing Title IX, support the Paycheck Fairness Act, and will urge ratification of the Convention on the Elimination of All Forms of Discrimination Against Women. (17)

We support the Employment Non-Discrimination Act because people should not be fired based on their sexual orientation or gender identity. (17)

We support the right of all families to have equal respect, responsibilities, and protections under the law. We support marriage equality and support the movement to secure equal treatment under law for same-sex couples. We also support the freedom of churches and religious entities to decide how to administer marriage as a religious sacrament without government interference. (18)

We support the full repeal of the so-called Defense of Marriage Act and the passage of the Respect for Marriage Act. (18)

Recognizing that gay rights are human rights, the President and his administration have vowed to actively combat efforts by other nations that criminalize homosexual conduct or ignore abuse. Under the Obama administration, American diplomats must raise the issue wherever harassment or abuse arises, and they are required to record it in the State Department's annual report on human rights. (31)

Employment Protection/Equal Pay:

We continue to fight for relief for the long-term unemployed, including a ban on hiring discrimination against the unemployed and a reformed and expanded universal worker training proposal to provide more training and job search assistance to all displaced workers regardless of how they lost their job. (3)

We will raise the minimum wage, and index it to inflation. (10)

We will fight for collective bargaining rights for police officers, nurses, firefighters, emergency medical technicians, teachers, and other public sector workers – jobs that are a proven path to the middle class for millions of Americans. We will continue to vigorously oppose "Right to Work" and "paycheck protection" efforts, and so-called "Save our Secret Ballot" measures whenever they are proposed. (10)

We are committed to ensuring that Americans do not face employment discrimination. We support the Employment Non-Discrimination Act because people should not be fired based on their sexual orientation or gender identity. (17)

We are committed to passing the Paycheck Fairness Act, and we will continue to battle Republican opposition to efforts to stop wage discrimination. (10)

We will continue to oppose all efforts to weaken the landmark Americans with Disabilities Act, and we will vigorously enforce laws that prevent discrimination. (15)

Democrats will continue to support efforts to ensure that workers can combat gender discrimination in the workplace and to protect women against pregnancy discrimination. And that's why we support passing the Healthy Families Act, broadening the Family and Medical Leave Act, and partnering with states to move toward paid leave.(17)

We will provide immediate relief to working people who have lost their jobs, families who are in danger of losing their homes, and those who – no matter how hard they work – are seeing prices go up more than their income. (6)

Global Women's Rights:

Ensuring full equality and providing women and girls the opportunity to learn, earn a livable wage, and participate in public decision-making are essential to reduce violence, improve economies, and strengthen democracy. To continue to make progress at home and advance women's rights and opportunities abroad, we will urge ratification of the Convention for the Elimination of All Forms of Discrimination Against Women. (31)

[We] are committed to advancing the rights of women and girls as a central focus of U.S. diplomatic, development, and defense interests. We will continue to promote the full engagement of women in the political and economic spheres. We will work to address underlying socio-economic problems, including women's access to health, education, and food security. And we will ensure that women are equal participants in reconciliation and development in areas affected by conflict. (31)

President Obama and the Democratic Party are committed to supporting family planning around the globe to help women care for their families, support their communities, and lead their countries to be healthier and more productive. That's why, in his first month in office, President Obama overturned the "global gag rule," a ban on federal funds to foreign family planning organizations that provided information about, counseling on, or offered abortions. (31)

The administration is also committed to taking action at home to fight trafficking, including the sex trafficking of young girls. (31)

Medicaid:

We will strengthen Medicaid and oppose efforts to block grant the program, slash its funding, and leave millions more without health insurance. (4)

The President and the Democratic Party will fiercely oppose the harsh cuts in Medicaid that would inevitably lead to no or significantly less health care for millions of Americans with disabilities, workers with disabilities, and families raising children with autism, Down Syndrome, and other serious disabilities. (15)

Medicare/Social Security:

We will find a solution to protect Social Security for future generations. We will block Republican efforts to subject Americans' guaranteed retirement income to the whims of the stock market through privatization. We reject approaches that insist that cutting benefits is the only answer. President Obama will also make it easier for Americans to save on their own for retirement and prepare for unforeseen expenses by participating in retirement accounts at work. (4)

Democrats adamantly oppose any efforts to privatize or voucherize Medicare; unlike our opponents we will not ask seniors to pay thousands of dollars more every year while they watch the value of their Medicare benefits evaporate. We will build on . . .reforms, not eliminate Medicare's guarantees. (5)

Violence Against Women:

Democrats enacted the Tribal Law and Order Act, support expansion of the Violence Against Women Act to include greater protection for women on tribal lands, and oppose versions of the Violence Against Women Act that do not include these critical provisions. (16) {These provisions were included in the reauthorization of the Violence Against Women Act passed in 2013.}

We will end the dangerous cycle of violence, especially youth violence, by continuing to invest in proven community-based law enforcement programs such as the Community Oriented Policing Services program. (20)

2012 Republican Platform

Abortion, Family Planning, and Sex Education:

We support a human life amendment to the Constitution and endorse legislation to make clear that the Fourteenth Amendment's protections apply to unborn children. (14)

We oppose using public revenues to promote or perform abortion or fund organizations which perform or advocate it and will not fund or subsidize health care which includes abortion coverage. We support the appointment of
judges who respect traditional family values and the sanctity of innocent human life. (14)

We urge Congress to strengthen the Born Alive Infant Protection Act by enacting appropriate civil and criminal penalties on healthcare providers who fail to provide treatment and care to an infant who survives an abortion, including early induction delivery where the death of the infant is intended. We call for legislation to ban sex-selective abortions – gender discrimination in its most lethal form—and to protect from abortion unborn children who are capable of feeling pain. (14)

We call for a ban on the use of body parts from aborted fetuses for research. We support and applaud adult stem cell research to develop lifesaving therapies, and we oppose the killing of embryos for their stem cells. We oppose federal funding of embryonic stem cell research. (14)

We seek to protect young girls from exploitation through a parental consent requirement; and we affirm our moral obligation to assist, rather than penalize, women challenged by an unplanned pregnancy. (14)

We call on the government to permanently ban all federal funding and subsidies for abortion and healthcare plans that include abortion coverage. (33)

We likewise support the right of parents to consent to medical treatment for their children, including mental health treatment, drug treatment, and treatment involving pregnancy, contraceptives and abortion. We urge enactment of pending legislation that would require parental consent to transport girls across state lines for abortions. (34)

We oppose school-based clinics that provide referrals, counseling, and related services for abortion and contraception. (36) We renew our call for replacing "family planning" programs for teens with abstinence education which teaches abstinence until marriage as the responsible and respected standard of behavior. (36) We will use the full force of the law against those who engage in modern-day forms of slavery, including the commercial sexual exploitation of children and the forced labor of men, women, and children. The principle underlying our Megan's Law— publicizing the identities of known offenders—should be extended to international travel in order to protect innocent children everywhere. (53)

Affirmative Action:

We reject preferences, quotas, and set-asides as the best or sole methods through which fairness can be achieved, whether in government, education, or corporate boardrooms . (9)

Children:

Any restructuring of the federal tax code should recognize the financial impact of the adoption process and the commitment made by adoptive families. (32)

We urge active prosecution against child pornography, which is closely linked to the horrors of human trafficking. (32)

[We support rejection of international treaties including] the U.N. Convention on Women's Rights, the Convention on the Rights of the Child, the Convention on the Rights of Persons with Disabilities, and the U.N. Arms Trade Treaty as well as the various declarations from the U.N. Conference on Environment and Development. (45)

Education:

While we encourage the retention and transmission of heritage tongues, we support English as the nation's official language, (26)

The Individuals with Disabilities Education Act (IDEA) has opened up unprecedented opportunities for many students, and we reaffirm our support for its goal of minimizing the separation of children with disabilities from their peers. (32)

School choice – whether through charter schools, open enrollment requests, college lab schools, virtual schools, career and technical education programs, vouchers, or tax credits – is important for all children (36)

We support options for learning, including home schooling and local innovations like single-sex classes, full-day school hours, and year-round schools. School choice – whether through charter schools, open enrollment requests, college lab schools, virtual schools, career and technical education programs, vouchers, or tax credits – is important for all children (36)

We support . . . block grants and the repeal of numerous federal regulations which interfere with State and local control of public schools. (36) We affirm the right of students to engage in prayer at public school events in public schools and to have equal access to public schools and other public facilities to accommodate religious freedom in the public square. (12)

Equal Rights

We consider discrimination based on sex, race, age, religion, creed, disability, or national origin unacceptable and immoral. We will strongly enforce antidiscrimination statutes and ask all to join us in rejecting the forces of hatred and bigotry and in denouncing all who practice or promote racism, anti-Semitism, ethnic prejudice, or religious intolerance. (9)

We reaffirm our support for a Constitutional amendment defining marriage as the union of one man and one woman. (10)

We condemn the hate campaigns, threats of violence, and vandalism by proponents of same-sex marriage against advocates of traditional marriage and call for a federal investigation into attempts to deny religious believers their civil rights. (12)

We will enforce and defend in court the Defense of Marriage Act (DOMA) in the Armed Forces as well as in the civilian world. (43)

We oppose government discrimination against businesses due to religious views. We support the First Amendment right of freedom of association of the Boy Scouts of America and other service organizations whose values are under assault and condemn the State blacklisting of religious groups which decline to arrange adoptions by same-sex couples. (12)

Employment Protection:

A Republican President will protect the rights of conscience of public employees by proposing legislation to bar mandatory [union] dues for political purposes. (8)

Use of the E-verify program – an internet-based system that verifies the employment authorization and identity of employees – must be made mandatory nationwide. (26)

Global Women's Rights:

The principle underlying our Megan's Law – publicizing the identities of known human trafficking offenders – should be extended to international travel. (8)

We affirm the Republican Party's long-held position known as the Mexico City Policy . . . which prohibits the granting of federal monies to non-governmental organization that provide or promote abortion. (45)

[We support rejection of international treaties including] the U.N. Convention on Women's Rights, the Convention on the Rights of the Child, the Convention on the Rights of Persons with Disabilities, and the U.N. Arms Trade Treaty as well as the various declarations from the U.N. Conference on Environment and Development. (45)

Medicaid/Medicare

We propose . . . block-granting the [Medicaid] program to the States, providing the States with the flexibility to design programs that meet the needs of their low income citizens. (22)

We propose to block grant Medicaid and other payments to the States; and to limit federal requirements on both private insurance and Medicaid. (33)

We will save Medicare by modernizing it, by empowering its participants, and by putting it on a secure financial footing. (21)

While retaining the option of traditional Medicare in competition with private plans, we call for a transition to a premium- support model for Medicare, with an income adjusted contribution toward a health plan of the enrollee's choice. (21)

We seek to increase healthcare choice and options, contain costs and reduce mandates, simplify the system for patients and providers, restore cuts made to Medicare, and equalize the tax treatment of group and individual health insurance plans. (32)

Military Women:

We support military women's exemption from direct ground combat units and infantry battalions. (43)

Social Security

Comprehensive reform should address our society's remarkable medical advances in longevity and allow younger workers the option of creating their own personal investment accounts as supplements to the system. (22)

Republicans are committed to setting [Social Security] on a sound fiscal basis that will give workers control over, and a sound return on, their investments. (23)

◊ NOTES ◊

1. Sullivan, Patricia. "Anne Gorsuch Burford, 62, Dies; Reagan EPA Director." *Washington Post,* July 22, 2004: B06.

2. Sydell, Laura. "Clarence the Credible, How Journalists Blew the Thomas Story." *Fairness and Accuracy in Reporting, Extra!*, 1992: Special Issue on Women.

3. U.S. Department of Human Services. *Donna E. Shalala, Ph.D., Secretary of Health and Human Services*. Retrieved November 15, 2007 from http://www.surgeongeneral.gov/library/youthviolence/shalala.htm

4. Barnes, Robert. "Over Ginsburg's Dissent, Court Limits Bias Suits." *Washington Post,* May 30, 2007: A01.

5. Lee, Christopher. "Birth-Control Foe To Run Office on Family Planning." *Washington Post*, October 17, 2007: A15 .

6. Berkowitz, Bill. " Wade Horn Cashes Out." *Media Transparency*, April 25, 2007. Retrieved December 1, 2007 from http://www.mediatransparency.org/story.php?storyID=190

7. Barnes, Robert. "Roberts Court Moves Right, But With a Measured Step." *Washington Post*, April 20, 2007: Page A03.

8. Risen, James. "White House Is Subpoenaed on Wiretapping." *New York Times*, June 28, 2007.

9. "DOJ Flinches, Skirts Drone Strike Subpoena Fight." *Legal Times*, April 17, 2013. Retrieved February 22, 2014 from http://legaltimes.typepad.com/blt/2013/04/doj-flinches-skirts-subpoena-fight-with-congress.html

10. Roberts, John. *Tobacco Executive Goes Public over Company Lies*. (February 3, 1996). Retrieved December 1, 2007 from http://www.bmj.com/cgi/content/full/312/7026/267/a

11. Milbank, Dana. "Sweeteners for the South." *The Washington Post*, Sunday, November 22, 2009.

12. "Fixing the Filibuster: Three Senators Offer a Solution." *The Nation*, December 16, 2010. Retrieved October 17, 2011 from http://www.alternet.org/news/149212/fixing_the_filibuster%3A_three_senators_offer_a_solution/

13. Sherr, Lynn. *Failure is Impossible: Susan B. Anthony in Her Own Words*. New York: Times Books, Random House, 1995.

14. Flexner, Eleanor. *Century of Struggle: The Woman's Rights Movement in the United States*. Cambridge, Massachusetts: The Belknap Press of Harvard University Press, 1959, 1975.

15. *Gender Differences in Voter Turnout, Fact Sheet*. Center for American Women and Politics, Rutgers University, New Brunswick, N.J. 2005. Retrieved January 15, 2008 from http://www.cawp.rutgers.edu/Facts/genderdiff.pdf

16. "The 2008 Presidential Election and Trends in Opinions on Education." Celinda Lake, Lake Research Partners, Public Education Network Annual Conference, November 16, 2008. http://www.docstoc.com/docs/5507993/The-2008-Presidential-Election-and-Trends-in-Opinions-on

17. Easley, Jonathan. "Gallup: 2012 Election Had the Largest Gender Gap in Recorded History." Washington, D.C.: *The Hill*, November 09, 2012. Retrieved February 20, 2014 from http://thehill.com/blogs/blog-briefing-room/news/267101-gallup-2012-election-had-the-largest-gender-gap-in-history

18. "Women in the 2006 Elections." Washington, D.C.: Lake Research Partners, November 17, 2006.

19. "Women Voters Made the Difference in 2006 Election." *Ms* magazine press release, November 17, 2006.

20. "2008 Election Gender Gap." Arlington, Va. Feminist Majority. http://www.feministmajority.org/elections/2008gendergap.asp

21. "2010 Exit Polls, U.S. House." CNN Election Center. Retrieved October 3, 2011 from http://www.cnn.com/ELECTION/2010/results/polls/#val=USH00p1

22. Kondik, Kyle and Geoffrey Skelley. "Mind the Gap: Gender Gap Present in Almost All Federal Statewide Races over Last Decade." September 12th, 2013

23. "The Independents," *The Washington Post*. Retrieved February 15, 2008 from http://www.WashingtonPost.com

24. "Women More Likely to Be Democrats, Regardless of Age," Gallup poll, June 12, 2009.

25. "Partisan Polarization Surges in Bush, Obama Years." Washington, D.C.: Pew Research, June 4, 2012. Retrieved February 21, 2014 from http://www.people-press.org/2012/06/04/section-9-trends-in-party-affiliation/

26. "Women in the House." *National Journal*. Retrieved Dec. 31, 2007 from http://nationaljournal.com/voteratings/pdf/06womenminorities.pdf

27. U.S. Senate, roll call votes, 108th Congress, 1st session. Retrieved December 15, 2007 from http://www.senate.gov

28. *The Global Gender Gap Report 2013*. Geneva, Switzerland: World Economic Forum, 2013. Retrieved January 23, 2014 from http://www.weforum.org/issues/global-gender-gap

29. Tripp, Aili Marie. "Debating Women's Rights and Customary Law in Africa Today." Conference paper, Indiana University School of Law, March 2007

30. Interparliamentary Union. *Women in National Parliaments*. (November 1, 2013). Retrieved January 23, 2014, from http://www.ipu.org/wmn-e/classif.htm

31. *International Database of Quotas for Women*. Stockholm, Sweden: International Institute for Democracy and Electoral Assistance Quota Project. Retrieved January 23, 2014 from http://www.quotaproject.org/aboutProject.cfm

32. "Women Presidents and Prime Ministers." England, UK: Centre for Women and Democracy. Retrieved January 24, 2014 from http://www.cfwd.org.uk/resources/women-presidents-prime-ministers

33. "Blacks Voted at a Higher Rate than Whites in 2012 Election – A First, Census Bureau Reports." Washington, D.C.: U.S. Bureau of the Census, May, 2013. Retrieved January 23, 2014 from http://www.census.gov/newsroom/releases/archives/voting/cb13-84.html

34. Hegewisch, Ariane and Williams, Claudia. "Fact Sheet, The Gender Wage Gap: 2012." Washington, D.C.: Institute for Women's Policy Research, September 2013. Retrieved January 25, 2014 from iwpr.org

35. Polochek, Soloman and Jun Xiang. *The Gender Pay Gap: A Cross-Country Analysis*. State University of New York at Binghamton, 2006. Retrieved November 2, 2011 from http://www.rand.org/content/dam/rand/www/external/labor/seminars/adp/pdfs/2006_polachek.pdf

36. *The Global Gender Gap Report 2013*. Geneva, Switzerland: World Economic Forum, 2013. Retrieved January 23, 2014 from http://www.weforum.org/issues/global-gender-gap

37. Robbins, Katherine Gallagher and Frohlich, Lauren. *National Snapshot: Poverty Among Women & Families, 2012*. Washington, D.C.: National Women's Law Center, September 2013. Retrieved January 25, 2014 from http://www.nwlc.org/sites/default/files/pdfs/povertysnapshot2012.pdf

38. Gebreselassie, Tsedeye and Sonn, Paul. "Women and the Minimum Wage," *The American Prospect* online, July 24, 2009.

39. Scheil-Adlung, Xenia & Lydia Sandner. "The case for paid sick leave." *World Health Report (2010) Background Paper* 9. Geneva, Switzerland, World Health Organization. Retrieved November 2, 2011 from http://www.who.int/healthsystems/topics/financing/healthre

port/SickleaveNo9FINAL.pdf

40. "The World's Women 2010, Trends and Statistics." United Nations, New York, 2010. Retrieved September 29, 2011 from http://unstats.un.org/unsd/demographic/products/Worldswomen/WW_full%20report_color.pdf

41. Heymann, Jody, Alison Earle, Jeffrey Hayes. "How Does the United States Measure Up?" Institute for Health and Social Policy, McGill University, 2007.

42. Shriver, Maria. *The Shriver Report: A Woman's Nation Pushes Back from the Brink*. Washington, D.C.: Center for American Progress, January, 2014.

43. *2013 Catalyst Census: Fortune 500 Women Board Directors*. New York: Catalyst, December 10, 2013. Retrieved January 28, 2014 from http://www.catalyst.org/knowledge/2013-catalyst-census-fortune-500-women-board-directors

44. Ivory, Danielle. "Women Lose More Ground in U.S. Small Business Contracts Race." *Bloomberg Online*, Jan 24, 2013. Retrieved January 28, 2014 from http://www.bloomberg.com/news/2013-01-24/women-lose-more-ground-than-men-in-small-business-awards-race.html

45. "The Military-Industrial Complex Leaderboard Since 10/30/06." MilitaryIndustrialComplex.com using information from the United States Department of Defense. Downloaded November 2, 2011 from http://www.militaryindustrialcomplex.com/contracts-leaderboard.asp

46. Carnevale, Anthony P., Jeff Strohl, and Michelle Melton. "What's It Worth?: The Economic Value of College Majors." Center on Education and the Workforce, Georgetown University, May 24, 2011. Retrieved November 2, 1011 from http://cew.georgetown.edu/whatsitworth/

47. Dey, Judy Goldberg and Catherine Hill. *Behind the Pay Gap*. Washington, D.C. American Association of University Women, 2007.

48. *Women, Minorities, and Persons with Disabilities in Science and Engineering: 2013*. Washington, D.C.: National Center for Science and Engineering Statistics Directorate for Social, Behavioral and Economic Sciences. Retrieved January 28, 2014 from http://www.nsf.gov/statistics/wmpd/2013/pdf/nsf13304_digest.pdf

49. *Business School Data Trends 2013*. Tampa, Florida: The Association to Advance Collegiate Schools of Business, 2013. Retrieved January 28, 2014 from http://www.aacsb.edu/publications/data-trends/2013.pdf

50. *A Current Glance at Women in the Law*. Chicago: American Bar Association, February 2013. Retrieved January 28, 2014 from http://www.americanbar.org/content/dam/aba/marketing/women/current_glance_statistics_feb2013.authcheckdam.pdf

51. Chen Vivia, "The Careerist: Women at Law Schools Decline," May 19, 2011. Retrieved November 2, 2011 from http://www.law.com/jsp/cc/PubArticleCC.jsp?id=1202494422378

52. "Medical School Applicants, Enrollment Reach All-time Highs," Washington, D.C.: Association of American Medical Colleges. Retrieved January 28, 2014 from aamc.org

53. Lo Sasso, Anthony T., Michael R. Richards, Chiu-Fang Chou, and Susan E. Gerber. "The $16,819 Pay Gap For Newly Trained Physicians: The Unexplained Trend Of Men Earning More Than Women." *Health Affairs*, February 2011. Retrieved November 2, 2011 from http://content.healthaffairs.org/content/30/2.toc

54. Organisation for Economic Co-operation and Development. *Can Parents Afford to Work? Childcare Costs, Tax-benefit Policies and Work Incentives.* (January 2006.) Retrieved November 15, 2007 from http://www.oecd.org/dataoecd/35/43/35969537.pdf

55. "Parents and the High Cost of Child Care 2013 Report." Arlington, Va: National Association of Child Care Resource and Referral Agencies. Retrieved January 28, 2014, from http://www.naccrra.org

56. "U.S. Child Care Seriously Lags Behind that of Europe." *American Sociological Association News*, November 18, 2002.

57. National Association for the Education of Young Children. *Child Care and Development Block Grant.* Retrieved January 15, 2008 from http://www.naeyc.org

58. Taxin, Amy. "State Child Care Cuts Force Hard Choice on Parents," *Associated Press*, December 29, 2011. Retrieved February 23, 2012 from http://www.newsvine.com/_news/2011/12/29/9806039-state-child-care-cuts-force-hard-choice-on-parents

59. *Women's Health USA 2011*. U.S. Department of Health and Human Services, Health Resources and Services Administration, Maternal and Child Health Bureau. Rockville, Maryland: U.S. Department of Health and Human Services, 2011. Retrieved November 2, 2011 from http://mchb.hrsa.gov/whusa11/hsu/pages/301hi.html

60. *Deadly Delivery: The Maternal Health Care Crisis in the USA*. London: Amnesty International, 2010, updated 2013. Retrieved January 28, 2014, from http://www.amnestyusa.org/sites/default/files/pdfs/deadlydeli very.pdf

61. "Abortion Facts,. National Abortion Federation, Washington, D.C. Retrieved November 2, 2011 from http://www.prochoice.org/about_abortion/facts/access_abor tion.html

62. *Women and Long Term Care*. Washington, D.C.: Older Women's League, 2007.

63. Ibid.

64. Ibid.

65. Tolchin, Martin. "Other Countries Do Much More for Disabled." *New York Times*, March 29, 1990.

66. Mukherjee, Sy. "Four Major Insurers Accused Of Discriminating Against Women In Long-Term Care Plans." thinprogress.org, January 16, 2014. Retrieved January 28, 2014 from http://thinkprogress.org/health/2014/01/16/3176091/major-insurers-discriminate-gender-long-term-care/

67. "Social Security Programs Throughout the World: Europe, 2006." Washington, D.C.: U.S. Social Security Administration Office of Policy, 2007.

68. Ibid.

69. "Rape Statistics." Washington, D.C.: U.S. Department of Justice, cited by Statistics Brain, research date June 18, 2013. Retrieved February 1, 2014 from http://www.statisticbrain.com/rape-statistics/

70. “Domestic Violence/Abuse Statistics,. Washington, D.C.: U.S. Department of Justice, cited by Statistics Brain, research date June 28, 2013. Retrieved February 1, 2014 from http://www.statisticbrain.com/ domestic-violence-abuse-stats/

71. Catalano, Shannan Ph.D., Erica Smith, Howard Snyder, Ph.D., and Michael Ran. *Female Victims of Violence*. U.S. Justice Department, September, 2009. Retrieved November 4, 2011 from http://bjs.ojp.usdoj.gov/content/pub/pdf/fvv.pdf

72. “The Campaign for U.S. Ratification of the Convention on the Rights of the Child (CRC).” Retrieved November 4, 2011 from childrightscampaign.org

73. “Help Ban Landmines.” Tacoma Park, MD: Handicap International. Retrieved February 1, 2014 from http://www.handicap-international.us/ landmine_petition

74. “Women in the 2006 Elections.” Washington, D.C.: Lake Research Partners, November 13,2006. Retrieved February 23, 2014 from http://www.lakeresearch.com/polls/pdf/Women%20in%20the%202006%20Elections%20_%20Lake%20Research.pdf

75. January 2011 political survey, Washington, D.C. Pew Research Center For The People & The Press. Personal correspondence.

76. Dugan, Andrew. “Women in Swing States Have Gender-Specific Priorities.” Princeton, NJ: Gallup, October 17, 2012. Retrieved February 20, 2014 from http://www.gallup.com/poll/158069/women-swing-states-gender-specific-priorities.aspx

77. "An Even More Partisan Agenda for 2008, Election Year Economic Ratings Lowest Since '92." Pew Research Center for People and the Press, January 24, 2008.

78. "Poll Findings: Understanding What Women Want In 2008." Peter D. Hart and Associates for the National Women's Law Center, August 5, 2008. Retrieved November 24, 2009 from http://www.nwlc.org/pdf /2008poll_whatwomenwantmemo.pdf

79. Burk, Martha. "The Myth of the Mancession." *Ms* magazine, Summer, 2011.

80. Results in this section from "Women's Movement Worthwhile," CBS News Poll, October 2005, partially updated February 11, 2009 CBS News Story "Women Strive to Find Balance." Retrieved October 14, 2011 from http://www.cbsnews.com/stories/2006/05/14/opinion/polls/main1616577_page2.shtml?tag=contentMain;contentBody.

81. "Women in the 2006 Elections." Washington, D.C.: Lake Research Partners.

82. "Women's Movement Worthwhile," CBS News Poll, 2005. Retrieved March 12, 2014 from http://www.cbsnews.com/news/poll-womens-movement-worthwhile/

83. "Gender Equality Universally Embraced, but Inequalities Acknowledged," Global Attitudes Project, Washington, D.C. Pew Research Center, 22 Nation Pew Global Attitudes Survey, July 1, 2010.

84. Opinion Research Corporation, national poll commissioned by the ERA Campaign Network, July 6–9, 2001.

85. "Three in Five Americans Say U.S. Has Long Way to Go to Reach Gender Equality," New York, N.Y.: Harris Polls, August 16, 2010. Retrieved February 20, 2014 from http://www.harrisinteractive.com/NewsRoom/HarrisPolls/tabid/447/mid/1508/articleId/452/ctl/ReadCustom%20Default/Default.aspx

86. "Poll Findings: Understanding What Women Want In 2008," Peter D. Hart and Associates for the National Women's Law Center.

87. "Poll Findings: Understanding What Women Want In 2008," Peter D. Hart and Associates for the National Women's Law Center.

88. "ABC News Poll." ABCNEWS.com, January 22, 2008.

89. Quinnipiac University poll, July 28 - 31, 2013. Retrieved February 20, 2013 from http://www.quinnipiac.edu/institutes-and-centers/polling-institute/national/release-detail?ReleaseID=1931

90. Ibid.

91. Lipka, Michael. "5 facts about abortion," Washington, D.C.: Pew Research Center, January 22, 2014. Retrieved February 20, 2014 from http://www.pewresearch.org/fact-tank/2014/01/22/5-facts-about-abortion/

92. "Less Opposition to Gay Marriage, Adoption and Military Service." The Pew Research Center for the People and the Press, March 22, 2006.

93. Newport, Frank. "For the First Time, Majority of Americans Favor Legal Gay Marriage," Gallup Organization, May 20, 2011. Retrieved October 3, 2011 from http://www.gallup.com/poll/147662/First-Time-Majority-Americans-Favor-Legal-Gay-Marriage.aspx

94. Saad, Lydia. "In U.S., 52 percent Back Law to Legalize Gay Marriage in 50 States," Princeton, N.J.: Gallup, July 29, 2013. Retrieved February 20, 2014 from http://www.gallup.com/poll/163730/back-law-legalize-gay-marriage-states.aspx

95. "Majority Continues To Support Civil Unions," The Pew Research Center for the People and the Press, Oct. 9, 2009.

96. "Gays In The Military Should Be Allowed To Come Out," Quinnipiac University National Poll, April 30, 2009. Retrieved November 24, 2009 from http://www.quinnipiac.edu/x1295.xml?ReleaseID=1292

97. Saad, Lydia. "Majority of Americans Still Support Roe v. Wade Decision." January 22, 2013. Gallup Politics. Retrieved February 25, 2014 from http://www.gallup.com/poll/160058/majority-americans-support-roe-wade-decision.aspx?utm_source=alert&utm_medium=email&utm_campaign=syndication&utm_content=morelink&utm_term=All%20Gallup%20Headlines

98. Dugan ,Andrew. "Women in Swing States Have Gender-Specific Priorities." Gallup, October 17, 2012. Retrieved February 24, 2014 from http://www.gallup.com/poll/158069/women-swing-states-gender-specific-priorities.aspx

99. Newport, Frank. "For First Time, Majority of Americans Favor Legal Gay Marriage." Gallup Organization, May 20, 2011. Retrieved October 3, 2011 from http://www.gallup.com/poll/147662/First-Time-Majority-Americans-Favor-Legal-Gay-Marriage.aspx

100. ABC News. "Most Oppose Gay Marriage; Fewer Back an Amendment." (May 31-June 4, 2006). Retrieved January 8, 2008 from http://abcnews.go.com/US/Politics/Story?id=2041689&page=3

101. "Majority Continues To Support Civil Unions." The Pew Research Center for the People and the Press, Oct. 9, 2009.

102. "Focus: Public Opinion & Polls." Gay & Lesbian Alliance Against Defamation, 2008.

103. Saad, Lydia. "In U.S., 52% Back Law to Legalize Gay Marriage in 50 States." Gallup Politics, July 29, 2013. Retrieved February 24, 2014 from http://www.gallup.com/poll/163730/back-law-legalize-gay-marriage-states.aspx

104. Dugan ,Andrew . "Women in Swing States Have Gender-Specific Priorities." Gallup, October 17, 2012.

105. NBC News/Wall Street Journal Poll conducted by the polling organizations of Peter Hart (D) and Bill McInturff (R). June 17-21, 2010. Retrieved October 3, 2011 from http://www.pollingreport.com/prioriti.htm

106. Preston, Julia."11.2 Million Illegal Immigrants in U.S. in 2010, Report Says; No Change From '09." *The New York Times*. Published: February 1, 2011.

107. Paral, Rob. *Playing Politics on Immigration: Congress Favors Image over Substance in Passing H.R. 4437*. (February 27, 2006). Retrieved December 30, 2007 from http://www.ailf.org/ipc/policybrief/policybrief_2006_playing politics.shtml

108. Preston, Julia. "In Report, 63% Back Way to Get Citizenship." *The New York Times*, November 25, 2013.

109. " Problems and Priorities." PollingReport.com compilation of 2013-2014 polls. Retrieved February 24, 2014 from http://www.pollingreport.com/prioriti.htm

110. Omero, Margie et. al. "What the Public Really Thinks About Guns." Washington, D.C.: Center for American Progress, March, 2013. Retrieved February 24, 2014 from http://www.americanprogress.org/issues/civil-liberties/report /2013/03/27/58092/what-the-public-really-thinks-about-gun s/

111. "Problems and Priorities." PollingReport.com compilation of 2013-2014 polls.

112. Table T10-0269, Taxable Estates, Estate Tax Liability, and Average Estate Tax Rate, By Size of Gross Estate, 2011. Washington, D.C. Tax Policy Center. Retrieved October 3, 2011 from http://taxpolicycenter.org/numbers/Content/ PDF/T10-0269.pdf

113. Johnson, David C. *The Attack on Trial Lawyers and Tort Law*. Menlo Park: The Commonweal Institute, October, 2003.

114. Peter D. Hart Associates. *Civil Justice Issues and the 2008 Elections*. (July 11, 2007). Retrieved Dec. 23, 2007 from http://www.atla.org/pressroom/CJSPollMemo.pdf

115. "Problems and Priorities: Compilation of National Polls on Possible Election Issues." Retrieved Dec. 18, 2007 from PollingReport.com

116. Krugman, Paul. "Dwindling Deficit Disorder." *The New York Times*, March 10, 2013. Retrieved February 24, 2014 from http://www.nytimes.com/2013/03/11/opinion/krugman-dwindling-deficit-disorder.html

117. *US Mortgage Defaults Leveling Off but Repos Rising.* Retrieved February 17, 2008 from http://www.researchrecap.com/index.php/2007/11/29/us-mortgage-defaults-leveling-off-but-repos-rising/

118. Leland, John. "Baltimore Finds Subprime Crisis Snags Women." *New York Times*, January 15, 2006.

119. Ibid.

120. Cornett, Brandon. "Subprime Mortgage Crisis Explained," Home Buying Institute, December 18, 2007.

121. Aversa, Jeannine. "Majority Believe US in Recession." Associated Press, Feb. 10, 2008.

122. "As Talk of Recession Grows, Republicans and Democrats Differ on Response.," *New York Times*, January 15, 2008.

123. Weisman, Jonathan. "Congress Approves Stimulus Package." *Washington Post*, February 8, 2008: Page A01.

124. Stevens, Allison. "Stimulus Plan Falls Short in Female-Friendly Audit." *Women's Enews*, Retrieved February 3, 2008 from http://www.womensenews.org/article.cfm?aid=3479

125. Ibid.

126. Burk, Martha. "Who Needs Money? You've Got Credit!" Ms. magazine, Summer, 2009.

127. Fenn, Peter. "Tea Party Funding Koch Brothers Emerge From Anonymity.," *U.S. News & World Report*, February 2, 2011. Retrieved December 6, 2011 from http://www.usnews.com/opinion/blogs/Peter-Fenn/2011/02/02/tea-party-funding-koch-brothers-emerge-from-anonymity

128. Dbug. "What Happened to The Tea Party in the 2012 Election?" The Daily Kos, December 29, 2012. Retrieved March 11, 2014 from http://www.dailykos.com/story/2012/12/30/1174753/-What-Happened-to-The-Tea-Party-in-the-2012-Election#

129. Lightman, David. "Talks Over Shutdown and Debt Ceiling Hold Risks for Tea Party and Its Influence.," Washington, D.C.: McClatchy News online, October 14, 2013. Retrieved March 11, 2014 from http://www.mcclatchydc.com/2013/10/14/205351/talks-over-shutdown-and-debt-ceiling.html

130. "Milwaukee Schools To Lay Off 354 Teachers.," CNN.com, June 29, 2011. Retrieved December 6, 2011 from http://articles.cnn.com/2011-06-29/us/wisconsin.teacher.layoffs_1_state-cuts-elementary-schools-federal-stimulus?_s=PM:US

131. "More Than 300,000 Women Drop Out of Labor Force as Sluggish Growth Continues.," press release. Washington, D.C., Institute for Women's Policy Research, December 6, 2011. Retrieved December 6, 2011 from iwpr.org

132. "Women Gained Over Half of the Jobs Added in February; Men Have Regained 82 Percent of Jobs Lost in the Recession. ," press release. Washington, D.C.: Institute for Women's Policy Research, March 7, 2014. Retrieved March 11, 2014 from iwpr.org

133. Berman, Jillian. "These 2 Stats Should Enrage Every Feminist In America," *The Huffington Post,* March 11, 2014. Retrieved March 11, 2014 from http://www.huffingtonpost.com/2014/03/11/low-wage-recovery-women_n_4941592.html

134. Dwight D. Eisenhower, speech, American Society of Newspaper Editors, 16 April 1953

135. *Statement on the Treasury Surplus - Brief Article.* Weekly Compilation of Presidential Documents. (September 21, 2000). Retrieved January 2, 2008 from findarticles.com

136. Belasco, Amy. *The Cost of Iraq, Afghanistan, and Other Global War on Terror Operations Since 9/11.* Washington, D.C. Congressional Research Service March 29, 2011.

137. Agiesta, Jennifer and Cohen, Jon. "Public Opinion in U.S. Turns Against Afghan War," *The Washington Post,* August 20, 2009.

138. Entmacher, Joan. "5 Reasons Why No Deal Is Better than a Bad Deal for Women," Washington, D.C., National Women's Law Center, November 21, 2011. Retrieved December 6, 2011 from http://www.nwlc.org/our-blog/5-reasons-why-no-deal-better-bad-deal-women

139. Estes, Ralph. *Who Pays, Who Profits?* Washington, D.C. IPS Books, 1993.

140. Ibid.

141. "Policy Basics: Where Do Federal Tax Revenues Come From?" Washington D.C.: Center on Budget and Policy Priorities, April 12, 2013. Retrieved March 11, 2014 from http://www.cbpp.org/cms/?fa=view&id=3822

142. "The Sorry State of Corporate Taxes.," Washington, D.C.: Citizens for Tax Justice,February 2014. Retrieved March 11, 2014 from http://www.ctj.org/corporatetaxdodgers/sorrystateofcorptaxes.php#Executive%20Summary

143. Peralta, Eyder. "Report: Many Large Corporations Are Paying No Income Taxes," National Public Radio, November 3, 2011. Retrieved November 29, 2011 from http://www.npr.org/blogs/thetwo-way/2011/11/03/141993927/report-many-large-corporations-are-paying-no-income-taxes

144. "Prime Numbers," *The New York Times*, November 29, 2009.

145. "400 Highest-Income Americans Paid an Effective Rate of 18.1% in 2008," Washington, D.C., May, 2011. Retrieved November 30, 2011 from http://www.ctj.org/pdf/irstop400may2011.pdf

146. Garofalo, Pat. "The Average Bush Tax Cut for the 1 Percent this Year Will Be Greater than the Average Income of the Other 99 Percent," Washington, D.C., Center for American Progress, November 23, 2011. Retrieved November 30, 2011 from http://thinkprogress.org/economy/2011/11/23/375654/bush-tax-cut-one-percent/

147. Weisman, Jonathan."Senate Passes Corporate Tax Bill." *Washington Post*,Tuesday, October 12, 2004: A01.

148. "Republican Myths about Costs of the Affordable Care Act," Congressional Budget Office figures cited by U.S. Senate Democratic Policy Committee, March 2011. Retrieved November 30, 2011 from http://dpc.senate.gov/dpcdoc.cfm?doc_name=fs-112-1-11

149. "Estimated War-Related Costs: Iraq and Afghanistan," Center for Defense Information. Retrieved November 30, 2011, from http://www.infoplease.com/ipa/A0933935.html

150. "Tax Cuts, Myths and Realities." Washington, D.C. Center on Budget and Policy Priorities, November, 2007.

151. "Europe's Welfare States." *The Economist*, April 1, 2004 .

152. Estes. *Who Pays, Who Profits?*

153. Table T10-0269 Taxable Estates, Estate Tax Liability, and Average Estate Tax Rate, By Size of Gross Estate, 2011. Washington, D.C. Tax Policy Center. Retrieved October 3, 2011 from http://taxpolicycenter.org/numbers/Content/PDF/T10-0269.pdf

154. Burk, Martha. "A Feminist Tea Party?" Ms. magazine, Spring, 2007.

155. Corbett, Christi. *The Simple Truth About the Gender Wage Gap 2014 Edition*. Washington, D.C.: American Association of University Women, March, 2014. Retrieved March 11, 2014 from http://www.aauw.org/research/the-simple-truth-about-the-gender-pay-gap/

156. AFL-CIO. *Working Women Fast Facts*. Retrieved October 25, 2011 from

http://www.aflcio.org/issues/jobseconomy/women/upload/women.pdf Pension data from Employee Benefit Research Institute, cited by AFL-CIO 2009.

157. Ibid.

158. *Working Families National Toolkit*. Washington, D.C.: Center for American Progress, March 2014. Retrieved Marrch 12, 2014 from http://workingfamiliessummit.org/pdf/white-house-summit-toolkit.pdf

159. Ibid.

160. Ibid.

161. *Women's Earnings and Income*. New York: Catalyst, September 18, 2013. Retrieved March 12, 2014 from http://www.catalyst.org/knowledge/womens-earnings-and-income

162. "Social Security is Important to Women." Social Security Administration, July, 2011. Retrieved October 25, 2011 from http://www.ssa.gov/pressoffice/factsheets/women.htm

163. Current Population Survey, Annual Social and Economic Supplement, 2010-2013, Washington, D.C.: United States Census Bureau. Retrieved March 12, 2014 from https://www.census.gov/cps/

164. Rose, Stephen J. and Heidi I. Hartmann."Still a Man's Labor Market: the Long-term Earnings Gap." Washington, D.C.: Institute for Women's Policy Research, May, 2004.

165. "Minimum Wage: Facts at a Glance." Washington, D.C.: Economic Policy Institute, April, 2007.

166. Filion, Kai. "Fact sheet for 2009 minimum wage increase – Minimum Wage Issue Guide." Washington, D.C. Economic Policy Institute, July 20, 2009.

167. *Behind the Pay Gap*, Washington, D.C: American Association of University Women, April, 2007.

168. Covert ,Bryce. "The Gender Wage Gap Between Unionized Workers Is Tiny – And Shrinking." Think Progress, January 27, 2014. Retrieved March 12, 2014 from http://thinkprogress.org/economy/2014/01/27/3206671/gender-wage-gap-unions/

169. "Status of the Social Security and Medicare Programs, Summary of the 2013 Annual Reports," Washington, D.C. Social Security Administration. Retrieved December 3, 2013 from http://www.ssa.gov/oact/trsum/

170. *The 2013 Annual Report of the Board of Trustees of the Federal Old-age and Survivors Insurance and Federal Disability Insurance Trust Funds.*Washington, D.C. Social Security Administration, Retrieved December 3, 2013 from http://www.ssa.gov/oact/tr/2013/tr2013.pdf

171. Jasmine V. Tucker, Virginia P. Reno, and Thomas N. Bethell. 2011. Strengthening Social Security: What Do Americans Want? Washington, DC: National Academy of Social Insurance.

172. United States Social Security Administration. *Social Security Is Important to Women.* (February, 2013). Retrieved December 3, 2013 from http://www.ssa.gov/pressoffice/factsheets/women.htm

173. Fischer, Jocelyn and Jeff Hayes, Ph.D. T*he Importance of Social Security in the Incomes of Older Americans Differences by Gender, Age, Race/Ethnicity, and Marital Status,* Washington, D.C.: Institute for Women's Policy Research,

August, 2013.

174. Ibid.

175. United States Social Security Administration. *Social Security Is Important to Women.*

176. Fischer and Hayes, *The Importance of Social Security in the Incomes of Older Americans Differences by Gender, Age, Race/Ethnicity, and Marital Status*

177. "Black Women and Social Security," Washington, D.C.: Institute for Women's Policy Research, May, 2011.

178. "Latinas and Social Security," Washington, D.C. Institute for Women's Policy Research, April 2011.

179. Krugman, Paul. "Good sense from the CBO," *New York Times Online*, November 9, 2007, 7:34 pm.

180. "Social Security Policy Options," Washington, D.C., Congressional Budget Office, July, 2010. Retrieved December 3, 2013 from http://www.cbo.gov/sites/default/files/cbofiles/ftpdocs/115xx/doc11580/07-01-ssoptions_forweb.pdf

181. Ibid.

182. *Reimagining America: AARP's Blueprint for the Future.*

183. Ibid.

184. *Strengthening Social Security for Women.* Washington, D.C.: National Task Force on Social Security and Women, National Council of Women's Organizations and The Institute for Women's Policy Research, 1999.

185. "Expanding Social Security Benefits for Financially Vulnerable Populations," National Council of Women's

Organizations and Center for Community Change, Washington, D.C., October, 2013.

186. "Chronic Disease Self–Management: Fact Sheet." National Council on Aging. Retrieved February 10, 2011 from http://www.ncoa.org/press–room/fact–sheets/chronic–disease.html

187. "Policy Briefing: Expanding Access To Affordable Health Care." Romney for President Campaign, Aug 24, 2007. Retrieved January 5, 2008 from http://www.mittromney.com

188. Davies, David Martin. "Foes of Obamacare Fight Policy by Discouraging Enrollment." Commerce, Texas, KETR-FM, September 23, 2013. Retrieved March 6, 2014 from http://ketr.org/post/foes-obamacare-fight-policy-discouraging-enrollment

189. *Voters Real Health Care Agenda*. Retrieved January 8, 2008 from http://justice.org/pressroom/CJSPollMe

190. Gallup poll, October 5-11, 2012. Most important issues among registered voters in 12 swing states.

191. Alonso–Zaldivar, Ricardo, "Health Care Spending Stabilized As A Percentage Of The Economy In 2010: Report." *Huffington Post*, January 10, 2012. Retrieved February 10, 2012 from http://www.huffingtonpost.com/2012/01/10/health–care–spending–report_n_1196315.html

192. *Affordable Health Care,* Washington, D.C.: AARP. Retrieved January 3, 2008 from DividedWeFail.org

193. “National Report: Women’s Access to Health Care Services.” Washington, D.C.: National Women’s Law Center, 2007.

194. Ibid.

195. Burk, Martha. “Astroturf War.” *Ms* magazine, Fall, 2009.

196. U.S. Department of Commerce, Bureau of the Census, Current Population Survey, 2007, 2008, and 2009 Annual Social and Economic Supplement (ASEC); and U.S. Department of Commerce, Bureau of the Census, "State Single Year of Age and Sex Population Estimates: April 1, 2000 to July 1, 2008 - RESIDENT," at <http://www.census.gov/popest/states/asrh/files/SC-EST2008-AGESEX-RES.csv>. Calculations by Children's Defense Fund, Washington, D.C.. November 29, 2009 from childrensdefensefund.org

197. *Child Health.*, U.S. Center for Disease Control, National Center for Health Statistics (2006). Retrieved January 4, 2008 from http://www.cdc.gov

198. Lowen, Linda. “ How Health Care Reform Benefits Women.” About.com, December 16, 2010. Retrieved February 10, 2010 from http://womensissues.about.com/od/womensbodiesminds/a/HealthCareReformWomen.htm

199. “State Bans on Insurance Coverage of Abortion Endanger Women’s Health and Take Health Benefits Away from Women.” Washington, D.C.: National Women’s Law Center, February 5, 2014. Retrieved March 6, 2014 from http://www.nwlc.org/resource/state-bans-insurance-coverage-abortion-endanger-women%E2%80%99s-health-and-take-health-benefits-awa

200. "Doctors Give Massachusetts Health Reform a Failing Grade." *North Denver News*, January 10 2008.

201. *Definition of Socialized Medicine.* Retrieved January 8, 2008 from Medicinenet.com

202. *Falling Through the Doughnut Hole.* Washington, D.C.:Institute for America's Future, June 2006. Retrieved January 8, 2008 from outfuture.org

203. *Lawmakers are Seeking Legislation That Addresses Medicare Part D Problems.* August, 2006. Retrieved January 8, 2008 from NeedyMeds.com

204. *2008 Part D Coverage – Major Changes Are Coming*, Washington, D.C.: Center for Medicare Advocacy. Retrieved November 1, 2007 from http://www.medicareadvocacy.org

205. *Medicare Advantage Coverage.* Financial Web. Retrieved January 8, 2008 from http://www.finweb.com

206. Rucker, Philip. " Hidden Costs of Medicare Advantage." *The Washington Post*, October 15, 2009.

207. Barry, Patricia. "Don't Fall for the Hard Sell." *The AARP Bulletin*, October, 2007.

208. "Lame Duck Budget." *The New York Times*, February 5, 2008.

209. "Lower Medicare Advantage Premiums Attract Seniors." *U.S. News and World Report*, February 7, 2012. Retrieved February 10, 2012 from http://money.usnews.com/money/blogs/the–best–life/2012/02/07/lower–medicare–advantage–premiums–attract–seniors

210. "Fiscal Year 2004 Federal MSIS Tables." Washington, D.C.: U.S. Centers for Medicare and Medicaid Services, June 2007.

211. Pear, Robert. "U.S. Curtailing Bids to Expand Medicaid Rolls." *The New York Times*, January 4, 2008: A1.

212. "Where the States Stand on Medicaid Expansion." The Advisory Board Company, February 2013. Retrieved March 10, 2014 from http://www.advisory.com/daily-briefing/resources/primers/medicaidmap

213. Lambrew, Jeanne M., Ph.D."The State Children's Health Insurance Program: Past, Present, and Future." The Commonwealth Fund, February 9, 2007, Volume 49.

214. Mallaby, Sebastian."Bush's Unhealthy Veto." *The Washington Post*, Monday, October 1, 2007: A19.

215. *1.8 Million Veterans Lack Health Coverage*. Physicians for a National Health Program. Retrieved November 30, 2007 from http://www.pnhp.org

216. "Over 2,200 Veterans Died in 2008 Due to Lack of Health Insurance." Press Release from Physicians for A National Health Program, November 10, 2009. November 29, 2009 from http://www.pnhp.org/news/2009/november/over_2200_veterans_.php

217. Daniel J. Kevles. "The Secret History of Birth Control." *New York Times*, July 22, 2001.

218. Rachel Benson Gold. "Federal Authority to Impose Medicaid Family Planning Cuts: A Deal States Should Refuse." *Guttmacher Policy Review*, Spring 2006: Volume 9, Number 2.

219. Go, Alison. "Spending Bill Reduces Cost of Birth Control Pills on Campus." *U.S. News and World Report* online, March 11, 2009. http://www.usnews.com/blogs/paper-trail/2009/03/11/spending-bill-reduces-cost-of-birth-control-pills-on-campus.html

220. Jackson, David and Kennedy, Kelly, "Obama backs restrictions on morning-after Pill." *USA Today*, December 8, 2011. Retrieved February 16, 2012 from http://yourlife.usatoday.com/health/story/2011-12-08/Obama-Morning-after-pill-decision-common-sense/51745132/1

221. Neergaard, Lauran, "FDA Approves Morning After Pill Over-the-counter Sales After Court Order." The Huffington Post, June 20, 2013. Retrieved February 18, 2014 from http://www.huffingtonpost.com/2013/06/20/fda-morning-after-pill_n_3475178.html

222. Rob Stein. "Pharmacists' Rights at Front Of New Debate." *Washington Post*, March 28, 2005: A01.

223. John Platner. *Planned Parenthood, Bush and Birth Control.* (2005). Retrieved February 18, 2008 from http://www.plannedparenthood.org/issues-action/birth-control/bc-bush-6516.htm

224. Kliff, Sarah. "The Future of Abstinence." *Newsweek* magazine online, Oct 27, 2009 newsweek.com

225. U.S. Social Security Act, §510(b)(2).

226. *Abstinence Only' Sex Ed Ineffective.* (April 2007). ABC News. Retrieved February 18, 2008 from http://abcnews.go.com/Health/Sex/story?id=3048738

227. Mike Stobbe."Teen Birthrate Makes Rare Rise." Associated Press, Thursday, Dec. 6, 2007.

228. Meckler, Laura. "Budget Widens Teen-Pregnancy-Prevention Efforts." *Wall Street Journal* online, May 7, 2009. http://online.wsj.com/article/SB124171750523696797.html

229. *History of Abortion in the U.S.*" Boston: Our Bodies, Ourselves Health Resource Center. Retrieved December 22, 2007 from http://www.ourbodiesourselves.org/book/excerpt.asp?id=27

230. *History of Abortion*. National Abortion Federation, Washington, D.C. Retrieved December 22, 2007 from http://www.prochoice.org/about_abortion/history_abortion.html

231. Ibid.

232. *NAF Violence And Disruption Statistics: Incidents of Violence & Disruption Against Abortion Providers in The U.S. & Canada*. Downloaded February 17, 2012 from http://www.prochoice.org

233. "Anti-Abortion Violence: America's Forgotten Terrorism." New York, N.Y: Anti-Defamation League, September 4, 2012. Retrieved February 20, 2014 from http://www.adl.org/combating-hate/domestic-extremism-terrorism/c/anti-abortion-violence-americas-forgotten-terrorism-1.html#.UwY3oLS7TId

234. "Ashcroft Seeks Hospital Abortion Records." Democracy Now, February 13, 2004. Retrieved December 22, 2007 from http://www.democracynow.org

235. "Court Battle Over Oklahoma's Strict Abortion Law." Associated Press, October 23, 2009

236. Ibid.

237. "Abortion Access in the United States." *Choice Voices*, Planned Parenthood of New York City, February, 2007.

238. *Abortion Policy in the Absence of Roe, State Policies in Brief*. Guttmacher Institute. Retrieved December 1, 2007 from http://www.guttmacher.org/statecenter/spibs/spib_APAR.pdf

239. "Timeline of Important Reproductive Freedom Cases Decided by the Supreme Court." American Civil Liberties Union. Retrieved December 31, 2007 from http://www.aclu.org/reproductiverights/gen/16463res20031201.html

240. Ibid.

241. Chokshi, Niraj. "State Abortion Rates Were Dropping Even Before the Recent Surge in Restrictions." *The Washington Post*, February 3, 2014. Retrieved February 18, 2014 from http://www.washingtonpost.com/blogs/govbeat/wp/2014/02/03/state-abortion-rates-were-dropping-even-before-the-recent-surge-in-restrictions/

242. Ibid.

243. Tillman, Laura and John Schwartz. "Texas Clinics Stop Abortions After Court Ruling." The New York Times, November 1, 2013. Retrieved February 18, 2014 from http://www.nytimes.com/2013/11/02/us/texas-abortion-clinics-say-courts-ruling-is-forcing-them-to-stop-the-procedures.html?_r=0

244. Ertelt, Steven. "Supreme Court: Arizona Can't Enforce Ban on Abortions After 20 Weeks." Washington, D.C.: LifeNews.com, January 13, 2014. Retrieved February 18, 2014 from http://www.lifenews.com/2014/01/13/supreme-court-arizona-cant-enforce-ban-on-abortions-after-20-weeks/

245. "Intimate Partner Violence," National Center for Victims of Crime, citing Federal Bureau of Investigation statistics, 2011. Retrieved February 28, 2014 from http://www.victimsofcrime.org/library/crime-information-and-statistics/intimate-partner-violence

246. Black, M.C., Basile, K.C., Breiding, M.J., Smith, S.G., Walters, M.L., Merrick, M.T., Chen, J., & Stevens, M.R. (2011). *The National Intimate Partner and Sexual Violence Survey (NISVS): 2010 Summary Report.* Atlanta, GA: National Center for Injury Prevention and Control, Centers for Disease Control and Prevention, November, 2011. Retrieved February 28, 2014 from http://www.cdc.gov/violenceprevention/pdf/nisvs_executive_summary-a.pdf

247. Ibid.

248. Ibid.

249. Ibid.

250. National Census of Domestic Violence Services, National Network to End Domestic Violence, September, 2012. Retrieved February 28, 2014 from www.nnedv.org/resources/census/3418-2012-report.html

251. "NY Group, University To Study Rape Kit Backlog," Associated Press, 9/19/ 2011. Retrieved November 4, 2011 from

http://www.foxnews.com/us/2011/09/19/ny-group-university-to-study-rape-kit-backlog/

252. "Put Volunteer Attorneys to Work for Domestic Violence Survivors," Washington, D.C.: National Organization for Women. Retrieved January 21, 2008 from http://www.capwiz.com/now/issues/alert/?alertid=10543461

253. HR 1286, Healthy Families Act, introduced by Rep. Rosa DeLauro, 113th Congress of the United States.

254. Williams Claudia, Robert Drago, Ph.D., and Kevin Miller, Ph.D. "44 Million U.S. Workers Lacked Paid Sick Days in 2010: 77 Percent of Food Service Workers Lacked Access," Briefing paper, Institute for Women's Policy Research, Washington, D.C. , January 2011.

255. Heymann, Jody, Alison Earle, Jeffrey Hayes. "How Does the United States Measure Up?" Institute for Health and Social Policy, McGill University, 2007.

256. Vestal, Christine. "Sick Leave Tops State Labor Agendas," Retrieved January 4, 2007 from http://www.stateline.org

257. Lafer, Gordon. "One by One, States Are Pushing Bans on Sick Leave Legislation," Economic Policy Institute, Washington, D.C., November 6, 2013. Retrieved January 6, 2014 from http://www.epi.org/publication/states-pushing-bans-sick-leave-legislation/

258. "The World's Women 2010, Trends and Statistics," United Nations, New York, 2010. Retrieved September 29, 2011 from http://unstats.un.org/unsd/demographic/products/Worldswomen/WW_full%20report_color.pdf

259. Jeffrey A. Mello. *Defining Hours of Service Under the Family and Medical Leave Act in Employment Disputes.* Retrieved February 16, 2008 from http://64.233.167.104/search?q=cache:Bmjax8tzhEsJ:www.cba.csus.edu/Partner/media/journal/FMLA%2520paper%2520for%2520Journal.doc+Family+Medical+Leave+Jeffrey+A.+Mello+Towson&hl=en&ct=clnk&cd=1&gl=us

260. Heyman et. al.

261. "Swedish Policy Supports Stay-at-home Dads," *Albuquerque Journal*, November 13, 2011. P. E4.

262. Heyman et. al.

263. Rockefeller/TIME poll commissioned by the Center for American Progress and Maria Shriver, September 2009. Retrieved September 29, 2011 from http://www.americanprogress.org/issues/2010/03/work_survey.html

264. "New Poll Shows Bipartisan Voter Mandate for Family Friendly Workplace Policies," National Partnership for Women and Families, Washington, D.C., December 3, 2012. Retrieved January 7, 2014 from http://www.nationalpartnership.org/news-room/press-releases/new-poll-shows-bipartisan-mandate.html

265. U.S. Department of Labor, Women's Bureau. *Mothers in the Labor Force.* Retrieved February 13, 2014 from http://www.dol.gov/wb/stats/recentfacts.htm

266. Mather, Mark. "U.S. Children in Single Mother Families," Population Reference Bureau Data brief, May, 2010. Retrieved September 25, 2011 from http://www.prb.org/Publications/PolicyBriefs/singlemotherfamilies.aspx

267. Organisation for Economic Co-operation and Development. *Can Parents Afford to Work? Childcare Costs, Tax-benefit Policies And Work Incentives*, January 2006. Retrieved November 15, 2007 from http://www.oecd.org/dataoecd/35/43/35969537.pdf

268. "Parents and the High Cost of Child Care 2013 Report," Arlington, Va: National Association of Child Care Resource and Referral Agencies. Retrieved January 28, 2014, from http://www.naccrra.org

269. *The State of Pre-School 2012, State Preschool Yearbook*, The National Institute for Early Education Research, Rutgers University Graduate School of Education. Retrieved February 13, 2014 from http://nieer.org/sites/nieer/files/yearbook2012_executivesummary.pdf

270. "Putting the Annual Cost of the War in Perspective," *The New York Times*. Retrieved Feb. 19, 2008 from http://www.nytimes.com

271. "Cost of War," National Priorities Project. Retrieved September 26, 2011 from http://costofwar.com/en/about/notes-and-sources/

272. Fottrell, Quentin. "How The Tax Code Is Squeezing Parents," *The Wall Street Journal*, November 12, 2013. Retrieved February 18, 2014 from http://www.marketwatch.com/story/why-the-child-care-tax-break-is-shrinking-2013-11-11

273. *Occupational Outlook Handbook, 2014-15 Edition, Childcare Workers*. Bureau of Labor Statistics, U.S. Department of Labor. Retrieved February 13, 2014 from on the Internet at http://www.bls.gov/ooh/personal-care-and-service/childcare-workers.htm

274. Smith, Kristin and Reagan Baughman. "Low Wages Prevalent in Direct Care and Child Care Workforce." Carsey Institute, University of New Hampshire, Summer, 2007.

275. Helburn, Suzanne W. and Barbara R. Bergmann. *America's Child Care Problem*. New York: Palgrave, 2002.

276. Ibid.

277. "Estimates of Child Care Eligibility and Receipt for Fiscal Year 2009," Washington, D.C.: U.S. Department of Health and Human Services, August, 2012. Retrieved February 17, 2014 from http://aspe.hhs.gov/hsp/12/childcareeligibility/ib.cfm

278. National Association for the Education of Young Children. *Child Care and Development Block Grant*." Retrieved January 15, 2008 from http://www.naeyc.org

279. Bornfreund, Laura. "FY11 Budget – Finally Passed – Brings Good News for Early Ed," Washington, D.C., New America Foundation, April 19, 2011. Retrieved September 26, 2011 from http://earlyed.newamerica.net/node/48826

280. Taxin, Amy. "State child care cuts force hard choice on parents," Associated Press, December 29, 2011. Retrieved February 23, 2012 from http://www.newsvine.com/_news/2011/12/29/9806039-state-child-care-cuts-force-hard-choice-on-parents

281. "Congress Approves Spending for FY 2014: Sequester Cuts Partly Replaced, but Many Programs Still Below Their FY 2010 Levels," Washington, D.C.: Coalition for Human Needs, January 24, 2014. Retrieved February 18, 2014 from http://www.chn.org/human_needs_report/chn-congress-approves-spending-fy-2014-sequester-cuts-partly-replaced-many-programs-still-fy-2010-levels/

282. "U.S. Child Care Seriously Lags Behind that of Europe." *American Sociological Association News*, November 18, 2002.

283. Fottrell, Quentin. "How The Tax Code Is Squeezing Parents," *The Wall Street Journal*, November 12, 2013. Retrieved February 18, 2014 from http://www.marketwatch.com/story/why-the-child-care-tax-break-is-shrinking-2013-11-11

284. Kim, Anne, Stovall, Tess and Donnell, Mark. "Double the Child Care Tax Credit," Idea Brief, Thirdway.org, February, 2010. Retrieved September 26, 2011 from http://content.thirdway.org/publications/230/Third_Way_Idea_Brief_-_Double_the_Child_Care_Tax_Credit.pdf

285. "National Parent Polling Results," Arlington, Va.: National Association of Child Care Resource & Referral Agencies, September, 2011. Retrieved February 18, 2014 from http://www.naccrra.org/sites/default/files/default_site_pages/2011/parent_polling_one_pager_healthsaf_sept_2011_0.pdf

286. Helburn, Suzanne W. and Barbara R. Bergmann. America's Child Care Problem. New York: Palgrave, 2002. (Helburn and Bergmann estimated the cost at $46 billion per year, with $26.6 in new money.)

287. Formulas provided by /Dr. Barbara R. Bergmann, personal communication.

288. Welch, David and Trudell, Craig. "GM Bailout Losses Worthwhile for Obama as IPO Shrinks Cost to $9 Billion." Bloomberg online, Nov 18, 2010. Retrieved September 27, 2010 from http://www.bloomberg.com/news/2010-11-19/gm-s-bailout-losses-worthwhile-for-obama-as-ipo-shrinks-cost.html

289. CNNMoney.com's bailout tracker, Retrieved September 27, 2011 from http://money.cnn.com/news/storysupplement/economy/bailouttracker/

290. Defense spending FY2010 $847.2 billion. USgovernmentspending.com Retrieved September 27, 2011 from http://www.usgovernmentspending.com/federal_budget_estimate_vs_actual_2010_88bs1n

291. U.S. Department of Health and Human Services, National Clearinghouse for Long-term Care Information, 2011. http://www.longtermcare.gov/LTC/Main_Site/Paying/Public_Programs/Veterans.aspx

292. Martin Tolchin. "Other Countries Do Much More for Disabled," *New York Times*, March 29, 1990.

293. Beth Baker. "Home, Sweet Nursing Home," Ms. magazine, Spring, 2007.

294. Ibid.

295. Efstathiou, Jim Jr. "Obama Extends Minimum Wage to 2 Million Home Health Aides," Bloomberg Politics, September 17, 2013. Retrieved February 18, 2014 from http://www.bloomberg.com/news/2013-09-17/obama-extends-minimum-wage-to-2-million-home-health-aides.html

296. "2010 Market Survey of Long-Term Care Costs," MetLife Mature Market Institute. Retrieved October 17, 2011 from http://www.metlife.com/mmi/research/2010-market-survey-ltcc.html#findings

297. Carrns, Ann. "Checking the Details on Gender for Long-Term Care Insurance," *The New York Times*, February 15, 2014.

298. Musil, Caryn McTigue."Scaling the Ivory Towers," *Ms* magazine, Fall 2007.

299. "Gender Differences in Participation and Completion of Undergraduate Education and How They Have Changed Over Time," National Center for Education Statistics. Retrieved February 27, 2014 from http://nces.ed.gov/pubsearch/pubsinfo.asp?pubid=2005169

300. "The Crossover in Female-Male College Enrollment Rates," Mark Mather and Dia Adams, Population Reference Bureau, February, 2007. http://www.prb.org/Articles/2007/CrossoverinFemaleMaleCollegeEnrollmentRates.aspx

301. Musil, above

302. "2010-11 Survey of Dental Education – Volume 1: Academic Programs, Enrollment, and Graduates," American Dental Association, May 2012. Retrieved February 20, 2014 from hhttp://www.ada.org/sections/professionalresources/pdfs/survey_ed_vol1.pdf

303. "Education Equality," Feminist Majority Foundation, January, 2008. http://feminist.org/education/

304. Sabo, Don and Philip Veliz. "The Decade of Decline: Gender Equity in High School Sports," D'Youville College, as reported by the Women's Sports Foundation. Retrieved February 27, 2014 from http://www.womenssportsfoundation.org/en/home/research/articles-and-reports/equity-issues/decade-of-decline

305. "Report Confirms Clarification Weakens Title IX," Washington, D.C.: National Women's Law Center, March, 2006.
http://www.nwlc.org/details.cfm?id=2681§ion=newsroom

306. Homer, Liz, Sue Klein, and Jan Erickson. "Dangers of Using Title IX to Increase Sex Segregation in U.S. Public Education," Washington, D.C. Feminist Majority Foundation, 2008.

307. Ibid.

308. Ibid.

309. Ibid.

310. Klein, Sue Ed. D. "State of Public School Sex Segregation in the United States," Washington, D.C. Feminist Majority Foundation, 2012.

311. "Trends in Political Values and Core Attitudes: 1987-2007," Washington, D.C.: Pew Research Center for People and the Press. Retrieved March 13, 2014 from http://www.people-press.org/2007/03/22/trends-in-political-values-and-core-attitudes-1987-2007/

312. Associated Press-GfK Poll conducted by GfK Roper Public Affairs & Media. May 28-June 1, 2009. Retrieved November 24, 2009 from
http://www.pollingreport.com/race.htm

313. USA Today Poll conducted by Princeton Survey Research Associates International. June 27-30, 2013 as reported by PollingReport.com. Retrieved February 20, 2014 from http://www.pollingreport.com/race.htm

314. *Adarand Construction v. Pena.* The Supreme Court ruled that the most rigorous type of constitutional review, "strict scrutiny," must be applied to federal affirmative action programs. At the same time it ruled that affirmative action programs are both legal and needed.

315. Moore, Mary and Jennifer Hahn."Contracting Connerly." *Ms.* magazine, Winter 2008.

316. Sacks, Mike, and Ryan Reilly. "Supreme Court Affirmative Action Decision: Sends UT-Austin's Race-Conscious Admissions Back For Review," Huffington Post, 06/24/2013. Retrieved February 12, 2014 from http://www.huffingtonpost.com/2013/06/24/supreme-court-affirmative-action-decision_n_3345534.html

317. Walker, Blair S. *Washington's Anti-Affirmative Action Vote Thrust Into Spotlight.* (July 13, 1999). Retrieved December 29, 2007 from Stateline.org

318. Kaufmann, Susan W. "The Potential Impact of the Michigan Civil Rights Initiative on Employment, Education and Contracting." The University of Michigan: Center for the Education of Women, June 2006.

319. Ibid.

320. Moore and Hahn.

321. News of the Nation. *Affirmative Action Setbacks* (1997). Retrieved December 29, 2007 from Infoplease.com

322. Ocampo, Carmina. "Prop 209: Ten Long Years." *The Nation*, December 11, 2006.

323. "UC Berkeley Fall Enrollment Data," UC Berkeley Office of the CFO, 2014. Retrieved February 12, 2014 from http://opa.berkeley.edu/statistics/enrollmentdata.html

324. Asimov, Nanette. "UC Minority Enrollment Among Lowest In Nation," SFGate.com, January 14, 2010. Retrieved November 16, 2011 from http://articles.sfgate.com/2010-01-14/bay-area/17828191_1_uc-berkeley-flagship-schools-latino-students|

325. Wilfore, Kristina. "Take the Initiative: A Feminist Guide To Ballot Measures That Will Impact Women's Lives," Ms magazine, Fall 2006.

326. "California Affirmative Action in Education Amendment (2014)," Ballotpedia. Retrieved February 12, 2014 from http://ballotpedia.org/California_Affirmative_Action_in_Education_Amendment_%282014%29

327. Goldberg Day, Judy and Catherine Hill. *Behind the Pay Gap*, Washington, D.C.: American Association of University Women Educational Foundation, 2007.

328. *2013 Catalyst Census: Fortune 500 Women Board Directors*, New York: Catalyst, December 10, 2013. Retrieved January 28, 2014 from http://www.catalyst.org/knowledge/2013-catalyst-census-fortune-500-women-board-directors

329. Ivory, Danielle "Women Lose More Ground in U.S. Small Business Contracts Race" *Bloomberg online*, Jan 24, 2013. Retrieved January 28, 2014 from, http://www.bloomberg.com/news/2013-01-24/women-lose-more-ground-than-men-in-small-business-awards-race.html

330. Zwahlen, Cyndia. "SBA Effort for Women Owners Stirs Outrage," *Los Angeles Times*, January 3, 2008.

331. "Women-Owned Small Businesses Suffer Largest Federal Contracting Opportunity Loss in History Date," Washington, D.C.: U.S. Women's Chamber of Commerce, August 24, 2009. Retrieved November 6, 2009 from http://uswccweb.squarespace.com

332. "SBA Releases Scorecard Showing Significant Progress in Federal Contracting Goal," June 2011, Small Business Trends press release. Retrieved November 2, 2011 from http://smallbiztrends.com/2011/06/sba-scorecard-federal-contracting.html

333. "The Military-Industrial Complex Leaderboard Since 10/30/06," MilitaryIndustrialComplex.com using information from the United States Department of Defense. Retrieved November 2, 2011 from http://www.militaryindustrialcomplex.com/contracts-leaderboard.asp

334. "Women-Owned Small Businesses," Washington, D.C.: U.S. Small Business Administration. Retrieved February 12, 2014 from http://www.sba.gov/content/contracting-opportunities-women-owned-small-businesses

335. "Procurement Statistics Revealed Great Gains for Women-Owned Small Businesses," Washington, D.C.: National Women's Business Council, November, 2013. Retrieved February 12, 2014 from http://nwbc.gov/research/procurement-statistics-revealed-great-gains-women-owned-small-businesses

336. Williams, Terry. "Small Businesses Owners Lose $30B as Federal Contracting Falls Short of Required Spending with Small Businesses in FY2008," August 24, 2009. Retrieved November 6, 2009 from http://www.nasbc.org/magazine

337. Dao, James. "Servicewomen File Suit Over Direct Combat Ban," *The New York Times*, September 28, 2012.

338. Tyson, Ann Scott."For Female GIs, Combat Is a Fact,." *Washington Post*, Friday, May 13, 2005.

339. Jelinek, Pauline. "Report: Too Many Whites, Men Lead U.S. Military," Associated Press, March 7, 2011. Retrieved November 27, 2011 from http://www.msnbc.msn.com/id/41955329/ns/us_news-life/t/report-too-many-whites-men-lead-us-military/#

340. Reske, Henry J. "75% Americans Want Women in Combat — Poll," ABC-Washington Post poll, March 16, 2011. Retrieved November 27, 2011 from http://www.newsmax.com/US/75percentAmericansWantWomeninCombat-Poll/2011/03/16/id/389638

341. Steinhauer, Jennifer. "Elite Units in Military to Admit Women," *The New York Times*, June 18, 2013.

342. Dao, James. "Servicewomen File Suit Over Direct Combat Ban."

343. "Confronting Rape in the Military," *New York Times*, March 12, 2004.

344. Mulrine, Anna. "Pentagon report: Sexual Assault In The Military Up Dramatically," The Christian Science Monitor, January 19, 2012. Retrieved February 1, 2012 from http://www.csmonitor.com/USA/Military/2012/0119/Pentagon-report-Sexual-assault-in-the-military-up-dramatically

345. Mulrine, Anna." Exclusive: 1 in 5 Air Force Women Victim Of Sexual Assault, Survey Finds," The Christian Science Monitor, March 17, 2011. Retrieved February 1, 2012 from http://www.csmonitor.com/USA/Military/2011/0317/Exclusive-1-in-5-Air-Force-women-victim-of-sexual-assault-survey-finds

346. *Annual Report on Sexual Harassment and Violence at the Military Service Academies, Academic ProgramYear 2012–2013,* United States Depart of Defense, January 8, 2014. Retrieved March 12, 2014 from http://www.sapr.mil/public/docs/reports/FINAL_APY_12-13_MSA_Report.pdf

347. McGreal, Chris. "Rape Case To Force us Defence Firms Into The Open," *The Guardian*, October 15, 2009. Retrieved November 27, 2011 from http://www.guardian.co.uk/world/2009/oct/15/defence-contractors-rape-claim-block

348. "Give Military Women the Health Care Coverage They Deserve," Washington, D.C.: National Women's Law Center, May 12, 2012. Retrieved March 12, 2014 from http://www.nwlc.org/resource/give-military-women-health-care-coverage-they-deserve

349. *Penalized For Serving Their Country: The Ban On Abortion For Women In the Military*, Washington, D.C.: Center for Reproductive Rights, June 2003. Retrieved January 2, 2008 from http://www.reproductiverights.org

350. Yeoman, Barry. "Women Vets: A Battle All Their Own," *Parade Magazine*, November 10, 2013.

351. Zucchino, David. "More Women Falling Into Ranks Of Homeless Veterans," *Los Angeles Times*, October 23, 2011. Retrieved November 29, 2011 from http://articles.latimes.com/2011/oct/23/nation/la-na-women-vets-20111024

352. Warren, Lizzie. "No Holidays Or Parades For Homeless Women Veterans," Salon.com, May 27, 2013. Retrieved March 12, 2014 from http://www.salon.com/2013/05/27/meet_americas_fastest_growing_homeless_population_women_veterans/

353. "RAND Study Finds Divorce Among Soldiers Has Not Spiked Higher Despite Stress Created By Battlefield Deployments," The RAND Corporation, April 12, 2007.

354. Washington Post-ABC News poll March 7-10, 2013. *The Washington Post*, March 2013. Retrieved February 10, 2014 from http://apps.washingtonpost.com/g/documents/politics/washington-post-abc-news-poll-march-7-10-2013/381/

355. "Gays In The Military Should Be Allowed To Come Out,"Quinnipiac University National Poll, April 30, 2009. Downloaded November 24, 2009 from http://www.quinnipiac.edu/x1295.xml?ReleaseID=1292

356. Jackson, Derrick Z."Optimism in the Hate Crimes Debate," *The Boston Globe*, May 26, 2007: A11.

357. "Discharges Under the Don't Ask/Don't Tell Policy: Women And Racial/Ethnic Minorities," The University of California School of Law Williams Institute, September, 2010. Retrieved February 11, 2014 from http://williamsinstitute.law.ucla.edu/wp-content/uploads/Gates-Discharges2009-Military-Sept-2010.pdf

358. "Gays In The Military Should Be Allowed To Come Out."

359. "Don't Ask, Don't Tell" Not Working," Zogby poll, December 18, 2006. Downloaded February 28, 2008 from http://zogby.com/news

360. Gallup poll, May, 2005, cited by *Focus: Public Opinion & Polls*.

361. Condon,Stephanie. "Supreme Court Strikes Down Key Part Of DOMA, Dismisses prop. 8 Case," CBS News, June 26, 2013. Retrieved February 10, 2014 from http://www.cbsnews.com/news/supreme-court-strikes-down-key-part-of-doma-dismisses-prop-8-case/

362. Mckinley, Jesse and Goodstein, Laurie "Bans in 3 States on Gay Marriage," *The New York Times*, November 5, 2008.

363. Mannix, Andy. "Thank Republicans for Gay Marriage in Minnesota," *Time* online, Aug. 01, 2013, Retrieved February 10, 2014 from http://nation.time.com/2013/08/01/thank-republicans-for-gay-marriage-in-minnesota/

364. Newport, Frank. "Americans Favor Rights for Gays, Lesbians to Inherit, Adopt," Princeton, N.J.: Gallup, December 17, 2012. Retrieved February 20, 2014 from http://www.gallup.com/poll/159272/americans-favor-rights-gays-lesbians-inherit-adopt.aspx

365. *Gay Marriage*. Pro-con.org Retrieved February 10, 2014 from http://gaymarriage.procon.org/view.resource.php?resourceID=004857

366. "Frequently Asked Questions Employment Non-discrimination Act," Washington, D.C.: Human Rights Campaign, Retrieved February 11, 2014 from hrc.org

367. *Global Gag Rule: A Flawed Policy That Sacrifices Women's Lives*. Washington, D.C.: NARAL Pro-Choice America, January 22,2007. Retrieved December 15, 2007 from http://www.prochoiceamerica.org

368. "Taliban Attacks on Afghan Girls' Schools Increase," *Feminist Daily News Wire*, July 12, 2006.

369. Starkey,Jerome, "Karzai's Secret U-Turn On afghan Rape Law," London: *The Independent*, August 15, 2009.

370. Rubin, Alissa, "For Afghan Woman, Justice Runs Into Static Wall of Custom," *The New York Times*, December 2, 2011. Page A1.

371. *A Way to Go:An Update on Implementation of the Law on Elimination of Violence against Women in Afghanistan*. Kabul: United Nations Assistance Mission in Afghanistan, December, 2013. Retrieved February 4, 2014 from http://unama.unmissions.org/Portals/UNAMA/Documents/UNAMA%20REPORT%20on%20EVAW%20LAW_8%20December%202013.pdf

372. "Iraqi Women: Prostituting Ourselves To Feed Our Children," CNN.com, August 16, 2007. Retrieved December 31, 2007 from http://www.cnn.com/2007/WORLD/meast/08/15/iraq.prostitution/index.html

373. "Women in Iraq Factsheet," New York: United Nations, March, 2013. Retrieved February 8, 2014 from http://unami.unmissions.org/LinkClick.aspx?fileticket=xqx9gxy7Isk%3D&tabid=2790&language=en-US

374. "Iraq: Security Forces Abusing Women in Detention," Baghdad: Human Rights Watch, February 6, 2014. Retrieved February 8, 2014 from http://www.hrw.org/news/2014/02/06/iraq-security-forces-abusing-women-detention

375. Salem, Mostafa, "Egyptian Women Aim For 100 Parliamentary Seats," *Daily News Egypt*, November 24, 2013. Retrieved February 3, 2014 from http://www.dailynewsegypt.com/2013/11/24/egyptian-women-aim-for-100-parliamentary-seats/#sthash.HVmGA7w3.dpuf

376. Wong, Kristine, "5 Ways Life Has Become Intolerable for This Country's Women," *takepart*, January 27, 2014. Retrieved February 3, 2014 from http://www.takepart.com/article/2014/01/24/women-syria

377. Muscati, Samer and Salah Hanan, "Women Face Challenges as Libya Moves Toward a New Constitution," *Globalpost*, May 31, 2013. Retrieved February 3, 2014 from http://www.globalpost.com/dispatches/globalpost-blogs/commentary/libya-women-constitution-gender-discrimination-politics

378. Abdul-Latif, Rola. *Libya Status of Women Survey 2013.* Washington, D.C.: International Foundation for Electoral Systems, September, 2013. Retrieved February 9, 2014 from http://www.ifes.org/~/media/Files/Publications/Survey/2013/Libya%20Status%20of%20Women%20Survey%20Report_final2.pdf

379. The information in this section comes from Arieff, Alexis, "Sexual Violence in African Conflicts," Congressional Research Service, November 30, 2010. Retrieved February 15, 2012 from http://www.fas.org/sgp/crs/row/R40956.pdf

380. Rassekh Milani, Leila (ed.). *Human Rights for All, CEDAW.* Washington, D.C.: Working Group on Ratification of the U.N. Convention on the Elimination of All Forms of Discrimination Against Women, 2001.

381. "Help Ban Landmines," Tacoma Park, Md: Handicap International. Retrieved February 1, 2014 from http://www.handicap-international.us/landmine_petition

382. *Convention on the Rights of the Child (CRC).* New York, UNICEF. Retrieved December 1, 2007 from http://www.unicef.org

383. The Campaign for U.S. Ratification of the Convention on the Rights of the Child (CRC). Retrieved November 4, 2011 from childrightscampaign.org

384. Burk, Martha. *Cult of Power: Sex Discrimination In Corporate America and What Can Be Done About It.* New York: Scribner, 2005, p. 83.

◊ INDEX ◊

Made in the USA
Charleston, SC
24 April 2015